# MEG, JO, BETH, AMY

ALSO BY ANNE BOYD RIOUX

*Constance Fenimore Woolson: Portrait of a Lady Novelist*

*Miss Grief and Other Stories* (editor)

*Writing for Immortality: Women and the Emergence of*
*High Literary Culture in America*

*Wielding the Pen: Writings on Authorship by*
*American Women of the Nineteenth Century* (editor)

# MEG, JO, BETH, AMY

## THE STORY OF
## ❧ LITTLE WOMEN ❧
### AND WHY
### IT STILL MATTERS

## ANNE BOYD RIOUX

**W. W. Norton & Company**

INDEPENDENT PUBLISHERS SINCE 1923

NEW YORK • LONDON

For information about permission to reproduce selections from this book, write to
Permissions, W. W. Norton & Company, Inc., 500 Fifth Avenue, New York, NY 10110

For information about special discounts for bulk purchases, please contact
W. W. NortonSpecial Sales at specialsales@wwnorton.com or 800-233-4830

Manufacturing by Quad Graphics, Fairfield
Book design by Brooke Koven
Production manager: Anna Oler

Library of Congress Cataloging-in-Publication Data

Names: Rioux, Anne Boyd, author.
Title: Meg, Jo, Beth, Amy : the story of Little Women
and why it still matters / Anne Boyd Rioux.
Description: First edition. | New York : W. W. Norton & Company, [2018] |
Includes bibliographical references and index.
Identifiers: LCCN 2018006602 | ISBN 9780393254730 (hardcover)
Subjects: LCSH: Alcott, Louisa May, 1832–1888. Little women.
Classification: LCC PS1017.L53 R58 2018 | DDC 813/.4—dc23
LC record available at https://lccn.loc.gov/2018006602

W. W. Norton & Company, Inc., 500 Fifth Avenue, New York, N.Y. 10110
www.wwnorton.com

W. W. Norton & Company Ltd., 15 Carlisle Street, London W1D 3BS

1 2 3 4 5 6 7 8 9 0

THIS BOOK IS DEDICATED TO
EMMA AND HER FRIENDS,
TODAY'S LITTLE WOMEN.

# Contents

# PROLOGUE

## "Our Book"

I FIRST READ *LITTLE WOMEN* in my early twenties, in a graduate course on American Literary Realism. I missed out on the formative experience of reading the novel as a child. As it turned out, though, it can have just as much impact on a young woman in her twenties who is still trying to figure out who she will be and whether she will find a way to have a family and a career. Jo inspired me not only because she had ambitions to be a writer but because she found a way to grow into adulthood without leaving those ambitions entirely behind. She was still on my mind ten years later when my daughter was born and I gave her the middle name Josephine.

As I worked on this book, I encountered numerous women who wanted to tell me their *Little Women* stories. They showed me nineteenth-century editions that had been passed down in their families like heirlooms, or they told me about the copy their grandmothers had given them and they had in turn given to their daughters. They recited passages to me from memory. They described their favorite scenes from the films. They told me, "I wanted to be Jo" or, simply, "I am Jo." Their stories are reflected in the one Elena Ferrante tells of two little girls growing up in 1950s Naples in her critically acclaimed novel *My Brilliant Friend* (2011). Lila and Lenú meet every day for months in the courtyard to read *Little Women* together, "so many times that the book became tattered and sweat-stained, it lost its spine, came unthreaded, sections fell apart. But it was our book," Lenú explains, "we loved it dearly."[1]

Something about *Little Women* has made it the paradigmatic book about growing up, especially for the female half of the population. Although it is set in Massachusetts in the years following the Civil War, it has transcended its time and place and been translated into over fifty languages. Writers from England, Chile, Pakistan, and Korea have invented their own March sisters and rewritten the story in new contexts. And *Little Women* has been adapted for television in many countries—from Mexico to Turkey to Japan. In its original form, it has inspired the devotion of readers of all ages. Countless readers report having pored over *Little Women* repeatedly, not content with just one read. And many speak of coming back to the book again as adults, sometimes yearly, as a ritual that centers them and returns them to their memories and dreams of childhood. What is it that has spoken to readers and audiences of all ages for the past 150 years and made *Little Women* the most widely beloved story of girlhood?

Perhaps it is the book's portrait of home. Images of the Marches nestled around the fire or the sisters performing plays for their neighbors make us yearn for quiet, candle-lit homes where pies are baking for dinner. The family bonds the Marches share—strong enough to survive war, marriage, overseas travel, and even death—make us nostalgic for a time before fragmented families became the norm. And the scenes of sisters curling each other's hair before a dance or fighting over who gets to go to the play with the cute boy next door remind us of our own siblings or make us wish that we had them.

More than cozy memories, though, *Little Women* evokes deep feelings of identification, especially in female readers. The March sisters are highly individualistic, lifelike characters in which girls can see themselves reflected. None is idealized. Meg, the dutiful oldest sister, is eager to make Marmee proud but also resents the family's poverty. Jo, the tomboy with literary ambitions and a fierce devotion to her family, struggles with an unruly temper. Beth loves music, plays mother to her broken dolls, and is excruciatingly shy. Amy, the youngest, aspires to be a great lady and a great artist but is also insufferably vain. Jo, especially, has fired the dreams of countless girls hoping to strike out on their own one day and do something exceptional. Readers as varied as Christine King Farris, Hillary Rodham Clinton, Carla Hayden, Simone de Beauvoir, Patti Smith, the Empress of Japan, Gloria Vanderbilt, Connie Chung, Gloria Steinem, J. K. Rowling, Cynthia Ozick, and Caitlin Moran have all been inspired by Jo March.[2] She was the girl inside of so many of us, the one who rebelled against convention and donned her glory cloak while genius burned in the garret yet wanted very much to love and be loved by her family.

While researching the history of how Alcott wrote *Little Women*, how generations of readers have thought about it and argued over it, as well as how others have adapted the story for new generations, I have discovered that Alcott's novel is not what it at first appears to be. What seems like a tale from a simpler time turns out to be the product of a difficult and sometimes troubled life. What appears to be a sweet, light story of four girls growing up is also very much about how hard it was (and is) to come of age in a culture that prizes a woman's appearance over her substance. And what may seem an idealized portrait of an intact home and family is also the story of a family in danger of being torn apart.

Once we look past the nostalgic glow on the surface of our memories of Alcott's classic, we can see that reading the novel raises questions still relevant today. What does it mean that this venerated story of girlhood centers on a girl who doesn't want to be one at all? How can we aspire to independence and also find love and support in the context of home? And is *Little Women* really a story only for female readers, or is it just as much about how we all have to make compromises as we grow into adulthood? Why have so many male readers, from Teddy Roosevelt to John Green, fallen in love with *Little Women* too, yet felt they had to hide or make excuses for it? And what are the implications of telling boys that the book is not for them, as happens with almost all books that center on girls?

Reading *Little Women*, talking about it, acting it out with friends, watching movies based on it, rewriting it ourselves, and being inspired by it are anything but simple acts of readerly affection. Alcott's classic has seeped into generations of lives and helped shape the way we think about what it means to grow up, what it means to be female, and what it means to live a fulfilling life. As *Little Women* celebrates its sesquicentennial, I have wondered, will it continue to matter to readers for another 150 years? Although younger readers are living in a much different world, they are still figuring out their relationships to family and friends and testing their independence. They can still find themselves reflected in the characters of Meg, Jo, Beth, and Amy as each sister finds her own way to grow up. Returning to *Little Women* reminds us of who we are and invites us to examine who we hope to be, making Alcott's classic as vital as ever.

# PART I

# THE MAKING OF A CLASSIC

# 1

# "PEGGING AWAY"

## The Road to *Little Women*

IN SEPTEMBER 1867, the publisher Thomas Niles of Roberts Brothers wrote to Louisa May Alcott to ask if she would write a girls' book. She wasn't wild about the idea. "Never liked girls or knew many, except my sisters," she wrote in her journal the following May, when she finally started writing the book that would become *Little Women*. She called it, at first, "The Pathetic Family," the name she had often used for her own family. When she sent the first twelve chapters to Niles, he thought them "dull," and she agreed. But she kept on with her story and after ten weeks had written an astonishing 402 pages. This would be what we now know of as the first part of *Little Women*. Niles came up with the title, which drew attention to the transitional period of the March sisters' lives as they matured from girls to women. Niles's opinion of the completed manuscript was much improved over his first impression. He had given several copies to girls to gauge their interest, and they declared it a success, so he was willing to offer Alcott a contract.[1]

Despite the young readers' encouragement, Alcott was unsure of what she had written. After publication of the first part on September 30, 1868, she confessed that she had written it quickly "to order" and had grave doubts about its success. She was happy that the critic and writer Thomas Wentworth Higginson thought her "little story was 'good, & American.'"[2] But she had no idea that thousands of girls around the country would feel the same way and make writing books for them more lucrative than any other kind of writing she had ever done.

By the end of that month, the first print run of two thousand copies had sold out and the printing presses were busy making more to fill the growing demand. Niles then asked Alcott to write a second volume. She set to work again, writing nearly a chapter a day, so caught up in weaving the futures of her four March girls that she barely stopped to eat or sleep. At the New Year, the manuscript of part two was delivered to the publisher, and Alcott was soon hailed across the country as "the children's friend."[3]

THE THIRTY-FIVE-YEAR-OLD Louisa May Alcott had not envisioned this career path for herself. She had grown up on the ideals of German and British romanticism and American transcendentalism, which promoted self-reliance and divinely inspired genius as the paths to literary success. Her neighbor and idol Ralph Waldo Emerson had written in his essay "Self-Reliance," "To believe your own thought, to believe that what is true for you in your private heart, is true for all men,—that is genius," and the young Louisa had copied those words into her scrapbook.[4] For a girl with such a mentor, and with a father who believed in the inherent divinity of every child, regardless of gender, it seemed quite possible to grow up and become a famous novelist one day—not unlike Nathaniel Hawthorne, another of her neighbors in Concord, Massachusetts.

Louisa's most unusual father, Bronson Alcott, was a close friend of Emerson's. Bronson had no sons on whom he could bestow his transcendentalist principles, but he felt that girls would do just as well. He believed that genius was a "flaming Herald" sent from God "to revive in Humanity the lost idea of its destiny." In his view, remarkable for his time, genius was innate in each child, male or female, but was stifled by fear and intolerance as the child grew. In his role as educator and father, he sought to counteract that process. No wonder that two of his four daughters grew up to pursue creative lives: Louisa as a writer and May, the youngest, as an artist. As a single-minded philosopher and writer himself, Bronson was thrilled by Louisa's intense devotion to her writing. He believed, when she was only twelve years old, that one day her "ready genius" would "make a way . . . in the world" and perhaps even grant her fame. On her fourteenth birthday, he gave her a book into which he had copied her own original poetry, sending her the clear message that he endorsed and took pride in her literary efforts. He brought apples and cider up to her garret while she was working intensely and later built her a desk, a wooden semicircle attached to the wall between the windows in her room at Orchard House, encouraging her, as her sister May put it, to "liv[e] for immortality." Bronson also read Louisa's letters—written when she was away from home—aloud to Emerson and passed them on to publishers in hopes they would print them. He told her he hoped she would "have the health, leisure, comforts, as you have the Genius" to write a book that would reach "the wider circle of readers." Her mother, Abigail, or "Abba," Alcott, was no less encouraging. After reading Louisa's poem "The Robin," written when she was only eight years old, Abigail told her daughter, "You will grow up a Shakespeare!" Many years later, when Louisa published her first book, she credited her accomplishment to her mother's unwavering support and interest "from the first to the last."[5]

Not many families in America had ever so thoroughly nourished and encouraged a girl's literary abilities. During the 1840s and '50s, when Louisa was growing up, girls and women were warned at every turn against picking up the pen. But they were doing so in ever greater numbers, which caused the *United States Review* in 1853 to call on "American authors [to] be men and heroes! . . . Do not leave literature in the hands of a few industrious females." In defense of the male-dominated sphere of literature, critics stood, in the words of now forgotten novelist Elizabeth Stoddard, "ready to sneer at every woman who aspires to make use of the talents with which God intended her to adorn the walks of literature or art." Even more perniciously, male family members were often ashamed of their sisters or daughters who dared to venture into print. Fanny Fern wrote in her 1854 autobiographical novel *Ruth Hall* of her brother, the famous editor Nathaniel Willis, telling her that she had no talent and had better find some "*unobtrusive* employment." Fern wrote her novel as a legitimation of her pursuit of a literary career, despite the overwhelming obstacles her family put in her way. Closer to home for Alcott, Hawthorne told his wife, Sophia, a gifted writer herself, that he was glad she had "never prostituted [her]self to the public" by becoming a published author.[6]

The message Louisa received from her family could not have been more different. To read her journals is to watch the slow budding of a writer who has the usual doubts and frustrations but not the crushing "anxiety of authorship" that most women writers experienced in the nineteenth century. She would write at the age of twenty-seven, astonishingly free of self-doubt or guilt, that she expected "the great authoress [Louisa] & artist [May] . . . [to] be 'an honor to our country & a terror to the foe.'"[7]

Alcott's earliest writings consisted of the exotic Italian-set short stories "The Rival Painters," published in 1852 when she was twenty years old, and "The Rival Prima Donnas," which appeared in 1854. Later that year, she published her first book, *Flower Fables*, a collection of stories about fairies and the flowers they befriend, based on the whimsical tales her teacher Henry David Thoreau had once told her, and that she, in turn, had told to the Emerson children when she was fifteen. With the encouragement and financial contribution of the Emerson family, she was able to convince a publisher to take a risk on the stories. It was a good bet; the book earned her a modest sum of $32. In a letter accompanying the copy of her "first born" that she gave to her mother for Christmas, Louisa indicated it was only a beginning, "for, with so much to cheer me on, I hope to pass in time from fairies and fables to men and realities."[8] This was but her literary apprenticeship that she hoped would lead to fame as a serious author.

Five years later, in 1860, Alcott was well on her way to that goal. The prestigious *Atlantic Monthly*, in which the work of Emerson,

Hawthorne, and Thoreau had previously appeared, had published two of her stories. She had reached the nation's utmost literary heights, it seemed, but that was not enough for her. One of her stories published in the *Atlantic* was "A Modern Cinderella," which anticipates *Little Women* in many ways. In the story, two sisters, Di and Laura—modeled on Louisa and May—abandon their household responsibilities when inspiration strikes them, while their sister Nan, modeled on the oldest Alcott daughter, Anna (who was also called Nan), picks up the slack. In time, Di learns to become a true artist not by neglecting her duty but by embracing it, telling Nan's fiancé, "I'll turn my books and pen to some account, and write stories full of dear old souls like you and Nan; and some one, I know, will like and buy them, though they are not 'works of Shakespeare.' I've thought of this before, have felt I had the power in me; *now* I have the motive, and *now* I'll do it."[9] The motive that inspires Di is the desire to support her family.

Money to augment the empty family coffers was Alcott's inspiration as well. After "pegging away all these years in vain," she wanted both recognition and her own literary fortune. Unfortunately, writing for the *Atlantic* wasn't turning out to be the path to get there, as she had hoped. The editors encouraged her to write a "flat sort of tale." In fact, they sought stories and poems by women as leavening for the weighty material by the magazine's illustrious male contributors. Deflated but not beaten, Alcott continued to send in her stories, writing primarily for money and earning between $50 and $75 for each one.[10] This pattern of letting out her ambitions and then drawing them in and claiming money to be her chief motivation would continue for many years.

Searching for a way to distinguish herself, Alcott also yearned for something important to do in the world. According to the transcendentalism of Emerson and Thoreau, only contact with the world would lead one to genius; locking oneself up at home or in the study was too limiting. In "Experience," Emerson wrote, "Of what use is genius, if the organ is too convex or too concave, and cannot find a focal distance within the actual horizon of human life?" Alcott longed for experiences that would fuel her writing, and soon after the first shots of the Civil War were fired at Fort Sumter in April 1861, she yearned to join the young men of Concord marching off to brave bullets and cannonballs. But she had to content herself with sewing bees and lint-picking parties, helping to outfit soldiers and prepare bandages for the casualties to come. At home there were also extra duties when John Brown's daughters came to board with the Alcotts, leaving Louisa no time to write down the story ideas simmering in her active brain. "I think disappointment must be good for me, I get so much of it," she wrote in her journal.[11]

As 1862 dawned, family friend Elizabeth Peabody suggested that Louisa start a kindergarten since Peabody's own, the first in America, had been so successful. The new editor of the *Atlantic Monthly*, James T. Fields, who wasn't interested in publishing her stories, encouraged her to give up writing and gave her $40 (worth over $1,000 today) to start a school. She dejectedly agreed. Unsurprisingly, life as a teacher dependent on the generosity of others did not suit Alcott. She "long[ed] for a crust in a garret with freedom and a pen."[12] By April she had given up the school as a failure, not having made enough money even to cover her own expenses.

Despite Fields's advice, Alcott decided that writing was her true calling and the surest way she had to make a living. Always at war with her desire to write great literature was her even keener desire to make money from it. For however much her parents encouraged her literary ambitions, they also needed her to help provide for their struggling family. Bronson was a dreamer with little concern for the practical necessities of life and utterly incapable of earning a living wage. As a child, Louisa once described a philosopher like her father as "a man up in a balloon with his family at the strings tugging to pull him down." When she later fictionalized the utopian community Bronson started with a friend at Fruitlands, she wrote humorously but also bitterly about how "some call of the Oversoul wafted all the men away" when it was time to harvest the crops.[13]

Bronson's self-reliant path to genius led to precisely the kind of neglect of others rejected by Louisa's alter ego Di in "A Modern Cinderella." She had grown up watching her father shift the burdens of everyday life onto the shoulders of his wife and daughters. The only occupations that did not compromise his principles were teaching and chopping wood. The former became impossible after the twin scandals of his unorthodox teaching methods and his acceptance of a black pupil, and the latter was not a reliable source of income. Louisa watched as her mother toiled to feed and clothe her four girls, and the two oldest went out to work as soon as they were able. As a result, for Louisa writing could never be a purely artistic affair. There was room in the Alcott family for only one self-absorbed genius.

Thus she turned away from writing for high cultural periodicals and toward the easiest path to financial reward: writing tales for the popular *Frank Leslie's Illustrated Newspaper*, known for its coverage of murder trials and sensational gossip. In 1862 she entered a contest held by the paper and won the $100 prize with her story "Pauline's Passion and Punishment." Set in Cuba, it is a melodramatic tale about a daring heroine who exacts revenge on the lover who cheats on her and jilts her. Two more similarly dramatic stories followed in 1863, "A Pair of Eyes" and "A Whisper in the Dark," which *Frank Leslie's* bought for $40 and $50, respectively. All were published anonymously. She called such stories "blood & thunder tales" and told her friend Alfred Whitman not to be shocked if he received a paper in the mail with one of her stories under a title such as "The Maniac Bride" or "The Bath of Blood. A thrilling tale of passion."[14] She once wrote that she thought her "natural ambition is for the lurid style," but she feared exposure. She didn't want her father or Emerson to know. What would they think of her? For all of their inspiring transcendentalist principles, they had also saddled her with "a chain armor of propriety."[15] She would in the coming years continue to write many such stories but either anonymously or under the gender-neutral pseudonym A. M. Barnard.

By the time "Pauline's Passion and Punishment" was published, however, Alcott had already taken another course that would lead her along a very different path as a writer. As the news from the battlefields worsened with defeats at the Second Battle of Bull Run and Antietam, Alcott's desire to join the boys who had marched off to war intensified. When she turned thirty years old and thus reached the age at which the Union nursing corps would consider applicants, she applied. She enjoyed nursing and needed an outlet for her considerable energy. Dorothea Dix, who had been an assistant at her father's school many years earlier and was now superintendent of the nursing corps, accepted her; and in early December 1862 Louisa got her orders, feeling like "the son of the house going to war."[16] She left the next morning and spent Christmas in the Union Hotel Hospital in Washington, D.C. There, over the next six weeks, she assisted with amputations, dressed wounds, and washed the hordes of battle-weary men whose naked bodies were rather alarming to her. In mid-January, however, her family was notified that she had come down with a dangerous case of typhoid pneumonia. When one of the other nurses died of the same disease, Bronson, who had already hurried to her bedside, rushed her back to Concord.

For three weeks Louisa's fever raged, and she had strange and sometimes frightening dreams. Her recovery from her illness lasted for two months, but the effects of the treatments of the time, which included a medicine containing mercury, would last a lifetime. Her strong frame was wasted, and her hair, which previously extended nearly to her ankles, had been cut off on doctors' orders. As soon as she could sit at her desk again, Alcott, wearing a small white cap, set to work revising the letters she had written home while she was nursing. They would soon be published in May and June 1863 as "Hospital Sketches," first in the antislavery weekly the *Boston Commonwealth* and then in book form. Thus the first writing that stemmed directly from her own life was published, and she got her first taste of the public's eagerness, particularly during the war, for stories of authentic experience. The sketches became an instant hit and showed her where her true talents lay. Her father, who was probably the one who first shared her letters with friends at the *Boston Commonwealth*, was proud of his daughter's first literary success.

Upon her next visit to Boston with her father, Louisa was surprised to see how celebrated she was, being more used to doing hard work than receiving the royal treatment. The up-and-coming writer William Dean Howells and the philosophical and theological author Henry James Sr. both sent her letters of praise. Fields admitted he was wrong about her giving up writing and now wanted some of her work for the *Atlantic*. He published her poem "Thoreau's Flute" as well as a wartime story, "The Brothers," for which he paid her $50. Then he proposed to send her to Port Royal, North Carolina, so that she could teach contraband slaves and write about her experiences for his magazine. They were to be called "Plantation Sketches," but she was not accepted for the enterprise.[17]

Meanwhile, Fields also said he wanted a novel from her for his publishing firm Ticknor and Fields, the most prestigious literary house in the United States. Did she perhaps have one in the works he could see? She did have a manuscript into which she had funneled countless hours and her greatest ambitions. She called it *Moods*. Having earned a highly respectable $600 for her writing in 1863, she felt she could take the time to nurture her novel into being, for this was a labor of love not business. *Moods* was an ambitious book about a volatile young woman who marries in haste and later regrets it. It was full of Louisa's youthful crushes on Emerson and Thoreau and her doubts about the wisdom of marriage for someone as willful and capricious as herself. But more than that, it was a serious bid for literary immortality, a psychological romance written in the vein of Charlotte and Emily Brontë's powerful works. Unfortunately, however, she was already under obligation to James Redpath, who had published *Hospital Sketches*. Redpath was willing to publish *Moods*, but he told her it was too long and she would have to cut it in half. She refused and sent it to Howard Ticknor, Fields's partner, who said he liked the book but felt they had too much in the works just then. Months later a friend of the family sent it to the publisher A. K. Loring. He also wanted it cut, particularly the long passages of description and analysis. Plot-driven works were in demand, he said. Alcott was disgusted and threw *Moods* back in the drawer where it had stayed for the past three years.

Eventually Louisa devised a new way to shorten *Moods*. Unable to eat or sleep for nearly two weeks, she slipped into her vortex, as she called it, revising and reshaping *Moods* for Loring. But after its publication in late 1864, she looked back with regret rather than satisfaction. It was not the book she had intended it to be, "for I followed bad advice & took out many things which explained my idea & made the characters more natural & consistent," she wrote to a friend.[18] It sold well, going into a second printing, and reviewers praised the writing but found its ideas about marriage unsettling and too free. Alcott was dismayed and swore that in the future she would leave out the ideas altogether.

She then went back to a new novel she had started, called "Success," but she soon set aside her ambition for serious recognition in order to contribute to her family's income. (The novel would become *Work*, published in 1873, five years after *Little Women*.) Her experiment with novel writing was not a failure, but it also was not the success she had hoped for. She went back to writing her "rubbishy tales." They paid better and were easy to write. She couldn't "afford to starve on praise," she wrote in her journal.[19] Alcott also gave up on the *Atlantic* when it started rejecting her stories again, probably because they dealt with antislavery themes. She went back to writing sensation stories for *The Flag of Our Union* and the newly launched *Frank Leslie's Chimney Corner*. She was satisfied to supply the demand for blood-and-thunder tales when, with little effort and much fun, she could crank out stories that garnered her between $50 and $75 apiece—and Leslie always wanted more.

In the summer of 1865, Alcott took an extended hiatus from writing when her long-cherished dream of traveling to Europe became a reality. Her reputation as a nurse had earned her an invitation to act as a paid companion to the wealthy invalid Anna Weld on a tour of the continent. Weld's half-brother, George, also joined them, but he often left them alone to go on his own adventures. Over the next year, the two women visited the principal sites throughout Germany and then stayed for a longer period in Vevey, Switzerland. There Anna suffered ill health, and Louisa was frustrated to be spending her time fluffing cushions and carrying shawls instead of seeing the sights. Fortunately for Louisa, she made a new friend in Vevey, the Polish youth Ladislas Wisniewski, whom she called "Laddie." She wrote something in her journal about a "romance with L. W." but later scratched it out and added, "Couldn't be." However, it seems they mostly walked, talked, sailed, and traded English and French lessons. When he finally left for Geneva and the women went to Nice, Louisa and Anna, who also seems to have taken a fancy to Ladislas, were despondent. A few months later, when Louisa decided to go home, she went first to Paris and spent two weeks there with Laddie, seeing the sights, attending readings, and listening to "my boy," as she called him, playing the piano for her.[20]

When Alcott came home in July 1866, she returned to a family as in need of money as ever. She set to work right away, writing tales for *The Chimney Corner*, *Youth's Companion*, the *Saturday Evening Gazette*, and any other magazine or paper that would take her wares. She managed to dash off twelve tales in three months. Meanwhile, Frank Leslie wanted her to write a story for him every month, for $50, which she agreed to, hoping she would be able to find the time between caring for her sick mother and helping with the sewing. By the end of the year, she was happy to have paid the bills, but new ones kept coming in.

Perhaps because of overwork, Louisa fell ill for the first half of 1867 and wasn't able to write again until June. When she was ready to resume her busy career, she discovered that a new market for children's literature had emerged. By that fall, about the same time Niles approached her about writing a girls' book, she was also asked to edit the children's magazine *Merry's Museum*, for $500 a year, an offer she could hardly refuse. While the book for girls wasn't going so well, she focused her energies on the magazine and used her new salary to get her own apartment in Boston. She was busy but happy, for she finally had the quiet and freedom to concentrate on her work. She was realizing her dual dreams of independence and supporting her family. At the end of the year, more work came in as the editor of the *Youth's Companion* asked her to contribute two stories a month. Thus, as 1868 dawned, Alcott counted her literary blessings and expected to make an unprecedented $1,000 in the coming year. When the white hyacinth bulb she had planted in her apartment bloomed, she took it as a sign that the new year would bring her the success and comfort she had long hoped for.

It didn't come right away, however. By March she was back in Concord. Her mother was becoming quite frail and needed Louisa as both nurse and housekeeper. Meanwhile, her father wanted her to get to work on the girls' story Thomas Niles wanted. As it turned out, Bronson had been negotiating with Niles for publication of a book of his own, and Niles had intimated that he would be more amenable to the idea if Bronson could encourage Louisa to write her book. Thus she returned to Concord and Orchard House and sat in her second-story room at the little desk Bronson had made for her. There she contemplated the new project while continuing to churn out the lucrative tales that provided for her mother's comfort, which was more important to her than anything else.

Alcott had delayed beginning the new book for so long because she didn't feel herself capable of writing it. "I could *not* write a girls' story, knowing little about any but my own sisters & always preferring boys," she wrote to a friend.[21] Finally she thought that perhaps her own childhood growing up with three sisters could provide enough material. She talked the idea over with her sisters and Marmee, as she referred to her mother. They were all in favor, so she decided to give it a try. She had already written a Christmas story for *Merry's Museum* about four sisters, whom she had given the nicknames of herself and her three sisters: Nan, Lu, Beth, and May. For the opening chapter of *Little Women*, she decided to use a scene from the story in which the girls give away their breakfast to a poor family.

Writing the novel felt like drudgery at first, and Alcott despaired of ever being able to complete it. She agreed with Niles that the first twelve chapters she sent to him were rather uninteresting—a surprising verdict considering that they contain some of the most memorable scenes of the book, such as Meg and Jo going to the ball and Jo's reaction to Amy burning her manuscript. Niles looked for a second opinion, and he soon wrote to Alcott that his niece had laughed until she cried over those same chapters. Alcott now began to look at the project in a new light, convinced that "lively, simple books are very much needed for girls." She wrote steadily for two months, descending into one of her vortexes, driven by Niles's assurance that "it will 'hit.'" In fact, so convinced was he that he encouraged her, against his firm's own self-interest, to sign a contract that would give her royalties on each copy sold instead of a higher advance without royalties. He also thought a sequel might be in order and suggested that she conclude the book by hinting that one could be written, if the public responded well.[22]

When the proofs came back in August, Alcott read them over with surprise. The book was better than she realized, not at all "sensational, but simple and true," and perhaps that would be its appeal.[23] By the time she was done with the first part of *Little Women*, she decided she would be happy to write more such stories, but she didn't expect they would pay as well as her blood-and-thunder tales.

When *Little Women or, Meg, Jo, Beth, and Amy* was published on September 30, 1868, it sold two thousand copies in two weeks. Niles's suggestion that Alcott conclude it with some hint to a sequel prompted her to insert these lines at the end: "So grouped the curtain falls upon Meg, Jo, Beth, and Amy. Whether it ever rises again, depends upon the reception given to the first act of the domestic drama, called 'Little Women.'" Readers got the hint and let her know they were clamoring for more. Their letters poured in with demands to know what would happen to the four March girls, or, most importantly, whom they would marry, "as if that was the only end and aim of a woman's life," the author grumbled.[24]

Niles promptly ordered a sequel, and after settling her mother with Anna and her family in Maplewood, north of Boston, for the winter, Louisa moved into a room in Boston and set to work again on November 1. Inspired by her success, she planned to write approximately a chapter a day and finish the whole thing within a month. She enjoyed launching the March girls into the future and allowing her imagination greater freedom, but she quickly faced a problem as the futures she envisioned did not match up with those her readers were expecting. On one particular she was adamant: "I *won't* marry Jo to Laurie to please any one." Yet she felt compelled by her publisher to marry off each of the girls, causing her to feel as if she had to finish the book "in a very stupid style."[25] She worked steadily all month, barely able to eat or sleep, stopping only for a run each day, her usual exercise.

The impression Alcott gives in her journals is that she wrote rapidly and with little or no revision. If not for the existence of two manuscript chapters of the novel, we might believe her. Although it was her practice to destroy the original drafts once the proofs were made, she saved these pages at her mother's request, apparently for sentimental reasons. Written on blue paper with dark ink that has faded to brown, the chapters cover Amy's trip to Europe and Laurie's ill-fated proposal to Jo. Both of them show how Alcott, more accustomed to writing sensational tales for adults, was learning to adjust her style and content for younger readers.

In "Our Foreign Correspondent," chapter seven of part two, Alcott made significant changes from the manuscript to the printed version, so many that there must have been an intervening draft. The original casts Amy's wealthy English suitor Fred Vaughn in a brief, minor role, leaving him behind in London. Amy never has a chance to make up her mind about whether she will marry him, if asked. Instead, an American she met on the ship to England, Captain Lennox, follows her to the continent and tags along on their travels, becoming immensely jealous at the male attention she receives. In her letter home, Amy claims she never had any interest in him and tries to convince her mother that she isn't a flirt toying with men's emotions. We can't know why Alcott trimmed down Amy's many admirers to one, Fred Vaughn, and made him a serious rival for Laurie's later affection, but it seems likely that she or her editor feared readers' censure of Amy's flirtatious behavior. Alcott also cut Amy's descriptions of her visit to a casino in Heidelberg where the women gambled as eagerly as the men.[26]

In the other surviving chapter, "Heartache," chapter eleven of part two, Alcott also felt the need to tone things down a bit, although here she made only a few minor changes, with one interesting exception. In the published version, after Jo finally convinced Laurie that she would never marry him, he got angry and turned away from her. Jo was frightened by his face and asked him where he was going. "To the devil!" was his answer, before he stormed off. But when she first wrote the scene, Alcott had a more dramatic exit in mind. Instead of simply turning away, Laurie "caught her in his arms and kissed her violently." Jo did not respond but was subsequently frightened by "his passion." Alcott later crossed out both references with a pencil. Apparently, she thought it prudent to remove Laurie's physical desire for Jo, although most of her young readers would still swoon over Laurie's intense love for Jo.[27]

On New Year's Day 1869, Alcott sent the second part of *Little Women* to Roberts Brothers. By then she was worn out with headaches and coughs that prevented her from working her usual fourteen hours a day. In April, when the book was published, Niles quickly asked her for another, but she was worried about going into her vortex again. This was the pattern of Alcott's writing life. She could rarely write at a leisurely pace. It was all or nothing. To write with such intensity again so soon would surely cause her to break down. With her family so utterly dependent on her, she couldn't afford to fall ill. To make things more complicated, her fame was growing and fans and reporters were beginning to show up unannounced at Orchard House, causing Louisa to flee out the back door whenever she could.[28] Meanwhile, she waited anxiously to hear from Niles about the second part of the book.

Sometime that spring, Louisa went into Boston to ask Niles directly how it was going. At the end of that day, upon returning to Concord, she regaled her parents and May—as well as her neighbors, the Hawthornes—with the story of what had happened during the visit to her publisher. Julian Hawthorne, son of the famous author who had died five years earlier, later recounted that Louisa held forth as Abba peeled apples for a pie, Bronson peeked in from his study, and May sat on the piano stool, occasionally twirling around to face the keyboard and provide a suitably dramatic chord. Louisa reported arriving at the Roberts Brothers offices to find boxes piled all around and deliverymen loading up wagons while clerks bustled in and out. Her first thought was that the publisher was going out of business and its wares were being carted off to pay its debts. When she finally pushed her way through to Niles's office, she found him bent over his ledgers and books in a state of near frenzy. He veritably leaped over his desk upon seeing her, in Julian Hawthorne's rather fantastical recounting, and grabbed her by the elbows. She was terrified and recoiled from his advance but was soon mollified by his excited cry that he had never experienced anything like it. "All else put aside— street blocked—country aroused—overwhelmed—paralyzed!" Just that day, Chicago bookstores had ordered two thousand copies, but that was nothing compared to the tens of thousands being shipped out. "Why, dearest girl, it's the triumph of the century!" he told her. He was just then writing her a check, in fact, and asked her to name her figure. She came home with $1,000, and for the first time in her life, she was able to invest it instead of paying off debtors.[29] That check was the beginning of the savings that would ensure her family would never want again. It was also the beginning of Louisa May Alcott's literary immortality.

# 2

# "WE REALLY LIVED MOST OF IT"

## Making Up *Little Women*

WHEN ASKED TO WRITE a novel for girls, Alcott had decided to base it on herself and her sisters, thinking, "Our queer plays and experiences may prove interesting." Upon completing the novel, she reflected, "we really lived most of it."[1] Having first discovered her "true style" while revising her letters for her book *Hospital Sketches*, she again wrote from her own life, creating the most lifelike book for children that had yet appeared. As a result, she became a celebrity not only as the author of *Little Women* but also as its protagonist, Jo March.

Early reviewers assumed that the novel drew on the author's life, and readers often wrote to Alcott as if she were Jo herself. The publisher also promoted the association of the Marches with the Alcotts, using one such fan letter as an advertisement. It begins, "Dear Jo, or Miss Alcott," and continues, "We were all so disappointed about your not marrying Laurie." Alcott even liked to call herself Jo and later added notations in her journal about which episodes had informed scenes in the book. For instance, next to a passage about living in a Boston apartment and writing to support herself, she wrote, "Jo in the garret."[2] In writing to fans, she referred to her family as "the Marches" and to each of her three sisters as the names of their fictional counterparts: Anna became Meg, Lizzie became Beth, and May became Amy. This connection between life and text would be carried through the many biographies and retellings of the Alcott story that began to appear immediately after her death.

It is safe to say that Alcott's family and her experiences inspired many of the characters and episodes in *Little Women*, especially in part one. However, the full story of their lives could not be represented in a book for young people, containing as it did extreme poverty, religious radicalism, marital strife, suicidal thoughts, and possible mental illness. Louisa had a much rougher time of it than Jo ever did. Still, the great charm of the book remains its realism, which is based on the pranks, dreams, and growing pains of four very real girls. As Alcott says in *Little Women* of even Beth, the most seemingly idealized of the novel's characters, she was "not an angel, but a very human little girl."[3]

PROBABLY THE MOST surprising fact about the Alcotts, contrary to the cozy ideal of home and family life immortalized in *Little Women*, is that the family moved incessantly—over thirty times before Louisa was in her midtwenties. Not only that, but the Alcotts were many times temporarily separated and occasionally in danger of being broken up altogether, due to her father's instability. In fact, the most conspicuously absent character in the book—Mr. March—is more or less based on the most formative person, for good and ill, in Louisa's life: her father.

Many have speculated about why Louisa chose to practically cut her father out of *Little Women*, sending him off to war in the first part and leaving him in the background in the second. But it is no wonder, considering how frequently Bronson was absent from the family in real life. When Louisa was just a baby, Bronson left a pregnant Abigail alone with two small children in Germantown, Pennsylvania, for eighteen months so that he could have his own

Bronson Alcott was largely excluded from *Little Women*. (Used by permission of Louisa May Alcott's Orchard House)

room near the library in Philadelphia where he studied literature and philosophy, making up for the substandard education he had received as the son of a poor farmer. He visited his family on weekends, but Abigail was depressed and endured her first of many miscarriages alone.[4]

In 1842, when Louisa was nine years old, Bronson's close friend Ralph Waldo Emerson wrote of him, "He is quite ready at any moment to abandon his present residence & employment, his country, nay, his wife & children, on very short notice, to put any new dream into practice which has bubbled up in the effervescence of discourse."[5] By then Bronson had already left on numerous travels, as he would many times more. Like his favorite character, Christian from John Bunyan's *Pilgrim's Progress*, he believed that spiritual awakening was more likely to be found away from home and family. And, like Christian, he hit the road in search of it.

Bronson's primary aim was to live a spotless spiritual life. He strove for serenity, goodness, and selflessness. He was not content to wait for Heaven to discover the pure source of divinity. He wanted the heavenly estate revealed here on Earth, and he was going to help make that happen through teaching, farming, or simply leading what he considered an exemplary life. A letter he wrote to his children in 1841 exhorted them to take Jesus Christ as their model, as he did: "He did not give himself to the indulgence of appetites or passions, but governed himself in all things. He ruled his own spirit: he obeyed his Conscience."[6] Bronson set the bar high for his daughters, but it was not, in his eyes, unreachable. Like his transcendentalist friends, he did not think of Jesus as exceptional. He believed that divinity was located in each of us and that it was our duty to resist any conditions that hindered our ability to discover and fully express it.

Adhering to no church's doctrine, Bronson was fanatical about following his own conscience, which prohibited the earning of filthy lucre and the amassing of goods for his own comfort or pleasure. He found some like-minded friends but very few who were as willing as he was to abandon all pursuit of material gain. His friend Henry David Thoreau perhaps best approximates his anti-materialist fervor, yet while Thoreau could leave civilization behind and create his own Eden on Walden Pond, Bronson had to figure out how to live an unencumbered existence with a wife and four daughters in tow. His friend and neighbor Ralph Waldo Emerson admired his ideas but had no intention of giving up his own family and comforts. Exasperated with Bronson's impractical idealism at times, Emerson nonetheless was a frequent benefactor of the Alcotts, surreptitiously slipping money under a book or behind a cushion, lest Abigail's pride be touched. He also helped them purchase their first stable home, Hillside, near him in Concord.

Bronson was happy to accept such charity, or reasonable payment for his lectures, teaching, or writing. The last two he failed at, however, at least in the sense that they earned him no money. The lectures brought in some income sporadically over the years, but he could never hang on to what he earned. Before he married, Bronson famously worked on and off as a peddler selling his wares all over the South, only to give up his business after five years, $600 in debt. Much later in life, after a long lecture tour out West essentially peddling his ideas, he came home to his wife and daughters with little more than the clothes on his back. One family story provides a glimpse of where the money went when it did come: Abigail once gave Bronson $10 to buy her a shawl for the winter while he was in town. He came back instead with a much-coveted book he had seen in a shop window, having entirely forgotten the shawl.[7]

Abigail had been at first drawn to Bronson's ideals, and she would continue to admire them throughout their forty-seven-year marriage. She was herself an ardent abolitionist and an advocate of all-around reform. She came from an elite Boston family, but she broke from their politics, like her brother to whom she was very close. Samuel Joseph May was a leading reformer, an early supporter of women's rights, and founder, with William Lloyd Garrison, of the New England Anti-Slavery Society. He was a minister who was called Mr. May, making him, quite possibly, another influence on Louisa's creation of Mr. March. The family name of the Marches clearly comes from the Mays.[8]

Yet Abigail also suffered under the weight of her husband's convictions, particularly as the family grew. Biographers and scholars of the transcendentalist circle have painted her as prone to harsh words and rancorous outbursts. One can hardly blame her. In one of *Little Women*'s most revealing passages, Marmee explains to Jo her difficulties in controlling her own anger. She "found it easy to be good" when she first married. "But by and by, when I had four little daughters round me, and we were poor, then the old trouble began again; for I am not patient by nature, and it tried me very much to see my children wanting anything."[9] In those few words are packed the years of extreme poverty the Alcotts endured and the anger Abigail felt about it.

Bronson has been called many unflattering things over the years, as the causes of the family's poverty became known. Some critics have chosen to overlook his negligence toward his family in a material sense, stressing the spiritual and intellectual gifts he bestowed on them. But for most of us, it is hard to overlook his refusal to do anything but the few types of work he considered honorable, at which he largely failed, even to support his family. He had no qualms about borrowing from others (usually Abigail's family members) or accruing insurmountable debts. The Alcotts were at times in so deep over their heads that they simply had to move away to escape their creditors. A common saying of Bronson's was "the Lord will provide." If He did not, then Bronson seemed, in Abigail's opinion, quite willing to starve. She once wrote to her brother, "No one will employ him in his way [as a teacher]; he cannot work in theirs, if he thereby involve his conscience. He is so resolved in this matter that I believe he will starve and freeze before he will sacrifice principle to comfort. In this, I and my children are necessarily implicated."[10] What could possibly make a man so obstinate that he was willing to allow his own family to starve? This is not a simple question to answer.

Despite later assessments by those who have found Bronson's character wanting, accounts from those who knew the family indicate that he was much beloved within and outside of his family. He famously possessed a guileless, childlike manner and "air of serene repose" that endeared him to many. His family shared his view that their era's "lack of reverence for goodness and wisdom" (Abigail's phrase) was primarily to blame for Bronson's inability to earn a living. Although Abigail grew frustrated with him at times (she once burst out, "I do wish people who carry their heads in the clouds would occasionally take their bodies with them"), she and her daughters stood by Bronson when the world turned against him.[11] He became an object of ridicule in 1837 after the publication of *Conversations with Children on the Gospels*, which was roundly criticized in the press as sanctimonious, blasphemous, even dangerous. Parents promptly removed their children from his Temple School in Boston, and his reputation was so tarnished that he could not simply move and open another.

In *Little Women*, there is a sense of an earlier golden age that has ended because Mr. March gave away his fortune to others needier than himself. In real life, it was less a fall from prosperity than a fall from grace. Bronson's supreme belief in himself and his views made others sneer at his self-righteousness. The Alcotts left Boston in 1839, broken in spirit and $5,000 in debt. The always supportive Emerson drew them to Concord, where they would live on and off for nearly the rest of their lives.

Bronson was known by all to be eccentric, another reason Louisa probably left him in the background of her novel, not wanting to expose him to further ridicule. But even more than simply eccentric, I think it fair to consider Bronson a kind of religious fanatic, forbidding his family to engage in many practices he viewed as sinful. While he was quite liberal in his encouragement of his daughters' talents and energies, he restricted them in other ways. For much of Louisa's childhood, she was improperly clothed and subsisted on little more than bread and water, making her "skinny, undernourished, and usually hungry," according to one of her biographers. The family's poverty was only partially to blame. Bronson would abide no meat at the table, or any other animal products: milk, butter, cheese, or eggs. Fruits and vegetables, preferably those that grew aboveground, were allowed when nature provided them. Bronson's reverence for animals also meant that no wool could be stolen from the sheep, and his abhorrence of slavery led him to forbid cotton. Linen was the only material fit for their backs, even during the cold Massachusetts winters. Similarly, "foreign luxuries," such as sugar, molasses, rice, tea, and coffee were also banished, recalled one friend of the family. These products not only polluted the body but corrupted the soul.[12]

Bronson's strict views reached their height in 1843 at Fruitlands, the utopian community he founded in Harvard, Massachusetts, with his English friend Charles Lane. Abigail watched as Bronson became ever stricter in his beliefs and even seriously considered breaking up the family in favor of communal living after the fashion of the Shakers, some of whom lived nearby. After seven months at Fruitlands, it became clear that the community was incapable of surviving through the winter. Abigail was determined to take her children away to prevent their being starved or frozen to death. Little Louisa, only eleven years old, wrote in her journal in December that the family had had a tearful talk. Afterward, "Anna and I cried in bed, and I prayed God to keep us all together."[13]

Finally, once all of the other Fruitlanders had left, Bronson lay down in his bed and turned his head toward the wall, refusing to eat and waiting simply to die. He believed, no doubt, that God had not deemed his enterprise worth providing for. This went on for days while Abigail and the girls tried to coax him back to life. Louisa describes the event at length in her later fictional account of the Fruitlands experiment, "Transcendental Wild Oats," but she does not describe how she and the rest of her family must have felt watching the captain of their ship abandon his post and all will to live. Fortunately, Abigail had been scouting out an alternative abode for herself and the girls. She did not want to leave her husband behind to die, though, so she mustered all of her strength and finally convinced him to eat and drink again. She got him and her four girls into a sled and brought them to a home in nearby Still River, where they regrouped and recommitted themselves to each other. The lesson that Fruitlands taught them was that the family unit was sacred and must stay together, no matter what, a lesson that permeates *Little Women*.

After the Fruitlands debacle (and possibly before), Bronson had periods of mental instability. His biographer John Matteson avoids using the word *insanity*, which earlier biographers have used, and instead settles on *manic depression*, which included, at various times, disturbing visions, nightmares, and delusions of being Christlike, a martyr, or "not merely God but, indeed, 'greater than God.'" These mental states were particularly acute during the family's time at Still River. But as he grew older, Bronson became a gentler, less fanatical father who did not worry his family as much. (However, his brother's suicide in 1852, which is barely mentioned in surviving documents, must have increased their concern of hereditary mental illness.) Bronson also gradually relaxed his strict beliefs, allowing the girls to wear warmer clothing and later to eat dairy and meat. Yet he never could contribute much materially to the family's welfare, believing simply that his gifts were not valued by his contemporaries and thus were not remunerable. He appears never to have considered becoming other than he was. His family would always think of him as the philosopher who "live[d] in the clouds" while they of the "earthly mould" took care of life's practical matters.[14] Over time, he became a kind of lovable misfit, out of place in the nineteenth century and therefore a man to be pityingly adored more than revered. Louisa called him Plato and joked in her letters about his utter lack of pragmatism, even telling the story of the forgotten shawl with a smile rather than bitterness.

Nonetheless, Louisa was deeply marked by these early experiences of poverty, family instability, and worry for her father's sanity. She watched her mother become the family's main support by taking in boarders, sewing, and other manual labor, and, as a result, losing her physical health and vigor. Louisa once said, in her father's presence, "It requires three women to take care of a philosopher, and when the philosopher is old the three women are pretty well used up." She understood her mother's failed hopes of an intellectual companionship with her father as well as her desperate need to idealize him while repressing her anger about his inability to provide for his family. Most of all, Abigail resented Bronson's inability to see her sacrifices, a failing she understood as not merely peculiar to him. Abigail possessed a vivid consciousness of the inequality of the sexes and the desire to redress women's wrongs, which she passed on to Louisa. During the Fruitlands episode, Abigail wrote in her journal, "A woman may perform the most disinterested duties. She may 'die daily' in the cause of truth and righteousness. She lives neglected, dies forgotten. But a man who never performed in his whole life one self-denying act, but who has accidental gifts of genius, is celebrated by his contemporaries, while his name and works live on, from age to age. He is crowned with laurel, while scarce a 'stone may tell where she lies.'" It is no wonder that as Louisa grew into womanhood, she had no inclination to marry. She learned early that "to be a woman in the world, particularly a married woman, was to be subservient and neglected."[15] Louisa also sought to redress the wrong of Abigail's life, making it her mission to honor her mother's legacy. If Mr. March is largely absent in *Little Women*, Marmee permeates every page.

Louisa also called her mother Marmee, which they likely pronounced "Mawmmy" or "Mommy," in the New England accent. Marmee is in many ways an idealized version of Abigail May Alcott, a reflection of her spirit without her sharp edges. Although Marmee admits to being "angry nearly every day of [her] life," she does not possess the bitterness that the real Abigail found it difficult to conceal.[16] Abigail's journals became an outlet for her true feelings, so much so that she requested they be burned upon her death. Louisa carried out her wishes to some extent, and Bronson heavily edited

Marmee is an idealized portrait of Louisa's mother, Abigail May Alcott. (Used by permission of Louisa May Alcott's Orchard House).

and excised them, destroying many, finding it painful to read how unhappy she had been, the extent of which he apparently had not realized.

If Abigail was angrier than the Marmee of *Little Women*, she did possess the same fierce belief in her girls, advising them, in biographer Eve LaPlante's summation, *"A woman can accomplish as much as a man,* . . . Educate yourself up to your senses. Be something in yourself. Let the world know you are alive. Push boldly off. Wait for no man." Abba, as she was called, did not pressure her girls to marry and regretted how much "girls are taught to *seem*, to appear—not to be and *do*."[17] She made sure her girls understood that their true worth lay in their minds and characters and not in their looks. She also wanted them to be able to support themselves. When Jo tells Professor Bhaer that she intends to work when they marry, she does not simply speak on principle but out of pragmatism. Depending on a husband for one's bread, Louisa learned from her mother, was foolish.

Unable to receive sufficient emotional and material support from her husband, Abigail instead looked to her daughters. None repaid her as well as Louisa, who was closest to her in looks and temperament. They shared, in LaPlante's words, a "marriage-like bond," an intimacy that exceeded all others. It is little wonder that as Louisa grew up she determined to provide for her mother. When she was only ten, her mother wrote to her, "In my imagination I have thought you might be such an industrious good daughter and that I might be a sick but loving mother, looking to my daughter's labors for my daily bread." Louisa would soon take up that responsibility in earnest, determining that one day she would provide for her a comfortable home without any debts hanging over her head. This aspect of Louisa's life, echoed in her father's characterization of her as "Duty's faithful child," would come to define Louisa in the popular imagination.[18] For many years after her death, as a number of (especially juvenile) biographies appeared, the perception of the self-sacrificial Louisa who rose through hardship and poverty to support her family as a famous author prevailed. Yet the real Louisa was much more complex, more so than could ever be contained in her most famous portrait of herself as Jo March.

JUST AS JO, short for Josephine, possesses a masculine nickname, so did Louisa, who was known as Lou, Lu, or Louie in the family. Her relatives considered her "an odd, grahamish, transcendental, half educated tom boy" who wouldn't amount to much, which sounds a lot like Jo in some respects. In her portrayal of Jo, Louisa was careful to avoid the "grahamish" (referring to the vegetarian beliefs of Sylvester Graham, inventor of the Graham cracker) and "transcendental" philosophical parts, both of which she inherited from her father. Like Jo, however, she was a bit of a misfit, much louder and more rambunctious than her sisters. She felt like the son or brother of the family. Many of the friends and relatives who wrote reminiscences of the Alcotts recall how much she acted like and wanted to be a boy. As one friend of Lizzie's later recalled, she was always scandalizing people with "her tomboyish, natural, and independent ways."[19]

Louisa also found it difficult to control her temper, as Jo does. A close childhood friend explained that she was subject to moods that could make her the most delightful companion when she was jolly, "but, if the opposite, let her best friend beware." She was known once to have hung a chair outside her window as a punishment for the chair being in her way when she was cleaning.[20] Louisa also had a difficult time containing her desires; she would never meet her father's ideal of Christ-like self-denial. She longed for food she was not allowed to eat, making her feel lustful and sinful, as if her character were to blame rather than her grumbling stomach. She wanted nice clothes and books to read, the same things all of the March girls yearn for. In short, she wanted no longer to be poor, a very natural desire that she was taught to see as pernicious. In life, Louisa learned to channel her selfish desires into selfless ones—a main theme in *Little Women* for all of the girls, but especially for Meg and the most covetous of the March girls, Amy. Patience and contentment were the most difficult lessons for Louisa to learn as a child. She was convinced that she was not "good," as her older sister, Anna, was, a perception her father reinforced in myriad ways, not least by equating his own and Anna's fairer coloring with angelic serenity and Abigail and Louisa's dark hair and complexions with passionate, disturbed minds.

Louisa found an outlet for her strong emotions, as she has Jo do, in performing theatricals and writing sensational stories. The pent-up anger, jealousy, and other errant emotions she experienced were channeled into stories she and Anna could act out for family and friends in a suitable environment: their home. Her mother also encouraged her journal writing as a way to examine herself and learn to control her emotions. It is not surprising that Louisa destroyed most of her journals from the 1840s and '50s, the most difficult years for the family and for Louisa herself as she grew from a willful child into an anxious young woman.

There were joyful times too, of course, particularly from 1845 to 1848 when Louisa, ages twelve to fifteen, lived in Concord at the home they called Hillside. (Nathaniel Hawthorne and his family would later live there and call it Wayside.) Louisa and Anna had, for the first time, rooms of their own. Louisa reveled in the freedom to read and write alone in her room or run in the woods behind the house. She loved to run so much that she imagined herself to have been a deer or horse in a former life. "No boy could be my friend till I had beaten him in a race," she explained, "and no girl if she refused to climb trees, leap fences and be a tomboy." She was the fastest runner around, her friend Clara Gowing recalled, and impressed everyone by running and climbing just like a boy. In *Little Women*, Jo enjoys running with Laurie but is scolded by Meg for it.[21]

While living at Hillside, the Alcott girls also made a "post office" out of a hollow tree stump and exchanged letters with Clara, as the March sisters do with Laurie. They also played Pilgrim's Progress and spent much of the day outdoors playing with friends, as the March girls do in the "Camp Laurence" chapter of *Little Women*. Those years were the happiest of her life, Louisa later reflected, so it is not surprising that she looked back to them for many of the episodes in the first part of *Little Women*. In fact, at the beginning of the novel, Jo is the age (fifteen) that Louisa was when they had to move away from Concord and Hillside.[22] By placing her story there, she imagined what it would have been like had they been able to stay.

While bucolic Concord and the frolics they enjoyed there made it into *Little Women*, Alcott whitewashed her family's poverty and the troubles they endured because of it. She later reflected that those were the days when her cares began and her "happy childhood ended." In the novel's opening, we hear the girls complaining about their lack of money: "'Christmas won't be Christmas without any presents,' grumbled Jo, lying on the rug." At least one Alcott Christmas, during the Civil War, was celebrated without any presents. We also see the March sisters give away their Christmas breakfast to the impoverished Hummels, a scene taken from life. Alcott described the same scene in a "true story" she wrote just before starting *Little Women*, and Abigail was known to give away what little they had to others who were suffering more.[23]

What Alcott didn't want to show, however, was how much her family depended on charity themselves. In *Little Women*, the Marches' wealthy neighbor, Mr. Laurence, bestows upon the girls a Christmas feast of cake, ice cream, and candy after he sees them giving away their modest breakfast, and he later gives Beth a piano. Accepting treats and the occasional luxury you can't afford is much less humiliating than being the recipient of necessities you are too poor to provide for yourself. In reality, friends and relatives gave the

Alcotts clothing, food, money, and rent-free accommodations and sometimes took in one of the girls. In 1847, for instance, fourteen-year-old Louisa spent part of the summer with friends near Boston, sixteen-year-old Anna spent the fall teaching in Walpole, New Hampshire, while living there with relatives, and twelve-year-old Lizzie was sent to stay with family in Boston during the winter.[24] The cozy nuclear family of the Marches (nearly) all under one roof was rarely a reality for the Alcotts. More typical were the separations we see in part two of *Little Women*, as the girls grow up. Jo goes to New York because she wants to spread her wings, but in real life, necessity often drove the girls away from home. Anna and Louisa spent much of their adolescence and twenties working in other towns, supporting themselves and sending money home when they could. Once, in the summer of 1848, even Abigail left home. Desperate to support her family, she took a job as the matron at a water cure spa in Maine for three months.

Even when the Alcotts were all together, they often weren't the only ones there. Sometimes one or more of Bronson's friends lived with them, as did boarders, many of them children who were being taught by Bronson, Anna, or Louisa and cared for by Abigail. For two years while they were at Hillside, Abigail cared for a mentally disabled child who boarded with them. Often they also took in strangers who needed help, with no concern for monetary return, including runaway slaves, one of whom Louisa recalled teaching to write. Louisa later wrote that they provided "shelter for lost girls, abused wives, friendless children, and weak or wicked men."[25]

When it became clear they could no longer support themselves in Concord, the Alcotts made the difficult decision to move to Boston. Hillside, which they had bought with Abigail's inheritance from her father, required too much upkeep, whereas in Boston they could rent rooms while Louisa and Anna looked for employment as teachers and Abigail worked as a "missionary to the poor." After the difficult family meeting that led to this decision, Louisa ran over the hill behind the house "for 'a good think'" and determined, "I *will* do something by-and-by. Don't care what, teach, sew, act, write, anything to help the family; and I'll be rich and famous and happy before

I die, see if I won't."[26] She would go on to do all of that and more in an effort to help support her family.

While the Alcotts lived in Boston, Abigail was one of the country's first professional social workers as well as director of an employment agency, jobs that barely earned enough for a small apartment without indoor plumbing in the city slums. They had to move so frequently in search of tolerable accommodations, and in and out of temporary homes loaned by absent relatives, that the girls didn't even bother to unpack their trunks.[27] The mixed feelings of resentment and gratitude that Louisa felt toward her mother's wealthy kin, on whom they were often dependent, are reflected in her portraits in *Little Women* of Aunt March and Mr. Laurence: the former provides her charity grudgingly, the latter is happy to help when he can without wounding the Marches' pride.

The Alcotts were not together in Boston for long before Bronson left to spend the summer with friends in Concord. Anna left to work as a nursery girl and then as a governess before moving to Syracuse, New York, to teach in a mental institution. She would live in Syracuse with Abigail's brother and his family for many years with only occasional visits to her own family. Louisa missed Anna terribly. She kept house and tried various teaching schemes while Lizzie and May went to school, something the older girls had not been able to do, except for one year while they lived in Concord.[28]

While trying to teach and to publish her stories and poems, Louisa once took a job as a live-in servant for a family she thought respectable. The experiment proved disastrous. She was made to do the most demeaning, backbreaking work in addition to enduring her male employer's advances. When she finally quit, she was paid a mere $4 for seven weeks of work. These degrading experiences would make their way into Louisa's adult novel *Work*, written earlier but published after the success of *Little Women*. In many ways, *Work* reflects Louisa's difficulties as a wage earner more accurately than *Little Women*, in which the worst Jo endures is Aunt March's crankiness. Yet Jo perfectly channels Louisa when she realizes "that money conferred power," and she resolves to have it "not for herself alone, but for those whom she loved more than self."[29]

At about this time, Louisa was even willing to sell her thick, dark hair, which hung down almost to the ground. When an onerous debt weighed upon her family, as she later told a friend, "I went to a barber, let down my hair, and asked him how much money he would give me for it. When he told me the sum, it seemed so large to me that I then and there determined I would part with my most precious possession if during the next week the clouds did not lift." Fortunately, a friend came to the family's aid and Louisa's hair was spared, but she would lose it during the war when she fell ill with typhoid fever after nursing in Washington, D.C. Louisa was terribly sad "about losing my one beauty."[30] All of this would make it into *Little Women*, where Jo sells her hair for $25 when they learn that Mr. March is ill and Marmee must make the journey to Washington to nurse him. And, of course, it was Louisa, not her father, who went to war and had to be brought home after falling seriously ill.

Particularly reflective of Louisa's experiences during these years are Jo's attempts to find her path to money and power through writing. Louisa said nothing to her family about her first publication, "The Rival Painters," in 1852, but simply read it aloud to them. Only when they praised the author did she reveal that it was herself, just as Jo does in *Little Women*. Under Louisa's direction, the Alcott girls also carried on a family newspaper irregularly from 1849 to 1851, whenever they could all be together to work on an issue. It was called at first *The Olive Leaf*, then *The Portfolio*, and then *The Pickwick* and was full of the stories and advertisements of which there is a sample in the March girls' *Pickwick Portfolio*. Not long after, when the family lived in Pinckney Street, in Boston, twenty-year-old Louisa wore a special cap and cloak her mother had made for her and went up into the garret to write. "I am in the garret with my papers round me," Louisa wrote (sounding a lot like Jo), "and a pile of apples to eat while I write my journal, plan stories, and enjoy the patter of rain on the roof, in peace and quiet."[31] Alcott also gave Jo her experiences of writing her first novel, *Moods*—going deeply into her vortex, having to cut the manuscript down to fit the publisher's specifications, and fretting over the conflicting reviews she received. And, as with Jo, sensation stories became her primary source of income.

Louisa May Alcott in her twenties, as she struggled to begin her literary career and help support her family. (Used by permission of Louisa May Alcott's Orchard House)

While Louisa's literary career developed, the family was again on the move. In 1855 the Alcotts were offered a home by Abba's brother-in-law in Walpole, New Hampshire. Louisa lived with her family there for a while before returning to Boston to work. It was after Louisa left that the two youngest daughters, Lizzie and May, contracted scarlet fever from a poor immigrant family, the Halls, whom their mother was helping to care for. (The Halls would become the Hummels in *Little Women*.) May got well quickly, but Lizzie, like Beth, almost died and never fully recovered.

Lizzie is a shadowy figure in her family's private writings, much as Beth is in the novel. She refused to read her journals aloud to the family as the other sisters did, an indication of shyness but also of unwillingness to reveal her deepest self, even to those closest to her. She also declined to perform in the girls' homegrown theatricals, limiting herself to making props and stage scenery. She loved to play the piano but had none of the artistic ambitions of her sisters. Bronson called her his "Little Tranquility." In fact, she among the four sisters seemed to have most inherited his serene disposition.

She also may have inherited the depression that hid behind it. Five years before, Abigail had written to Bronson, then away in Cincinnati, that Lizzie seemed to suffer from "some collapse of the brain," which could be her way of describing depression. "At times she seems almost immoveable—almost senseless. . . . There is a great struggle going on in her mind about something," Abigail wrote. Similarly, in *Little Women*, Marmee is worried about Beth's "spirits" as much as she is about her health. In her journals, Louisa once mentioned Lizzie having "a little romance" (perhaps echoed in Jo's suspicion that Beth is in love with Laurie), but otherwise her references to Lizzie are unremarkable: glimpses of her going to school, teaching a little, and being the "the home bird" and the "little Cinderella" of the house.[32]

After she became ill, however, Lizzie became an object of much concern. Louisa wrote in June 1857 that she feared Lizzie would "slip away; for she never seemed to care much for this world beyond home." By October, Lizzie was little more than "a shadow." During her time in Walpole, the ill Lizzie also received a piano from a wealthy bene-

The only known portrait of Lizzie Alcott, immortalized as Beth in *Little Women*. (Used by permission of Louisa May Alcott's Orchard House)

factor, as Beth does from Mr. Laurence in *Little Women*, and Abigail took her to the seaside in hopes of restoring her health. When she didn't improve, they finally took her to Boston to consult a doctor. The family greatly distrusted the medical establishment, and with good reason. Physicians had a poor record of accurately diagnosing and treating disease. The Alcotts put their faith in an alternative medicine then quite popular: homeopathy, based on the idea that "like cures like" or that very small doses of substances producing the same symptoms already suffered can combat a disease. Lizzie may have been given belladonna in the early stages of her illness, as Beth is in *Little Women*, since it was considered an effective homeopathic treatment for scarlet fever.[33]

It is not clear what Lizzie's long-term malady was. Alcott biographers have conjectured that it was rheumatic fever, which can follow scarlet fever and lead to heart failure, or psychological causes, including that she may have been starving herself. What is clear is that she was slowly wasting away, hence one doctor's diagnosis of consumption, or tuberculosis. Another doctor diagnosed "atrophy or consumption of the nervous system with the great development of hysteria," nineteenth-century lingo for what we would call chronic depression and/or anxiety. We know that she suffered from "weight loss, weakness, stomach pains, nausea, vomiting, sweating, hair loss, depression, irritability, drowsiness, and restlessness." Depression seems to have made her resign herself to, or even wish for, death. She was convinced, she told her mother, that she could "best be spared of the four."[34]

Louisa nursed her sister in her final months and weeks. She watched as Lizzie sewed little presents to drop out of the window to passing schoolchildren until, like Beth, she could no longer hold her needle. On March 14, 1858, Lizzie drew her last breath. Afterward, Abigail and Louisa dressed Lizzie's body, "a form chiseled in Bone, held by a mere integument of skin, no flesh perceptible," Abigail wrote in a letter to her brother. Although only twenty-three, she looked as if she were forty, Louisa thought. Moments after her death, they also witnessed a mist rise from her, which the doctor told them was but the visible manifestation of her life leaving her body. Louisa chose not to include this remarkable event in *Little Women*, nor did she describe the extent of Lizzie's wasting away, choosing to omit as well that she had lost all of her hair. Beth dies peacefully, while poor Lizzie endured intolerable pain in the end. Having long refused medicine, she nonetheless cried out for something to relieve her pain. A poem Bronson wrote after her death begins, "'Ether,' she begged, 'O Father give['],'" and continues, "We had it not," indicating how helpless her family felt in the face of her painful death.[35]

After Lizzie's death, Louisa suffered a serious emotional crisis that was compounded by her sister Anna's engagement to be married. In the novel, Meg marries many years before Beth dies. In real life, however, Anna became engaged only a few months after Lizzie's death, sending Louisa into a tailspin. She fled Concord, where the Alcotts had recently purchased Orchard House, and tried unsuccessfully to find work in Boston. Without the mooring of her family, which seemed to have broken apart, Louisa found herself one day contemplating jumping into the swirling waters of the Charles River. She told her family, "My courage most gave out, for every one was so busy, & cared so little whether I got work or jumped into the river that I thought seriously of doing the latter."[36] She would later describe the episode in her adult novel *Work*, but the depth of her despair was not fit for a novel for young people.

In May 1860, after a two-year engagement, Anna ("Nan") married John Pratt, who had lived as a child at Brook Farm, a far more successful utopian community than Fruitlands was. (Thus he becomes John Brooke in *Little Women*.) However, while Anna's fictional counterpart, Meg, meets John Brooke at the age of seventeen and marries him at twenty, Anna was twenty-nine on her wedding day, an event that bore many similarities to the one described in the novel. Louisa had been very close to Nan and must have thought they were both destined to stay unmarried and grow old together.

Anna had dreamed of being an actress, just as Louisa had dreamed of becoming a famous author and May a famous artist. No hint of Anna's ambition made it into *Little Women*, perhaps because of the great stigma attached to acting for women. Louisa explored the theme in another precursor to *Little Women*, the story "The Sisters' Trial," in

Anna "Nan" Alcott, who became Meg in *Little Women*, dreamed of becoming an actress. (Used by permission of Louisa May Alcott's Orchard House)

which four orphaned sisters have to find work to support themselves. One, Nora, lives by her pen; Ella becomes a governess; Amy will be a paid companion on a tour of Europe, where she hopes to develop her skill as an artist; and Agnes decides to try her luck on the stage. After one year, all of the girls but Agnes have prospered. Nora and Ella are to marry, Amy is to be an artist, and Agnes has worked hard only to discover that the man she loves has spurned her because she makes her living on the stage. She therefore leaves acting behind and "endeavor[s] to become what *he* would have me: not an actress, but a simple woman, trying to play well her part in life's great drama."[37] Interestingly, Anna had met John Pratt while performing together in the Concord theatricals. But participating in community theater for fun or charity was a far cry from professional acting, which required an exposure both physical and emotional that was deemed to compromise a woman's morals and make her unfit for private domestic life. In her portrait of Anna, Louisa therefore chose to limit Meg's interest in the theater and make her "castle in the air" about having a "lovely house, full of all sorts of luxurious things."[38] Louisa also emphasized Anna's traditionally feminine qualities of docility and domesticity and made Meg a conventional beauty. Louisa felt she had to make at least one of the March sisters pretty.

Louisa gradually accepted her older sister's choice to marry, but as Anna left the family, the primary responsibility to maintain those left behind fell to Louisa. After a short period of freedom in Boston, Louisa had in 1859 returned to Concord and Orchard House, which she called "Apple Slump" because the floors sloped. It would be the Alcott family home for the next eighteen years. It was where Anna would marry, the family would live through the war, Louisa would write *Little Women*, and the youngest daughter, May, would become an artist. While Louisa struggled to establish her literary career, the money she earned from her sensation stories went to buy household necessities, comforts for her mother, and art lessons and supplies for May.

May was named Abigail May Alcott, after her mother. Her family called her Abby, although starting in her adolescence she asked

Orchard House, the home in Concord, Massachusetts, where Louisa wrote *Little Women*, with the Alcott family in the foreground. (Used by permission of Louisa May Alcott's Orchard House)

them to call her May. Eight years younger than Louisa, she was raised by her older sisters as well as her parents. In personality, May was much like Amy in *Little Women*: a social butterfly with many "fashionable friends," a girl who yearned for beautiful things and was the pet of the family. She could be, according to one family friend, "childishly tyrannical." She had a happier childhood than Louisa simply by virtue of having missed the Temple School scandal and having been only three years old during the Fruitlands debacle. May's greatest dream was to be rich and go to Europe to study art and become a famous artist. As a teenager she was often exempted from housework and allowed to go to school. When in 1864 a family friend offered to pay May's way in art school, Louisa felt much as Jo does when Amy is chosen to go to Europe instead of her. Louisa was resigned in her jealousy, however, convincing herself that it was better to make her own way than have others readily help her, as May did. Years later, she wrote of May, "She always had the cream of things."[39] These comments make it easy to suspect that Louisa's negative portrayal of Amy was motivated by her jealousy of May.

May was not entirely pleased with her sister's portrait of her in *Little Women*, writing to their close friend Alfred Whitman, "Did you recognize . . . that horrid stupid Amy as something like me even to putting a cloths pin on her nose?" Yet, she more or less admitted to

Louisa's portrait of Amy in *Little Women* did not sit well with her youngest sister, May. (Used by permission of Louisa May Alcott's Orchard House)

being like Amy: "so superficial & career[ing] about with such noo-
dles as Frank Wheeler." She further reflects, "I used to be so ambitious, & think wealth brought everything," but she had learned how
to find happiness in hard work and in her pursuit of a career in art.⁴⁰
In fact, May would do the illustrations for the first part of *Little
Women*, itself a kind of sanction of her sister's novel, and the two sisters became quite close after Nan married, living together for periods
in Boston while Louisa wrote and May painted.

Louisa couldn't help noticing how much more the amiable May
was liked by family members and friends than her blunt self, and her
portrait of Amy and Jo's visits to neighbors in part two of the novel
pokes perhaps more fun at herself than at May. She also had Amy go
to Europe, whereas it was Louisa who was able to travel abroad and
witness the scenes that would form the backdrop of Amy's adventures in *Little Women*. (After its publication, May would get to go to
Europe with Louisa, thanks to the novel's royalties.) At the time of
the novel's creation, May had, like Louisa, chosen art over a family
of her own. Ten years later, however, May had established herself as
a successful artist in London and Paris and decided, at age thirty-
seven, to marry. The following year, after the birth of her daughter,
she died suddenly, cutting short the experiment in love and art that
Louisa had watched closely. The little girl, Lulu, named after her
aunt, was sent to America to be raised by her famous relative.

Louisa's first trip to Europe in 1865 contributed more than the
background to Amy's tour. It was also there that Louisa met the
Polish Ladislas Wisniewski, whom she later claimed was her model
for Laurie. In *Little Women*, Theodore Laurence's Europeanness, his
poor health, his lack of parents, and his talent as a pianist all come
from Ladislas. The impossibility of a romance between Louisa and
the younger Pole, whom she called Laddie, also comes through in the
way Jo rejects Laurie, seeing him more as a brother than as a lover.

Ladislas was not the only model for Laurie, however. Three
other young men also laid claim to that title. The most prominent
was Julian Hawthorne, son of the novelist, who lived next door to
Orchard House (at Wayside, formerly Hillside) and had a prodigious
crush on May. Yet Louisa specifically said he was not Laurie. Bron-

son and Anna (but not Louisa, apparently) both told Frederick L. Willis he was Laurie, probably because the March girls' romps with Laurie outdoors reminded them of the times Frederick, Anna, and Louisa played at the Bare Hill Pond near Still River. Frederick was an orphan whom Abigail had taken under her wing and treated as a son, and the girls felt sorry for him, as the March sisters do for Laurie. Willis recalled their first meeting as awkward, since he was a city boy and they were from the country. But Louisa proposed they go outside and play, and "we were comrades from that time forth." Years later, when he visited at Hillside in Concord, they would run and climb trees together. And when he finally went away to college, she wrote him letters full of "frolicsome and serious advice and admonition," much as Jo helps keep Laurie out of trouble during his college years.[41]

Alfred Whitman, who came to live in Concord when the Alcotts moved back there in 1857, was another motherless boy the family befriended. Nine years younger than Louisa—fifteen to Louisa's twenty-four—he was a student at Frank Sanborn's school and found in the Alcotts a replacement family. For many years after he moved to Kansas, Louisa, Anna, and May all kept up a correspondence with him. In her letters, Louisa called him "my boy," as she has Jo call Laurie. Alfred later described the beneficent influence Louisa had over boys like himself, providing a glimpse of Jo not only in *Little Women* but also in the sequels, in which she mothers many boys and young men at Plumfield: "She never scolded, and scarcely ever preached" but molded their lives through affection and "*silent* influence." After *Little Women* came out, Louisa wrote to Alfred Whitman that he and her Polish friend were combined in her creation of Laurie. "You are the sober half & my Ladislas . . . is the gay whirligig half." She remembered Alfred as the serious boy "who used to come and have confidences on the couch, a la Laurie, & be very fascinating without knowing it."[42]

None of the real-life candidates for Laurie was wealthy. By making Laurie heir to a great fortune, Louisa indulged her fantasy of an Alcott gaining the riches that she and her sisters had always dreamed of one day possessing. Such inheritances were common in her sensational fiction, where she regularly allowed wish fulfillment to reign. In life, none of the Alcott girls married rich men.

Jo's marriage to Professor Bhaer, however, was not the product of fantasy but the result of pressure from Alcott's publishers. They "insist on having people married off in a wholesale manner which much afflicts me," Louisa wrote to a friend. "'Jo' should have remained a literary spinster but so many enthusiastic young ladies wrote to me clamorously demanding that she should marry Laurie, *or* somebody, that I didnt dare to refuse & out of perversity went & made a funny match for her. I expect vials of wrath to be poured out upon my head, but rather enjoy the prospect." Louisa herself never wished to marry. Although in *Little Women* Jo begins to soften toward marriage and family after spending time with Meg and her babies, Louisa was not similarly moved by Anna's domestic bliss. After visiting newlyweds Nan and John in their new home, she wrote, "Very sweet and pretty, but I'd rather be a free spinster and paddle my own canoe."[43]

Louisa seems to have had two opportunities to marry. There was a "funny lover" she met on a train in the month before Anna's wedding. He professed to have "lost his heart" almost immediately. Lou-

Louisa was happy to grow into adulthood without marrying, although she felt pressured to marry off her alter ego, Jo March. (Used by permission of Louisa May Alcott's Orchard House)

isa thought him handsome but odd. He was older, about forty, and from the South. She kept him at bay, although he wrote her letters and once attempted to visit her at Orchard House. She declined to see him, so he wandered the road like a forlorn ghost. Finally, he got the message. "My adorers are all queer," she wrote in her journal. Another man, a Mr. Condit, offered her his hand in 1860. The fact that he was a "prosperous manufacturer of silk hats," writes biographer Harriet Reisen, seems to have tempted Louisa. But her mother counseled her not to marry where there was not love, even for the comfort she could gain for herself and her family. It was about a month later that she decided she was content "paddl[ing] her own canoe." Similarly, Marmee in *Little Women* tells Meg and Jo, "Better [to] be happy old maids than unhappy wives."[44]

In choosing a mate for Jo, Alcott seems to have drawn on her attraction to older men like Thoreau and Emerson. Her great affection for them was most fully expressed in her earlier novel *Moods*, where the characters Adam Warwick and Geoffrey Moor can be recognized as idealized portraits of the two men. In *Little Women*, she seems to have particularly had Emerson in mind when she created the character of Professor Bhaer. Louisa called the transcendentalist philosopher "my beloved 'Master'" and in her teens wrote chaste love letters to him, modeled after those Bettina von Armin wrote to Goethe and published in *Goethe's Correspondence with a Child*, a book that Emerson loaned to her. Louisa also once sang Mignon's song from Goethe's *Wilhelm Meister* up to Emerson's window. In *Little Women*, Jo overhears Bhaer singing the same song, *Kennst Du Das Land?* ("Do You Know the Land?"), and later they sing it together.[45]

Writing *Little Women* gave Alcott the opportunity to immortalize some aspects of her life while concealing others. It would take over a century for readers to learn just how difficult and troubled her real life was. As Reisen has put it, "Her life was no children's book."[46] But out of that life grew her tremendously successful book for children, which owed its popularity almost entirely to how much it seemed to resemble real life and real people. No wonder Alcott felt, as readers devoured the two parts of *Little Women* and wrote her countless fan letters, that they just might devour her as well.

# 3

# "FRESH, SPARKLING, . . . FULL OF SOUL"

### The Phenomenon of *Little Women*

W HEN *LITTLE WOMEN* first appeared, readers and reviewers were astonished by how new and original it was. There had been nothing like it before, they felt, at least not for girls. A few entertaining books for boys had been published in recent years, but the vast majority of literature for children, a growing segment of the literary marketplace, was so stilted and pious that it failed to capture the attention of young readers. Most of these books, as one reviewer wrote, "consist of puling, do-me-good copy-book morality, calculated to turn the stomach of any sensible child."[1] These so-called Sunday-school books were written with one goal in mind: to convince children of God's justice. Characters were stereotypical and flat, either good or bad with little or no moral growth, and the predictable outcome was reward for the good and punishment for the bad, which usually meant illness or occasionally death. The stories were told by wise adult narrators talking down to children, warning them to be obedient to their elders if they wanted to grow up virtuous and in one piece.

To get a sense of how *Little Women* must have seemed to the children and adults who picked it up in 1868, we can compare it to some of the other books that were then popular with young readers, particularly girls. One very widely read book was British author Charlotte Yonge's *The Daisy Chain* (1856), whose bookish heroine is seen by some as a precursor to Jo March. (Jo cries over Yonge's other famous novel, *The Heir of Radcliffe*, in chapter two of *Little Women*.) *The Daisy Chain* starts off with lots of lively dialogue, although it is nearly impossible to keep everyone straight in the family of eleven children plus parents, servants, and visitors. A middle daughter, Ethel, seems somewhat vivacious and interesting, although she is not nearly as compelling as Jo. Rather than assert her right to go to school, for instance, she quietly tries to keep up with her brother in his classical studies (as girls received virtually no education). Her siblings tease her mercilessly simply for wearing glasses, without which she is virtually blind. And daily Bible reading and her class-conscious mother have convinced Ethel that "fame is coarse and vulgar," as is ambition.[2] No wonder Jo was more interested in the gothic thriller *The Heir of Radcliffe*. By the end of chapter three in *The Daisy Chain*, a carriage accident kills off the mother and paralyzes the oldest sister, and from there the story becomes a somber affair with the father reeling from grief and the older girls wondering how they are going to take their mother's place. All of this is underscored by regular references to scripture and the religious ceremonies of the Anglican Church, which form the foundation of the family's life. It's not hard to see why *Little Women* has enjoyed more lasting fame than *The Daisy Chain*.

Then there was American author Adeline D. T. Whitney's *Faith Gartney's Girlhood* (1863), with which *Little Women* was sometimes compared, especially by British reviewers. The novel follows Faith from age fourteen to twenty and was one of the most popular books of its time. Just reading the opening sentence, however, gives us an idea of why audiences were so thrilled with Alcott's relaxed prose:

> East or West, it matters not where,—the story may, doubtless, indicate something of latitude and longitude as it proceeds,—in the city of Mishaumok, lived Henderson Gartney, Esq., one of those American gentlemen of whom, if she were ever canonized, Martha of Bethany must be the patron saint,—if again, feminine

celestials, sainthood once achieved through the weary experience of earth, don't know better than to assume such charge of way-ward man,—born, as they are, seemingly, to the life-destiny of being ever "careful and troubled about many things."[3]

Perhaps nineteenth-century audiences could make some sense out of that, but I doubt those of any subsequent generation could pick up the book without throwing it across the room.

In contrast, readers who opened the plain little volume—available in red, green, or brown—with "Little Women" on the cover wreathed in gold, were electrified from the start after reading the famous opening lines. The novel immediately draws the reader in with four young voices, each expressing her own wishes and desires and hinting at her unique personality:

> "Christmas won't be Christmas without any presents," grumbled Jo, lying on the rug.
>
> "It's so dreadful to be poor!" sighed Meg, looking down at her old dress.
>
> "I don't think it's fair for some girls to have plenty of pretty things, and other girls nothing at all," added little Amy, with an injured sniff.
>
> "We've got father and mother and each other, anyhow," said Beth contentedly, from her corner.
>
> The four young faces on which the firelight shone brightened at the cheerful words, but darkened again as Jo said sadly,—
>
> "We haven't got father, and shall not have him for a long time." She didn't say "perhaps never," but each silently added it, thinking of father far away, where the fighting was.[4]

The first part of *Little Women* was greeted with nearly unanimous praise and predictions that it would remain on bookstore shelves much longer than most of the volumes then being published. The earliest reviewers struck a theme that would never fade away: in the words of one critic, *Little Women* was "fresh, sparkling, natural, and full of soul." The same words—*fresh, natural, healthy, simple, sincere, realistic,* and *unaffected*—were repeated again and again in the reviews. As another reviewer put it, the story "is related with so much naturalness and vivacity that we predict for it a much more permanent success than usually falls to the lot of modern story-books."[5] The novel's naturalness came from a narrator who didn't talk down to children but seemed to be one of them herself, or, at times, a former child who looks back with compassion on her younger self. When she preaches to her readers, she often does it through Marmee or one of the four girls themselves, rather than through a moralizing narrator.

Meanwhile, the English publisher Sampson Low noticed the book's initial reception in America and arranged to publish an edition in England. It appeared in December 1868 under the title *Four Little Women*. *The Spectator*, a British periodical, found the book full of "genuine humor and pathos" and particularly praised the portrait of Jo. Noting that Alcott suggested there was more to come, the reviewer concluded, "By all means let us have it."[6]

However, the book's informal language left a sour taste in the mouths of some British reviewers, who regretted that Alcott's little women didn't express "themselves in a more lady-like language." Over the years there would occasionally be some high-toned snobbery about the girls' lack of gentility and the rather unfashionable home they came from, but what seemed to trouble Brits was the way Alcott had her young women speaking a "rough and uncouth" language rife with "Americanisms." The novel was "slightly tainted by vulgarity," one reviewer wrote. "The language is sometimes not such as we should care to hear from the lips of English girls."[7] It could be argued that the novel's language more than anything else makes it an American book. What Alcott brought to children's—and American—literature was the fresh language of American colloquialism, a departure from the stiffness of Yonge and Whitney, and a precursor to the even more "vulgar" speech of the lower-class Huck Finn, who would appear sixteen years later, in 1884.

There was also something revolutionary about a narrator who spoke directly to girls without correcting or admonishing them. As the young critic Henry James Jr. observed, with considerable discomfort, Alcott had "a private understanding with the youngsters she depicts, at the expense of their pastors and masters." There is no denying that Alcott's fiction wrote around and essentially supplanted—James would say undermined—patriarchal authority as it was manifested in churches, schools, and the home. Another very popular novel, Martha Finley's *Elsie Dinsmore*, published the year before *Little Women*, exemplifies the type of children's literature that satisfied the "pastors and masters," featuring as it did a heroine so good and meek that she seems not quite human. Her chief function is evangelical, pointing the way to a virtuous Christian life for all around her. Her main struggle, to the point of suffering a nervous breakdown, is over whether to obey God or her father, the latter of whom threatens to whip her whenever she refuses to follow his wishes when, say, she won't play a secular song on the Sabbath. Eventually, of course, she reforms even her own father, so that she can comfortably obey all the patriarchal authorities. One reviewer determined that the book "would be peculiarly attractive to all persons who believe that children seven years old love moral tales better than candy, and obedience to their parents better than dolls and pretty pictures."[8] Apparently there were plenty of such people. The book was so popular that Finley continued to publish sequels—twenty-seven of them—until 1905.

While Christian authorities approved of the piety of *Elsie Dinsmore*, they found *Little Women* wanting. Specifically, they objected to the lack of overt religiosity in the book. The *Zion's Herald* refused to recommend the book, for "it is without Christ." *The Ladies' Repository* declared, "It is not a Christian book. It is religion without spirituality, and salvation without Christ." Both reviewers advised Sunday school librarians against purchasing the book. The Sunday school portion of the market was considerable enough that Alcott's publisher, Thomas Niles, was mildly concerned. "Some very good & pious people," as he put it, objected to the novel's portrayal of Christmas Day. On the holiest of Christian holidays, not only do the Marches not go to church, but the daughters even perform a play that has no religious content whatsoever. When a new edition of the novel was in the works, only three weeks after the first print run, which was selling rapidly, Niles wondered if perhaps Alcott wanted to replace that scene, although he thought it "about the best part of the whole book.

Why will people be so *very good*," he wondered.[9] The scene stayed and sales continued to climb, even without the support of the pious.

The illustrations, done by Louisa's youngest sister, May, also lent a certain charm to the first edition of *Little Women* (copies of which, incidentally, are now priced somewhere between $15,000 and $20,000). As illustrator, May didn't want to be identified as one of the "Little

Frontispiece illustration by May Alcott from the first edition of *Little Women* (Roberts Brothers, 1868).

Women," Alcott told Niles, but simply as "May Alcott." Her illustrations—there are four of them—have gotten a bad rap over the years and are often mentioned as having been ridiculed in early reviews. I found, however, that most reviewers liked them, calling them "vigorous and impressive," "very creditabl[e]," and "clever." Only the review in *The Nation* was critical, saying that "Miss May Alcott betrays . . . a want of anatomical knowledge" in her illustrations.[10] We might agree today, yet most of them possess a simplicity and immediacy, a kind of childlike innocence, particularly the frontispiece and the portrait of Beth welcoming home her father, that none of the subsequent illustrators was quite able to capture.

While part one of the book sold rapidly and went into multiple new editions, the public eagerly awaited part two. When it was announced in the spring that the printing would be delayed a bit, readers got anxious. "The curiosity to learn the denouement of 'Little Women' amounts to an epidemic," one newspaper claimed. By this time, 55,000 copies of part one had been sold, and 3,000 advance orders for part two had already been taken. Alcott wasn't sure what to call the next installment. A friend had suggested "Wedding Marches," in light of all the "pairing off." All she could come up with was "Little Women Act Second" or "Leaving the Nest. Sequel to Little Women." On April 14, 1869, part two appeared under the simple title *Little Women or Meg, Jo, Beth and Amy, Part Second*. Within a month, Sampson Low published it in England as *Little Women Wedded*, more obviously catering to readers' expectations.[11]

Again, reviewers were nearly unanimous in their praise. This time, however, critics weren't entirely sure whether the new volume qualified as a children's book. *Harper's New Monthly Magazine* thought it "a rather mature book for the little women, but a capital one for their elders," and wondered, "do not her children grow rather rapidly?" Most didn't seem to mind, however. The *Boston Post* declared, "the author has taken eminent possession of that domain in fiction on the border line of what pleases the young and what engages the mature." Indeed, many of the reviews of parts one and two commented on the book's interest to readers both young and old. According to an Alcott family friend, Frank Preston Stearns, *Little Women* was "the rage in '69," when everyone from children to grandparents was reading it. He

Although May Alcott was not happy with her illustrations, this one of Beth welcoming home Mr. March for the first edition of *Little Women* (Roberts Brothers, 1868), captures a childlike innocence no subsequent illustrator was able to approximate.

describes merchants and lawyers, clerks in his office, and the elevator boy all merrily asking each other, "Have you read 'Little Women?'" In short, *Little Women* was a cultural phenomenon that knew no boundaries of age, gender, or class. Its ubiquity is reflected by the reviews that appeared not simply in periodicals for children (of which there were a few) but in newspapers and serious literary magazines, such as *The Nation* and *Putnam's*. The dividing line between adult and children's literature was not yet clearly drawn, and *Little Women* benefited from the crossover then possible. As the book's fame grew, more and more reviewers took notice. Even two years later, the *British Quarterly* noted that *Little Women* could still be found "upon every American book-stall, and . . . in almost every American home."[12]

As for the religious press, the *Zion's Herald* again had its objections, especially that Beth's death scene made no reference to God and her ascent to Heaven. Conservative Christians generally saw nothing to admire in the vaguely transcendentalist spiritualism of the March family. In response, Alcott lampooned the field of pious children's books when Jo tries her hand at writing a story for children. Jo finds that she cannot "consent to depict all her naughty boys as being eaten by bears, or tossed by mad bulls, because they did not go to a particular Sabbath-school, nor all the good infants who did go, of course, as rewarded by every kind of bliss, from gilded gingerbread to escorts of angels, when they departed this life, with psalms or sermons on their lisping tongues." Never shy to criticize beloved institutions where she saw hypocrisy or injustice, Alcott let the pious gatekeepers of children's literature know what she thought of them, and they responded in kind. Even three years later, the *Christian Union* would designate Alcott's works as "wholly *bad*" and unfit for Sunday school libraries.[13] Her readers didn't mind. America was becoming increasingly secular, and Americans no longer required that books for children preach the Bible. Marmee gives her girls a book to guide them in their efforts to become better people, but the book is not specified. Scholars today believe it was the New Testament, although many have believed it was *Pilgrim's Progress*. Either way, it is significant that Alcott didn't name it.

Also unnamed was the book's illustrator, Hammatt Billings. May Alcott was either removed from the project or unwilling to continue, and the more professional Billings—illustrator of the most famous American book before *Little Women*, Harriet Beecher Stowe's *Uncle Tom's Cabin* (1852)—was enlisted. While we don't know what Louisa thought of May's drawings, she hated those by Billings and promptly sent them back. On the proof of a portrait that was designed for the frontispiece and showed Amy and Laurie together in Europe, she wrote, "Oh, please change em!" Neither of the likenesses lived up to her ideal. Amy looked too old and was not nearly "picturesque" enough, while Laurie looked too young and unattractive. Alcott was more explicit in a letter she wrote to her friend Elizabeth Greene. Billings had made Amy "a fat girl with a pug of hair, sitting among weedy shrubbery with a light-house under her nose, & a mile or two off a scrubby little boy on his stomach in the grass looking cross, towzly, & about 14 years old!"

Alcott was not happy with Hammatt Billings's first attempt at this illustration of Amy and Laurie in Europe. (Princeton University Library)

Niles set Billings to work again, and when the new picture came, Alcott thought it an improvement. Amy was "pretty," but now Laurie, who looked like "a mixture of Apollo [and] Byron [was] no more like the real Teddy than Ben Franklin." She couldn't delay the book any longer, however.[14]

Billings's biographer calls his illustrations "adequate if not inspired."[15] Undoubtedly they have a stiff refinement that robs the characters of their vitality. Amy, who is supposed to be seventeen, looks almost matronly. Alcott's complaints notwithstanding, Laurie more or less matches what he seems to be in the text; but his expression is blank, giving him no personality. Much more successful, and one of the very best illustrations ever done for *Little Women*, was Billings's "Jo in a vortex." Here Jo, with her hair in rags, looks a bit like a Medusa and has the kind of wild look that seems just right for Jo. The picture captures, in what could have been a static scene, the intense energy of creative work, complete with pages fluttering to the floor. The picture almost looks like it is moving, with Jo scratching away, then crossing out a passage,

Alcott was much happier with Billings's second drawing, which became the frontispiece for the first edition of *Little Women*, Part Two (Roberts Brothers, 1869).

Billings's image of Jo in her vortex is one of the most successful illustrations ever done for *Little Women* (Roberts Brothers, 1869).

and finally tossing the paper aside as she comes up with a new idea. Billings's biographer calls it "the perfect visualization of creative genius at work."[16] Billings also did two more illustrations: one of Professor Bhaer playing with Tina (one of Jo's charges) and one of Beth and Jo at the seaside.

*Little Women*'s publication history does not end with the appearance of volume two; the text would take on many forms over the years. Throughout the 1870s, the two parts of the novel were offered as a two-volume set. The only differences were minor textual corrections and two new illustrations by Billings for part one that replaced the original ones by May. But in 1880, the novel would change dramatically when Roberts Brothers decided to publish a one-volume version. This would not be merely a repackaging of the two parts but a newly revised, illustrated edition, released in time for the holiday season. Niles wanted to enshrine *Little Women* as a book of lasting value for families to keep and turn into family heirlooms. It was a "sumptuous edition," as one rapturous reviewer put it, with its green and gold cover and gilded edges. The first children to have read the novel had by then entered adulthood, another reviewer wrote, and "the memory of this [fascinating] story has become a little dim." Indeed its sales had begun to slip, but they would pick up again with the 1880 edition.[17]

The new edition contained an astonishing two hundred new illustrations by Frank T. Merrill, a competent journeyman illustrator whose most famous work would be this edition of *Little Women*. Alcott was again involved in proofing the illustrations, writing notes on the backs of Merrill's drawings where they fell short of how she imagined her characters. Jo was "always made to look too old for her years." Laurie was sometimes too stiff or too old, at other times too young and wearing the wrong expression. On the back of one portrait of Professor Bhaer, she wrote, "Eyes too starring. Bhaer was not frightened of Jo." Merrill took her advice and gave him a whole new head and made similar alterations of other drawings she objected to. Most of Merrill's drawings Alcott heartily approved of, however, writing "Capital," "Lovely," or "Jolly" on the back. She wrote to Niles, probably after the revisions were complete, that they were "all capital, and we had great fun over them."[18]

The illustrations are sprinkled throughout the volume's 586 pages and become rather overwhelming, but a few stand out. The frontispiece, an echo of May Alcott's, is one of the most elaborate drawings. It shows Marmee with the girls gathered around her, this time with Mr. March's letter as the focus. It would become a central scene for illustrators and film directors for decades to come.

Most of the illustrations, however, look rather stiff and idealized. Professor Bhaer looks a bit like Santa Claus and all of the girls something like Gibson girls, although the real Gibson girls popularized by

In an echo of May Alcott's frontispiece, Frank Merrill captured
what would become the iconic scene of Marmee reading Mr.
March's letter to the girls (Roberts Brothers, 1880).

Charles Dana Gibson didn't start showing up until the 1890s. Merrill's girls have pointy noses and long lashes and look more like man-
ikins than real girls. His portraits of Jo, besides making her look too
old, give little sense of her character, for the most part. She looks
like any other proper young woman of the period, not the rough-
and-tumble personality readers love. But Merrill does deserve credit

Merrill's illustration of Jo writing is his most successful portrait of her
(Roberts Brothers, 1880).

for the wonderful drawing of Jo wearing her writing cap, which has become iconic.

Just as Merrill's drawings flatten and standardize the novel, so the text of the new edition smoothed the rough edges of Alcott's original creation. The text was extensively altered, mainly to get rid of the slang and colloquialisms, clean up the grammar, and make the whole sound more genteel and proper. No correspondence has survived to indicate whether Alcott was involved in making the changes, but she must at least have approved of them. It is likely that she let the publisher take charge, having little patience for those who tried to tame her boisterous prose. In response to critics of her informal language, she had written these words in her next novel, *An Old-Fashioned Girl*, published in 1870:

I deeply regret being obliged to shock the eyes and ears of such of my readers as have a prejudice in favor of pure English, by expressions like the above but, having rashly undertaken to write a little story about Young America, for Young America, I feel bound to depict my honored patrons as faithfully as my limited powers permit. Otherwise, I must expect the crushing criticism, "Well, I daresay it's all very prim and proper, but it isn't a bit like us," and never hope to arrive at the distinction of finding the covers of "An Old-Fashioned Girl" the dirtiest in the library.[19]

Alcott didn't care a fig for her adult readers. She wrote solely for the nation's youth.

Niles, on the other hand, wanted *Little Women* to be treasured by youngsters while also gaining the respect of elders who had the power to confer on it the status of a classic. So he had his copy editors clean up the text, resulting in dozens of changes, some minor, some more significant. The girls don't stay at the New Year's Eve dance until *past ten*, but only until "past nine"; *ain't* is changed to "am not" or "are not" throughout; *grub* and *peg* become "work"; *spandy* becomes "new"; *I guess not* is changed to "I think not"; and *red as a beet* is now "red as a peony." Jo is no longer allowed to say that Aunt March "worries you till you're ready to *fly out of the window or box her ears*"; instead, she says "fly out of the window or cry." As with the illustrations, the text also begins to portray the characters as much more flawless in their appearance. Whereas the narrator tells us that Marmee "wasn't a particularly handsome person" in the original, in 1880 we are told, "She was not elegantly dressed, but a noble-looking woman." Even Laurie gets a makeover. No longer as tall as Jo and possessing a "long nose," he is now taller than Jo and has a "handsome nose."[20]

Overall, the changes tone down the original text's lively language and tame its playful spirit. It was as if, writes critic Susan Gannon, the publishers were "anxious to provide readers with a polished, established, suitably improving 'classic text.'" The changes came at a time when Americans were increasingly anxious about regional dialects and informal slang and sought to impose a more regularized language on the nation. Niles thought the "change in style," as well as the illustrated, one-volume packaging, were the reasons for the increase in sales over the next few years. In 1881, Roberts Brothers issued this revised version in a smaller, cheaper, one-volume edition with only four illustrations. It would become the standard version of *Little Women*, the one read through the generations. Only in the twenty-first century would a few publishers resurrect Alcott's original text and restore the vibrant language for which it was first known, thereby restoring the novel's distinct realism.[21]

In England, the new version of *Little Women* also became the standard, with the added alteration of English spelling (*grey* instead of *gray*, *labour* instead of *labor*, etc.). However, Alcott's novel has had a very different publication history in Britain than in the United States. Alcott was not able to secure copyright in England; to do so required her to be present in the country when it was first published. As a result, multiple pirated editions appeared. The publisher, Sampson Low, was so aggrieved by this siphoning off of its profits that it included a "Special Notice to the Public and to Booksellers" at the back of its edition. While Sampson Low had merged the two parts into one volume in 1871, its competitors were still selling them in two separate volumes, giving the public the impression "that they were buying two distinct works—that they got in paper covers for one shilling the same volume which Messrs. Low sell for 3s. 6 d., in cloth, gilt edges." In retaliation, Sampson Low decided to compete directly by offering the volumes at a cheaper price, using the titles *Little Women* and *Little Women Wedded*, while continuing to produce the more expensive one-volume edition. That book was called *A Story of Four Little Women*, but it never really caught on.[22]

The English public preferred two books instead of one. While part one remained *Little Women*, different publishers gave a variety of titles to part two, including *Little Women Married*, *Little Wives*, and *Nice Wives*. The most enduring was *Good Wives*, which first appeared in 1872 in the Lily Series of cheap, one-shilling editions of American books, published by Ward, Lock, and Tyler.[23] The net result of this confusion and piracy is that readers in the U.K., Ireland, Canada, and Australia to this day find in their libraries and bookstores both *Little Women*, which includes only part one, taking the story up to Meg and John Brooke's engagement, and *Good Wives*, which continues the story up to Jo and Professor Bhaer's running of the Plumfield school. Therefore, I've found readers from England happy that Beth didn't die in *Little Women* or blissfully unaware that Jo rejected Laurie and married Professor Bhaer. For many British children, in other words, *Little Women* has been a very different book.

WHETHER IT APPEARED in two volumes or one, *Little Women* undoubtedly changed the shape of children's literature. A host of imitators cropped up, eager to ride the wave Alcott had created. The popular novelist Elizabeth Stuart Phelps, for instance, published "Our Little Woman" in the children's magazine *Our Young Folks* in 1872.[24] But the most successful imitation was *What Katy Did*, by Susan Coolidge (the pen name for Sarah Woolsey), also published in 1872. The heroine, Katy Carr, is another Jo, eager to be famous one day and unwilling to settle into proper young womanhood. She is tamed, however, in a rather cruel way. An accident paralyzes her and forces her to become an invalid. (The influence of *The Daisy Chain* is, regrettably, also obvious.) Over the years as Katy is forced to watch life rather than participate in it, she learns to live for others rather than for herself. Despite the morose plot, the novel spawned four sequels.

Alcott's pervasive influence is also visible in the career of another writer who was just starting out when *Little Women* first appeared: Constance Fenimore Woolson, who would become one of the most popular and critically acclaimed American authors, compared to Henry James and George Eliot. Early on, however, Woolson felt obligated to imitate Alcott, after one of her mentors gave her "fully an hour's eulogy of Miss Alcott's 'Little Women.'" It was the "fashion," she wrote to a friend, to "exalt . . . stories for children to a place which it did not seem to me belonged to them. I thought that they had their own sphere, and that it was a very high one. But Shakespeare still existed, and Milton; the great historians, the great essayists, the great writers of fiction. But in the U.S. at that time, one would almost suppose to hear the talk . . . that the writers for children were greater than all these." And Alcott above them all. Despite her misgivings, Woolson tried her hand at writing for children and produced *The Old Stone House* (1873) under the pseudonym Anne

March, an obvious nod to Alcott's work. The novel won top prize in a competition for D. Lothrop's Sunday School series, suggesting how much *Little Women* had affected even the religious portion of the literary market. One of Woolson's characters, Bess, wants to become a famous artist and clearly shares some of Jo's and Amy's qualities. (She loves to ride horses, like Amy, and is a bit of a tomboy, like Jo.) Imitation did not ensure success, however. Not having achieved even a small portion of the sales Alcott had, Woolson gave up on writing for children.[25]

Chief among those pressured to imitate Alcott's success was Alcott herself. Roberts Brothers wanted her to start writing another similar novel as well as a sequel as soon as possible, to "make hay while the sun shines." Despite her concerns about breaking down again from overwork, she cranked out *An Old-Fashioned Girl*. It began its serial run in *Merry's Museum* in July 1869, only three months after the appearance of part two of *Little Women*. The novel is about Polly Milton, a girl from the country who visits her sophisticated cousins in the city and teaches them the virtues of being old-fashioned. When the story ended in December, letters poured in again from fans wanting to know what would happen to Polly when she grew up. For the book version, therefore, Alcott satisfied their curiosity, adding another twelve chapters to the edition hurriedly prepared by Roberts Brothers, who published it in March 1870.[26]

As soon as she was finished, Alcott put down her pen and planned an extended rest from writing. In April she took May to Europe, accompanied by May's friend Alice Bartlett. They lingered in France until the fall, when they crossed the Alps for Italy and decided to spend the winter in Rome. While there, news arrived just before Christmas that Anna's husband, John Pratt, had died suddenly after a short illness. Learning that he had left Anna and their two boys with no debts but also with no income, Alcott began work on the promised sequel to *Little Women*. While May sketched and absorbed all she could of Italian art, Louisa devoted herself to her writing, this time to provide for her widowed sister and nephews. "I must be a father [to them] now," she felt. After a month in London in the spring, Louisa came home to Concord, arriving in June 1871 to find

*Little Men: Life at Plumfield with Jo's Boys* just out and 50,000 copies already sold.[27]

In the novel, set not long after the conclusion of *Little Women* at Plumfield, a boys' boarding school, Alcott was able to indulge her love of boys and to fictionalize many of her own exploits as a child. Jo March was fifteen at the start of *Little Women*, but many of the characters in *Little Men* are much younger and at the right age for the larks that Louisa indulged in before the advent of puberty. The twelve boys and two girls at the school play the same pranks and get in the same scrapes she recalled from her days in Still River and Concord when they lived at Hillside. In chapter eight, Alcott insisted that "most of the incidents are taken from real life, and the oddest are the truest; for no person, no matter how vivid an imagination he may have, can invent anything half so droll as the freaks and fancies that originate in the lively brains of little people." Just as the young Louisa was known to wander off and get lost, a tomboy named Nan, a younger version of Jo, wanders off confidently with one of Jo's young sons and proceeds to get them lost. Mrs. Jo, as she is now called, also relates Louisa's own story of putting little stones up her nose when she was young. She got the idea from her mother, who told her of the children who never dreamed of putting beans up their noses until their mother warned them one day as she left, "don't let baby fall out of the window, don't play with the matches, and don't put beans up your noses." As soon as their mother left, "they ran and stuffed their naughty little noses full of beans." Louisa couldn't resist either. Unable to find any beans, she used pebbles, which only the doctor was able to remove after hours of pain. Jo tells the story to her son Rob, who, thankfully, "[takes] the warning to heart" and is not compelled to imitate it.[28]

Alcott also found a use for the story of the transcendentalist writer (and former assistant at Temple School) Margaret Fuller's visit to Hillside in the 1840s. Just when Fuller asked to see the "model children" Bronson was raising, the Alcott children came barreling around the corner, baby May in a wheelbarrow, Louisa playing horse and being driven by Anna, and Lizzie pretending to be a dog and barking loudly. In *Little Men*, Mrs. Jo is boasting to Mr. Laurie about the children's improvement when "they came up in a cloud of dust, looking as wild a set of little hoydens as one would wish to see." Mr. Laurie laughs and says, "So these are the model children, are they? It's lucky I didn't bring Mrs. Curtis out to see your school for the cultivation of morals and manners; she would never have recovered from the shock of this spectacle."[29]

With her popularity, Alcott didn't have to worry anymore about her audience being overly shocked by her characters' antics. The most outrageous—and humorous—is when the children decide that the vengeful spirit they have conjured, "The Naughty Kitty-mouse," demands that they make a sacrifice, and they proceed to make a bonfire of their favorite toys. Even Daisy, Meg's demure daughter, is persuaded to throw the beautiful paper dolls Aunt Amy made for her onto the fire. Then little Teddy, Jo's youngest, gets involved: "The superb success of th[e] last offering excited Teddy to such a degree, that he first threw his [toy] lamb into the conflagration, and before it had time even to roast, he planted poor dear Annabella [a noseless doll] on the funeral pyre. Of course she did not like it, and expressed her anguish and resentment in a way that terrified her infant destroyer. Being covered with kid [leather], she did not blaze, but did what was worse, she *squirmed*." Her arms proceed to rise above her head, her glass eyes pop out, and finally she collapses in a heap of ash, "frighten[ing] Teddy half out of his little wits." He runs toward the house screaming for his "Marmar."[30]

As these scenes suggest, life at Plumfield, including plenty of free time and exercise outdoors, was drawn straight from Louisa's childhood. Her father's educational theories, which he had been prohibited from using with other children, had been thoroughly carried out at home with his own, especially the oldest two, Anna and Louisa. He opposed the standard practices of teaching by rote, preferring the Socratic method of questioning students and encouraging self-discovery and self-expression. In *Little Women*, Mr. March had been relegated to the background and given the quasi-profession of a respectable minister. But his presence is fully felt in *Little Men*, in the character of Professor Bhaer, who runs the educational side of Plumfield. The students receive an unconventional education, relying less on books and more on conversation. "Latin, Greek, and mathematics were all very well, but in Professor Bhaer's opinion, self-knowledge, self-help, and self-control were more important," the narrator explains, directly echoing Bronson Alcott. Every afternoon, Bhaer takes the children out for walks, believing that the body as well as the mind must be exercised, and finding, like a good transcendentalist (and borrowing a somewhat mixed-up quote from Shakespeare), "sermons in stones, books in the running brooks, and good in everything."[31]

If she had felt that she had to keep her freethinking father largely out of *Little Women*, Alcott had no such worries by the time she wrote *Little Men*. The first novel's popularity had made not only the daughter famous but also the father. Forever after, Bronson would be known as the father of the "little women." Suddenly his lectures were crowded, and afterward people gathered eagerly around to ask questions about Louisa and the rest of his family. Now when he returned from his lecture tours in the West, his pockets were full of money, and he was eager to spend it on the daughter who had made him a celebrity. When Louisa came home from Europe, she was delighted to see that he had fixed up her room with his earnings.[32]

With *Little Men*, Alcott was able to take her father's rehabilitation even further. So successful was her redemption of his reputation as an educator that Roberts Brothers published a revised version of *Record of a School*. The book contained the reports of Bronson's conversations with his students at Temple School, compiled by his assistant, Elizabeth Peabody, that had caused all of the trouble back in the 1830s. Louisa was quoted in the preface, explaining that Plumfield was modeled on Temple School, and that "not only is it a duty and a pleasure, but there is a certain fitness in making the childish fiction of the daughter play the grateful part of herald to the wise and beautiful truths of the father."[33] In some ways Plumfield, as its name suggests, also reflects the utopian experiment of Fruitlands. In fiction, however, Alcott could temper the extremism of her father's ideas and focus on the practical application of his theories. By doing so, she brought him the fame he and Abigail had always believed he deserved. When he thereafter founded the Concord School of Philosophy in the front room of Orchard House, the crowd exceeded the house's capacity. Eventually a building, which still stands, was erected on the grounds to accommodate the growing numbers of people who came each summer from all around the country.

While Bronson enjoyed his new fame, Louisa was uneasy with hers, and each book only added to her discomfort. There were eighteen more, including the six-volume series *Aunt Jo's Scrap-Bag* as well as two other girls' stories, *Eight Cousins* and *Rose in Bloom*, and her adult novels *Work* and *A Modern Mephistopheles* (the latter a sensation novel published anonymously). She also had the chance to revise her first novel, *Moods*, in 1882. One of her last works was the concluding volume in the *Little Women* trilogy, *Jo's Boys: And How They Turned Out*, published in October 1886. Picking up ten years after the end of *Little Men*, it shows the boys and girls of that book coming into adulthood and attending Laurence College, a legacy left by Laurie's uncle. Mrs. Jo is now a famous author, having, in answer to a request from a publisher looking for a book for girls, "hastily scribbled a little story describing a few scenes and adventures in the lives of herself and her sisters." She enjoys having been able to make her mother's final year comfortable, as Louisa did in real life, but Jo is no less accepting of the intrusions of her many admirers than her creator, whose journals show her sneaking out a back window when strange visitors arrive demanding to see her. "This sight-seeing fiend is a new torment to us," Louisa wrote in the summer of 1872. Living in Concord on one of the main thoroughfares surely didn't help. Literary tourists could stop by Orchard House, peek at Hawthorne's former house next door, swing by the Emersons across the road, and then head up the hill to the Sleepy Hollow cemetery to see the final resting places of Hawthorne and Thoreau (although Thoreau's fame was still in its infancy). Alcott mercilessly lampooned the autograph seekers, journalists, and nosy readers who regularly knocked on her door in a letter she wrote to the *Springfield Republican* in 1869. A new hotel called "The Sphinx's Head" was opening in Concord to cater to the "pilgrims to this modern Mecca," she jested. They would be provided with telescopes to view the Oversoul on its overhead flight and lassoes to apprehend the literary lions roaming their natural habitat. Emerson could be seen out walking at 4, William Ellery Channing at sunset, and Bronson Alcott (ever eager to meet his fans) would "converse from 8 a.m. till 11 p.m." Meanwhile, "one irascible spinster, driven to frenzy by twenty-eight visitors in one week," was considering using a garden hose to keep unwelcome visitors away.[34]

In *Jo's Boys*, Alcott took the satire even further, portraying one day in Jo's busy life when she is trying to finish some writing that is due at a magazine. First the mail comes, full of requests for autographs, donations, advice, even the use of her name to help get one aspiring writer published. Then come the knocks on the door. First is an impertinent newspaperman who wants to write an article about her. Next are a mother and three girls from Oshkosh, hoping to meet her and get a memento, in a scene inspired by a woman who once told Alcott, "If you ever come to Oshkosh, your feet will not be allowed to touch the ground," a prospect she found rather uninviting. And finally, before lunch, a young ladies' seminary picnics on the lawn, having been denied entrance. Jo has a particular horror of young female admirers, Alcott herself having once been nearly "kissed to death by gushing damsels" at a women's convention. In the afternoon, seventy-five college boys arrive at Plumfield in the rain and tramp with their muddy boots throughout the house. An hour after their departure, a strange lady arrives wanting an old piece of Jo's clothing to weave into a rug she is making with the remnants of famous authors' clothes. Not much writing gets done that day. More than anything, Jo/Louisa lamented the lack of privacy. "I cannot shut my doors even in free America," Jo protests.[35]

Alcott was not always unresponsive to her fans, however. She carried on a correspondence with some readers, most notably the five Lukens sisters from Brinton, Pennsylvania. In 1871 the Lukenses had started their own manuscript newspaper, called *Little Things*, patterned after the March girls' *Pickwick Portfolio*. They carried it on for two years and turned it into a typeset paper that had over a thousand subscribers. Alcott was one of them. She also gave the Lukens sisters advice for their budding writing careers and even invited them to visit her. She retained an interest in them over many years, writing to sister Maggie Lukens as late as 1886.[36] Sadly, virtually none of her other fan letters survive.

*Little Women*'s admirers had other ways of recording their devotion. Alcott's novel was, for instance, the book most frequently mentioned in the diaries of late-nineteenth-century young women. And, as scholar Barbara Sicherman writes, "Girls not only read themselves into *Little Women*, they elaborated on it and incorporated the story into their lives." M. Carey Thomas, future president of Bryn Mawr College, was reading *Little Women* in her teens in the 1870s and took on the persona of "Jo" in her journals. Jane Addams, future founder of Hull House, similarly read *Little Women* over and over again. Countless girls and young women started their own Alcott or Little Women clubs and took on the identities of the March sisters. Many wrote to Alcott about how their group of friends had formed their own "March family." Students at Vassar planned to dress up as Meg, Jo, Beth, and Amy for a photograph they wanted to send to her.[37] In 1905 the phenomenon made its way into literature with Marion Ames Taggart's *The Little Women Club*, a novel about four girls who not only adopt the March sisters' names and personalities but also try to reenact the story of Alcott's novel. By then, Little Women clubs were common across the United States.

The popularity of *Little Women* continued unabated in those years, even though its author was no longer living. In fact, new readers often didn't know she had died and kept writing her fan letters, as many as fifty a year, until at least 1933. Louisa May Alcott had died on March 6, 1888, apparently of a stroke, at the young age of fifty-five. Her health had never fully returned after her nursing stint during the war. Some scholars believe that the mercury poisoning she had then suffered aged her prematurely, as she herself believed. Others think she died from lupus. Her death came only two days after her father's. The two had shared a birthday (November 29) as well as nearly a death date, something that was much remarked in the notices and obituaries. The papers made clear, however, that Louisa's significance rested on one novel alone. The *New York Times* claimed, "There was probably no writer among women better loved by the young than she," *Little Women* having "endeared her to so many hundred thousands in this country and Europe alike." The popular writer Harriet Prescott Spofford eulogized her as "the writer better loved by the children of America than Shakespeare himself." For many decades to come, Alcott would be known solely as "the children's friend," the subtitle of the first biography of her that appeared within a year of her death.[38]

WHILE ROBERTS BROTHERS controlled the novel's publication until the firm was bought out by Little, Brown in 1898, the valuable copyright of *Little Women* had been extended beyond Alcott's lifetime through her heir, John Pratt Alcott, Anna's younger son, whom Louisa adopted so that he could continue collecting royalties. Her will stipulated that he share the proceeds with the remaining family: his mother, brother, and May's daughter, Lulu. It also instructed the executor of her will, Anna, to destroy her remaining papers, letters, and manuscripts, or what was left over from the fires she had regularly stoked before her death. Anna destroyed some of them, but not all. She gave a number to a family friend, Ednah Cheney, who published them, with alteration (she had Anna remove passages they thought too personal or injurious to Louisa's reputation), and then never returned them. It was not until 1950 that independent scholar Madeleine Stern published the first comprehensive biography and revealed to the world that the author of their beloved childhood books was also the writer of opium-laced sensation stories.[39]

By then, very little could have harmed the reputation of *Little Women*. After Alcott's death, the novel thrived as editions proliferated and numerous illustrators reimagined the novel's key scenes for new generations of readers. In 1915, Little, Brown published the first edition with color illustrations by Jessie Wilcox Smith, a prolific and highly regarded magazine and book illustrator. Many readers still prize this edition as their favorite, and many subsequent editions used Smith's plates. They introduced a new, highly stylized look to *Little Women*, turning the March sisters into fashion plates with rosy cheeks and fancy dresses they hardly would have been able to afford.

Jessie Wilcox Smith's illustration of Laurie proposing to Jo, who
has been turned into a fashion plate (Little, Brown, 1915).

Between 1898 and the expiration of *Little Women*'s copyright in
1924 (part one) and 1925 (part two), Little, Brown sold 1.5 million
copies of the novel.[40] Thereafter, as new versions by other publishers proliferated—including cheap reprints, newly illustrated gift
editions, collector's editions signed by the illustrator and printed in
small numbers, as well as countless abridged editions for younger
readers—it became difficult if not impossible to track the novel's
actual sales.

Fully half of Smith's eight illustrations were love
scenes, including this portrait of Professor Bhaer and
Jo, moments before his proposal (Little, Brown, 1915).

One of the earliest of the unauthorized editions was published by
John Winston Company in 1926. It was illustrated by Clara Burd, a
prolific children's book artist who also designed stained glass windows for Tiffany. Although the edition was rather cheaply produced
using paper that feels like newsprint, the cover contains a stunning color illustration. Inside is a gorgeous frontispiece of the Busy
Bee Society and two more color plates as well as a number of line
drawings.

In Burd's portraits, Marmee and the girls are for the most part busy with their hands; in the portrait on the cover, all the girls except for Amy are engaged with themselves, not with us. They are grouped in aesthetic poses, but they also look as if they are just busy living and we happened to come upon them, just as Laurie does when they are all sitting outside conducting their Busy Bee Society meeting. Yet they are still much too beautiful to be realistic. Like Smith's illustrations, Burd's are intended to turn *Little Women* into a pretty dream of Victorian life rather than make the story real to us.

The increasingly doll-like portraits of the March sisters also may have inspired the actual dolls that began to appear in 1933, when Madame Alexander created her series of Little Women dolls. (Since then the company has released new dolls annually.) Shortly thereafter, the most famous illustrator to tackle *Little Women* took his turn—not in a book, but in the pages of *Woman's Home Companion*. Under the title "The Most Beloved American Writer," the magazine ran a lengthy biographical essay on Alcott from December 1937 to March 1938.[41] Accompanying the four-part essay were illustrations by Norman Rockwell, who produced a number of line drawings and four-color paintings for the series. The subdued colors and natural poses are a nice compromise between the overly decorative images in some illustrated editions and the simple line drawings published in the earliest ones. Since then, Rockwell's paintings have enlivened posters and various *Little Women* memorabilia over the years.

Just after World War II, in 1946, one of the most remarkable editions of *Little Women* was released by World Publishing Company. The illustrations by Hilda van Stockum consist of striking silhouettes, more conventional woodcuts, and a few color plates produced with vibrant acrylics. Van Stockum interspersed her domestic, stylized groupings (in color) with dynamic images of the girls that convey their bustling energy better than any other illustrations I've seen. It is interesting how the most abstract style (the silhouettes) yields the liveliest images, allowing the reader to imagine the scene not as a picture but as a living thing.

Other notable editions of the period were illustrated by Louis Jambor (1947); Salomon van Abbé (1948); Rene Cloke (1949); Albert de

Mee Jousset (1950); Reisie Lonette (1950); the comic artist of World War II–era "Girl Commandos," Jill Elgin (1955); and Caldecott Honor winner Tasha Tudor (1960). Most of these illustrators, however, took the opportunity to pose the girls in their colorful, voluminous dresses, accentuating fashion over storytelling. Thereafter, newly illustrated editions become impossible to track because more than one appeared each year.[42] One noteworthy edition, from 1967, is the Limited Editions Club's very fine quarto-sized edition of 1,500 copies, each signed by the illustrator, Henry C. Pitz, with a floral tapestry cover and a slipcase. A copy now resides in the Special Collections of the Library of Congress. Pitz, an educator and authority on book illustration in addition to being a prolific illustrator himself, decorated the volume with dozens of line drawings and colored prints in a subdued palette. While maintaining the nineteenth-century atmosphere, he managed to give the book a midcentury feel.

Henry C. Pitz's artistic rendering of Jo and Beth at the seashore, a popular scene for illustrators (The Heritage Press, 1967). (©MBI, Inc. Used by permission.)

Since its original publication, *Little Women* has never gone out of print. Over one hundred newly illustrated editions have appeared in English. Foreign illustrated editions come to roughly two hundred. The total number of editions, however, which includes many that simply recycle the illustrations of previous volumes, is difficult to estimate. Currently about 320 versions of *Little Women* in English, which includes adaptations retold by other authors, reside in libraries around the world.[43] These numbers don't include the picture books and early readers, of which there have been dozens as well.

The phenomenon has not merely been an American or English-language one. By the mid-1870s *Little Women* had appeared in German, Dutch, and French. Soon it was also translated into Russian, Swedish, Danish, Greek, and Japanese. The title was often altered in these translations. In Dutch it becomes "Under Mother's Wings," and in French, "The Four Daughters of Dr. Marsch."[44] In France, a largely Catholic nation, Mr. March's profession as a pseudo-minister would have been unsettling, so he became a doctor instead. The title is still used in French translations today.

Up through the 1960s, *Little Women* was translated into at least fifty languages. Several Chinese translations appeared, as well as Arabic, Bengali, Indonesian, Urdu, Spanish, and Korean. In Moscow it was one of the most popular books in the 1920s, and its popularity extended to rural Russian villages as well. Between 1977 and 2009, a further three hundred translated editions of *Little Women* appeared in over thirty-seven languages. More than a dozen editions of the novel were printed in each of seven countries: Chile, China, Greece, France, Italy, Japan, and Spain. It has been particularly influential in Japan ever since it first appeared there in 1891 as "A Story of Young Grass," which signifies adolescence. During the next century, legions of schoolgirls read it, and many women were influenced by Jo's example to become writers. It remains today the second most popular book among Japanese girls, according to one educator, and is a popular subject of literary scholarship. Most professors in Japan find that their students already know the book well, having grown up reading it and its many adaptations, including several anime versions.[45]

The popularity of *Little Women* around the world only grew throughout the twentieth century. The novel's sales went up and down over the years, but it has never faded from view. While it is impossible to know how many copies have sold since its first publication, considering the vast number of editions from multiple publishers, it is safe to estimate that they approach 10 million.[46] But *Little Women* was much more than a book. The story of the March sisters lived on in many other forms as well, from radio and film to television drama and anime, spreading its influence well beyond the written page.

# PART II

## THE LIFE OF A CLASSIC

# 4

# "SEE HER . . . *LIVING* . . . THE IMMORTAL JO!"

### *Little* Women **on Stage and Screen**

THROUGHOUT THE HISTORY of radio, television, and film, adaptations of *Little Women* kept the Marches alive for generations of readers and nonreaders alike, revealing what each era saw as the story's most important elements. Adaptations transformed the story in subtle and not so subtle ways, emphasizing some plotlines and neglecting others, simplifying characters, and putting new dialogue into characters' mouths. Despite adapters' avowals of fidelity to the original text, each one reinvented *Little Women* for a new generation, sustaining Alcott's story as a living text growing and changing with time.

The first adaptations appeared on the stage. With home theatricals built into the novel, it was a natural progression. Amateur productions in school and community theaters had flourished since the novel was first published, but in the first decade of the twentieth century, bringing *Little Women* to Broadway was first proposed. There was serious resistance, however, to the idea of moving the story of the March sisters from the intimate pages of a book to the public, commercial setting of the stage. A writer for *Woman's Home Companion* summed up fans' concerns: "To see the ideals of your girlhood, womanhood, and motherhood massacred by a Broadway stage manager who never, never kept a dog-eared and tear-stained copy of 'Little Women' on the bedroom stand . . . seems more than you can endure!"[1] *Little Women* was much more than a story. It was a sacred object, anointed with tears and marked with the signs of an engaged reader's passionate interest. Would the play evoke the same reverence and deep feelings that the book did? Or would it be turned into a comic farce or melodramatic spectacle? For those who had cried over Beth's death, cheered on Jo's ambition, or smiled over Meg's mishaps as a new wife, a new version could do irreparable damage to their fond memories.

No wonder it took eight years for the director, Jessie Bonstelle, to convince Alcott's descendants to approve the plan of putting *Little Women* on Broadway. With the book still in copyright, Bonstelle conducted a long, concerted siege on John Pratt Alcott, Louisa's heir and executor of the Alcott publishing empire, for permission to write a script and stage the play. He feared—as did his brother, Frederick, and his cousin, May's daughter Louisa, or Lulu—that the play would "make a sacrilege of our home." They thought of *Little Women* as their family's story, making it "too intimate for the publicity [of] the stage." Even after Bonstelle was able to assure the family of her reverence for the story, others remained skeptical of her plan. When she approached Broadway theater manager William A. Brady, his response was, "What! . . . That girls' book?" There was no way it could make a successful play, he believed. Four weeks later she returned with a script covertly titled "The Four Sisters," and he loved it. Only afterward did he learn that it was in fact the story of *Little Women* (parts one and two, as all significant later adaptations would be).[2]

The play premiered in October 1912 at the Playhouse on Broadway, with the Alcott descendants in attendance. They were pleased with the result, agreeing with the reviewer from the *New-York Tribune* that "the 'real people' of the book" were there on the stage. The script by Marian de Forest remained largely faithful to the novel, telling the

Jo lies on the rug and complains, "Christmas won't be Christmas without any presents," the line that opened the 1912 Broadway play and brought the house down. From *Little Women,* Players' Edition (Little, Brown, 1912).

story of four sisters who make their way through life's ups and downs. Bonstelle believed that the play's appeal would depend on its ability to replicate the experience of reading the book. "The moment we get away from the spirit of the author," she wrote, "we lose the interest of the public," particularly those who had grown up loving the book. Audiences agreed. At least one performance was reportedly stopped by the audience's gasps and fervent applause when the actress playing Jo started the play with the novel's familiar opening line: "Christmas won't be Christmas without any presents."[3]

Of course, the story had to be significantly compressed for a two-hour play, meaning that the girls mature rather quickly. The romances between Meg and John Brooke and between Laurie and Amy develop rapidly with little suggestion that Jo and Laurie might be romantically paired off at all. Only slight attention is paid to Jo's writing or Amy's art, resulting in "a glorification of domesticity above such careers as writing or painting," as one reviewer put it.[4] Nonetheless, most of the play comes more or less directly from the book and established a framework followed by many of the adaptations to come.

The family play was tame in an era known for melodramatic and sensational entertainment. Vaudeville and minstrelsy reigned supreme, while dramas were full of damsels in distress and stereotypical heroes and villains. One critic, who generally liked the play, warned theatergoers, "There are no smashing 'dramatic' moments; there is no 'emotional' acting; there is no 'grip,' no 'thrill.'" An antidote to Broadway's usual fare, it provided wholesome entertainment whose emotional pull seemed genuine rather than manipulative. As the *Brooklyn Eagle* reviewer put it, the play avoided "the conventional stage tricks, [making] us live for a few brief hours, the sweet and simple lives of simple folk, to share their sorrows and to delight in their happiness. Art can do no more." Much as the novel itself had, the play made audiences feel they were experiencing real life transfigured into art. The play ran for 203 performances on Broadway and toured the country for two years. In 1914, it was the most highly valued theatrical property in the country because it drew audiences of all ages. Theatergoers must have felt much as the *New York Times* reviewer Adolph Klauber did: "Our hearts go out to Jo and Beth and Amy and the rest of them quite as much as they did in the old days when we begged for 'five minutes more to finish the chapter.'"[5]

HOT ON THE HEELS of the Broadway play's success, two new adaptations appeared in the 1910s: a silent film opened in Britain in 1917 and another in the United States in 1918. Sadly, both are lost. The U.S. film, made by William A. Brady and based on the De Forest play, was filmed in Concord, using Orchard House, by then a historic home open to the public, for exterior shots and as the model for interior shots. In addition, Bonstelle again staged the play in New York and in London in 1919. During the 1920s, although the copyright expired in 1925 and the novel ranked above the Bible in popularity, adaptations of *Little Women* dried up.[6] During the Roaring Twenties, the era of flappers and all things new and young, audiences weren't particularly interested in looking backward. Nostalgia had become passé.

However, as the worldwide economy faltered in the 1930s, *Little Women* regained its prominence. With the Depression weighing heavily on their minds, readers and audiences yearned for an escape to simpler times and wanted to recapture the lost innocence exemplified by the March family. During the 1930s *Little Women* was a perpetually best-selling book in England and America. Revivals of De Forest's play were staged on Broadway in 1931 and 1932, and in 1939 it appeared in the newly minted medium of television. Meanwhile, community productions flourished across the United States and Britain, and six new theatrical adaptations appeared. These again tended to downplay Jo's writing and independence while placing the girls' romances center stage. Nonetheless, the story's themes of deprivation and women's work made *Little Women* newly relevant during the 1930s.[7]

The revival was nowhere more apparent than when the first sound film adaptation of *Little Women* appeared in 1933. Made by RKO and directed by George Cukor (who would later direct *The Philadelphia Story*), it starred a newly famous Katharine Hepburn. The project was initiated by the head of production, David O. Selznick (of later *Gone with the Wind* fame), who wanted to modernize the story and thus save on period costumes and sets. RKO was having financial troubles. Cukor, however, was adamant that historical accuracy was crucial to the film's success, so Selznick conducted a poll to find out what the public preferred. Authenticity won by the ratio of three to one. About this time, Selznick left RKO in a dispute with its corporate president, and one of Selznick's assistants, Merian Cooper (producer and codirector of *King Kong* that same year) was put in charge of the film. Cukor was happy to find Cooper willing to let him make the film he wanted.[8]

Although filming took place in the San Fernando Valley outside of Los Angeles, Orchard House again served as a model for the set. Exact reproductions were made of every picture and piece of furniture. The costumes were made to look as if handed down among the sisters, and the dress cuffs were sandpapered to look worn.[9] Yet there were nods to contemporary circumstances, namely the Great Depression. In the opening, Marmee provides aid to a poor man who has lost three of his four sons to the war (an incident only briefly mentioned in the novel), and one scene shows the severe poverty of the Hummels, whom the sisters and their mother visit on Christmas morning. Later adaptations would gloss over the deprivation and hardship alluded to in Cukor's film.

By sticking with the original setting, the screenwriters also had to capture the tone and feeling of the book. After rejecting various screenplays that made the story too sentimental or that diverged from the plotline of the original book, Cukor settled on one written by Sarah Mason and Victor Heerman. In Hepburn's opinion, they had produced a "brilliant script, . . . simple and true and naïve but really believable."[10]

Publicity posters for the 1933 film, directed by George Cukor,
played up its association with Alcott's beloved novel.
(Photo 12/Alamy Stock Photo)

Despite RKO's money troubles, the film was allowed to go over schedule and over budget. Filming was briefly complicated by a strike of the sound men, who were replaced by an inexperienced crew. Multiple takes, due to the poor sound, of Beth's tearful deathbed scene finally caused Hepburn to throw up. "Well, that's what I think of the scene too," Cukor announced, and he called off filming for the day. He was initially worried that Hepburn wasn't professional enough. When she spilled ice cream on her dress, despite his warning that they didn't have a replacement, he hit her and called her an amateur. "You can think what you want," she shot back.[11] Soon the breach was healed, however, and they would become great friends while working together on ten films, including *Holiday*, *The Philadelphia Story*, and *Adam's Rib*.

*Little Women* was only Hepburn's fourth film, and it made the twenty-six-year-old a star. Although she earned her first Academy Award for Best Actress for her performance earlier that year in *The Morning Glory*, she always insisted she had won for the wrong film. Full-page newspaper ads trumpeted her ability to capture "the best loved heroine ever born in a book. See her . . . *living* . . . the immortal Jo!" Hepburn had felt a special kinship with the book. She *was* Jo, her brother and Cukor both said. She once boasted, "I could outdive, outswim, outrun most of the boys around me." She completely empathized with Jo's desire to be a boy—when Hepburn was ten, she had shaved her head, worn boy's clothes, and changed her name to Jimmy.[12]

Cukor took a risk in letting Hepburn play the tomboy to the hilt. Her earlier performance in *Christopher Strong* as an independent woman aviator was not well received. Hepburn essentially played Jo as herself. As scholar Beverly Lyon Clark points out, Hepburn's Jo is a modern version of Alcott's heroine who leaps fences, slides down banisters, and crosses swords with Laurie—none of which Jo does in the book. But Cukor's risk paid off, and the public fell in love with Hepburn. Reviewers almost uniformly gushed over her performance. *Variety*'s reviewer summed up the wide approval, writing that Hepburn "endows the role with awkwardly engaging youth, energy that makes it the essence of flesh and blood reality."[13]

A rough-and-tumble Jo, played by Katharine Hepburn, fences
with Laurie in the 1933 film. (AF archive/Alamy Stock Photo)

For many fans there will never be another Jo like Hepburn's, yet
what felt realistic to her contemporaries now seems over the top. I
have to agree with critic Kate Ellis, who notes that Hepburn emphasized Jo's masculine traits at the expense of her nurturing ones.
"Apparently a tomboy . . . must be constantly swaggering, stomping,
thrusting out her chin and exclaiming 'Christopher Columbus!'"
Hepburn herself understood the character as requiring an exaggerated, theatrical performance.[14] The result is that she overwhelms the
role rather than disappearing into it. Her transformation from an
unnaturally boyish young woman with an affected low voice into a
wistful, dewy-eyed girl with a high, soft voice swooning over Professor Bhaer is also jarring. Neither Jo rings true.

The professor was played by Hungarian Paul Lukas, who makes
him rather suave and vaguely Italian-sounding instead of German.
Perhaps Hitler's rise to power earlier that year had already made Ger-

mans suspect. Amy, who is supposed to be twelve years old, was played by twenty-three-year-old and secretly pregnant Joan Bennett. When she could no longer hide her condition, her costumes had to be altered and she had to be filmed from the waist up. Douglass Montgomery makes a much-too-polished Laurie, who is supposed to be fifteen; Montgomery was twenty-six and looked thirty. Jean Parker, who played Beth, also looked too old but still captured the childlike simplicity of the March sister who hides at home with her kittens. Frances Dee, at twenty-three, played Meg and was probably the most suited to her role. Yet as a prim, scolding Meg, she doesn't make a lasting impression.

As filming wrapped up, it became clear the film could be a hit. Merian Cooper felt it might even be bigger than *King Kong*. After seeing the rushes, he thought the four March sisters "as charming

Katharine Hepburn, as Jo, instructs a noticeably pregnant Joan Bennett, as Amy, how to act in her play. (SilverScreen/Alamy Stock Photo)

as anything that has ever been on screen." Critics were less sure of the film's success. The story's simplicity could make it a hard sell in "these practical, hard boiled times," as one put it. Yet audiences weren't as hardened as all that. When the film opened in November at Radio City Music Hall, it broke box office records. Three thousand people crowded into the theater, and another thousand gathered outside. Thirty mounted policemen had to be called in to manage the crowds.[15]

Ultimately, Cukor's *Little Women* was the fourth-highest-grossing film of 1933, netting a profit of $800,000 though it cost only $424,000 to make. Moviegoers also ranked it as their favorite of the year. It was nominated for three Academy Awards—Best Adapted Screenplay, Best Director, and Best Movie—and won for the screenplay. Distributed to at least eleven foreign countries, *Little Women* also played to full houses across Europe. Critics raved, calling it "a perfect picture," "an amazing triumph," and "a masterpiece of Americana." It proved to be a nice break for audiences tired of the racy content of movies overpopulated with gangsters and hardened dames. (Strict enforcement of the Hayes Code, censoring risqué or violent content, would begin the following year.) A reviewer for the *Indianapolis Star* admitted that he was expecting to scoff at the "painfully prim" film but found instead that this love story without sex "actually got the raucous ring of 'come up and see me sometime' out of our ears," an allusion to Mae West's famous sexual invitation to Cary Grant in *She Done Him Wrong* earlier that year.[16]

The film's success caused a spike in sales of the original novel and spawned a range of new commercial products. Little, Brown brought out "Orchard House" editions of *Little Women*, *Little Men*, and *Jo's Boys*, with pictures of the Alcotts' home in Concord. Whitman Publishing produced a "Big Little Book" edition of *Little Women*, written from the script and featuring a still from the movie on every other page. RKO also made souvenir playing cards and an embroidery sampler featuring each of the March sisters—Jo holding a pen, Meg knitting, Beth playing the piano, and Amy twirling an umbrella. Madame Alexander, independently, also began producing her *Little*

*Women* dolls. And fashions for women, according to the United Press correspondent from Paris, were being influenced by the film. "Old-fashioned loveliness" was in style once again.[17]

The 1930s and 1940s were also the heyday of radio, when families huddled around large consoles listening to quiz shows, variety hours, soap operas, detective series, and radio plays, including dramatizations of classics like *Little Women*. It is impossible to know how many radio adaptations there were, since broadcasts were not routinely recorded until the 1940s. One of the earliest aired on NBC in 1932, and two years later, Jack Benny spoofed the novel and the film in his skit "Miniature Women," or "Small Dames." In act one, when Beth complains of being sick while her mother waxes on about her being so good, Benny quips, "Maybe that's why she's sick." In act two, his Laurie proposes to Marie Livingstone's Jo, who responds, "I am a genius and I have a career that I must strive and work hard for. Someday I'm going to be famous, and then I'll come back and marry you. It might be five years, it might be ten years, . . . it might be forty years. . . . Will you still want me in forty years?" Benny says, "In forty years even RKO won't want you."[18] Although the themes of career versus family were subdued in the RKO film, clearly audiences were aware of the tensions that Jo's character represented.

Between 1935 and 1950, at least eight dramatizations of *Little Women* were aired on radio shows such as *Lux Radio Theater, American Novels*, and *Tell It Again*. In 1947, *Favorite Story*, which retold stories chosen by celebrities, featured Shirley Temple's pick, *Little Women*. Ranging from thirty minutes to an hour, the radio plays sadly diluted Alcott's story. They tended to skip Jo's literary attempts, Amy's adventures in art, the girls' plays, school, and work, focusing almost entirely on the girls' romances and Beth's illness. Some radio versions of *Little Women* featured the stars of the RKO film. Katharine Hepburn appeared in one in 1934 and reprised her role in 1945 for *Theater Guild on the Air*. In that version, Jo dismisses her literary success after Beth's death. She tells her parents that what she wrote was "nothing," while Professor Bhaer conveniently arrives and proposes to Jo as a crescendo of music abruptly closes the show. In 1949, when another film of *Little Women* was released, its stars would also appear in a radio adaptation.[19] In the years between films, radio plays helped to keep *Little Women* alive, making the story a staple in the entertainment diet of Americans throughout the first half of the century.

As THE COUNTRY emerged from the Depression and plunged into World War II, *Little Women*'s popularity continued to soar. Its Civil War setting and portrayal of women on the home front, making do while the family patriarch is away at war, made the story relevant in a new way. *Little Women* appeared onstage in London in 1941 and in New York on Broadway in 1944 and 1945, and was produced across Britain and the United States in community and school theaters.[20]

In the aftermath of the war, Hollywood again turned its eye toward *Little Women*. David O. Selznick, who had recently formed his own company, still regretted not being at the helm of the RKO film and decided in 1946 that he wanted another go at it, this time in Technicolor and starring his future wife, Jennifer Jones. He had Mason and Heerman adapt their 1933 script and hired Mervyn LeRoy, producer of *The Wizard of Oz*, to direct. Selznick failed to enlist Cukor, who saw no point in a remake without Hepburn. The "magic simply wouldn't be there," he felt.[21] Filming lasted for only three weeks before budget cuts and the threat of a strike closed the production. LeRoy, still keen to move ahead, convinced Louis B. Mayer, head of MGM, to buy the rights from Selznick, including the screenplay and sets, and to rehire him as director. A new cast was assembled with June Allyson as Jo.

Allyson, who had a girl-next-door image, was known primarily for musical roles in films such as *Two Girls and a Sailor* and *Good News*. (She would star with James Stewart in *The Stratton Story*, released just two months after *Little Women*.) Although Allyson was thirty-one when she played Jo, she quite naturally captured Jo's refusal to grow up. Not only boyish in voice and mannerisms, Allyson was also delightfully off balance much of the time. In the novel, Alcott described Jo as "a colt; for she never seemed to know what to do with her limbs, which were very much in her way." Pretty without being Hollywood beautiful, Allyson also more accurately approximated a character who isn't supposed to stand out for her physical appearance. Nonetheless, Allyson's performance has generally been seen as not up to the benchmark set by Hepburn. Critic Carol Gay writes, for instance, that Allyson "indicated [Jo's] tomboy qualities, . . . but she brought little else to the role. (Her films, on the whole, have actually epitomized the whole artistic failure and moral vapidity of the popular films of the 40s and 50s.)" Allyson herself complained that she didn't get many substantial roles and cited Jo as her favorite. "Jo is a fantastic character," she said, because "she is determined to do something more than bake cookies."[22]

Meg was played by Janet Leigh, a relative newcomer who wouldn't become famous until *Psycho* (1960), while the other sisters were played by two of the most popular child stars of the era. Eleven-year-old Margaret O'Brien, who was Beth, had already been in a string of films, most memorably opposite Judy Garland in *Meet Me in St. Louis* (1944). Elizabeth Taylor played Amy, although she turned eighteen on the set and had to don a blond wig for the part. This was her last child role (*National Velvet* had been five years earlier), and she played the worldly innocent to the hilt, looking more like a Madame Alexander doll than a real girl. (In fact, all of the actresses wore too much makeup.) Interestingly, the birth order of the sisters was changed, making Beth the youngest and thereby allowing Amy to more naturally grow into a fancy young lady during the course of the story. Although it took a tremendous liberty, the move makes sense, since Beth never has to grow up.

The four actresses became quite close during the filming, eating lunch together and gossiping about costar Peter Lawford, who played Laurie. The tanned Hollywood heartthrob had previously costarred with each actress, except O'Brien. The silliness that ensued irritated Mary Astor, who played Marmee. While shooting the scene where Lawford was supposed to say that a newly shorn Allyson looked like a porcupine, he kept pronouncing it "porky-pine." Astor stood stiffly by as the young actors guffawed at every botched take. She was especially aggravated

This publicity photo for the 1949 film places June
Allyson, as Jo, on top, with a gussied-up Elizabeth
Taylor, as Amy, on the left. (Moviestore Collection Ltd/
Alamy Stock Photo)

with Taylor, who giggled on the phone with her boyfriend while
the entire company waited for her to finish. "I had never before
encountered such a brazen attitude of a child actor," she later said.
Astor had been playing a string of mothers, including O'Brien's in
*Meet Me in St. Louis*, and she wasn't happy about it. She had previously starred with Humphrey Bogart in *The Maltese Falcon* and been
nominated for an Academy Award for Best Supporting Actress for
her performance in *The Great Lie* (both 1941). Being cast as Marmee felt like being put out to pasture.[23] Her lack of enthusiasm for
the role or rapport with the other actors shows in her rather stern
performance.

MGM basically wanted to remake the RKO film in color, so it reused the score and slightly altered the screenplay. Some of the same scenes even reappear, most noticeably the one in which Amy is reprimanded by her teacher at school. In fact, Amy's drawing of her teacher was spliced in from the earlier film. As in the earlier adaptations, the so-called little women grow up awfully fast. There is no Pickwick Club or Castles in the Air, no dreams of the future, only a quick march to the altar for three of them and a sad death, of course,

Posters for the 1949 film emphasized the love plots
in part two of *Little Women* over the novel's
domestic and coming-of-age themes.
(AF archive/Alamy Stock Photo)

for Beth. The girls are turned into romantic objects pretty much from the outset. Laurie tells Jo the first time he meets her of Brooke's interest in Meg and is clearly in love with Jo at first sight. Not surprisingly, MGM billed the movie as its "New Technicolor Romance" and "World's Greatest Love Story!"

In one important way, however, LeRoy's film is very different from Cukor's. It opens with Jo jumping the fence on her way home while her sisters watch from the window, rather than with the montage of soldiers heading off to the Civil War as in the 1933 film. By 1949, audiences didn't want to be reminded of war or deprivation. Instead, they wanted a colorful rendition of the home as a haven and source of plenty. The studio even added an elaborate shopping scene. Having received Christmas money from Aunt March, the girls head downtown and savor the offerings at the general store. They linger over the gifts they most want but end up buying presents for Marmee instead. The movie thus supported the idea that consumerism was

The March sisters look through the store window in this shopping scene created for the 1949 film. (Moviestore Collection Ltd/Alamy Stock Photo)

the patriotic duty of American women after the war. They were to rebuild the population and the economy by marrying, having babies, and filling their homes with new products.

It is perhaps not surprising, then, that in this version Laurie dismisses Jo's literary ambitions. Whereas in the book he calls her stories "works of Shakespeare compared to half of the rubbish that's published every day," here Laurie complains, "I just don't understand you, cooping yourself up in that garret, missing a lot of fun with me, working. And for what? For one measly little dollar." His attitude makes Jo's later refusal of his proposal (in part because he wouldn't like her writing) more plausible, but her interest in Professor Bhaer is made even more puzzling in this film. The Italian Rossano Brazzi makes a very handsome Bhaer, but in a slick, Hollywood sort of way. He is nothing like the endearingly absentminded professor that Alcott tried to make him. And he sounds even more Italian, at a time when everything German was tainted with Nazism.

The biggest difference from the 1933 film was the use of color. In some ways it aids the storyline, highlighting the difference between an unornamented Jo, in her simple brown and blue dresses, and Meg and Amy in bright colors and frills. In their pink brilliance, Meg and Amy reflect the over-the-top femininity that came into vogue after World War II, which their performances also accentuate. Clearly aware of the image they are creating, Leigh and Taylor self-consciously tuck in their chins, widen their eyes, and talk in soft, babyish voices. Allyson's Jo, on the other hand, is perfectly unconcerned with how she looks to others. She raises her chin, looks men directly in the eye, and speaks in a more natural voice.

Critics were not impressed with this color version of *Little Women*, however. They especially objected to its sentimentality, a charge scarcely leveled at the 1933 film. The emotions evoked by Cukor's film, which stressed authenticity to the original era and story, seemed like wholesome nostalgia. But the showiness of LeRoy's film smacked of mawkish sentiment. For the *New York Times* critic, the rainbow that arches over the Marches' home at the end symbolized everything that was wrong with the film. Technicolor had been around for a while, but it made a story that audiences were used to thinking of as "real" seem false, reminding them of movies such as 1939's *The Wizard of Oz*. Under the headline "Somewhere Under the Rainbow Lies Louisa May Alcott's 'Little Women,'" one critic asserted that color was "the principal fault" of the film. "Wash it clean of its phony colors, and you would also wash it clean of its phony emotions." Nonetheless, some reviewers were charmed by the film's old-fashioned focus on family. For the *Los Angeles Times* critic, it was "a gracious and warming glance backward at a way of life that is gone forever." In Australia, the Melbourne *Age* reviewer, apparently overlooking Jo entirely, approved of the film's portrayal of an era when families were tight-knit and "girls were girls and did not try to pose as half-baked men."[24]

The consumerism highlighted in the film also spilled over into the new market of movie-related products. Some of the tie-ins included Hallmark cards—one of each sister—a jewelry box shaped like the book with the stars' photos inside, and a scarf with each of the four actresses splashed across it. Clothing manufacturers created *Little Women*–inspired dresses and coats, while advertisers used the film to sell milk, soap, and breakfast food.[25] Ultimately, LeRoy's film did well in the United States and abroad, where it was distributed to at least thirteen countries. And, presumably because it was in color, it would become the standard movie version of the popular book, the one replayed on television for each new generation of fans.

As TELEVISION ROSE to prominence, *Little Women* also moved into the new medium. In all, twelve adaptations of *Little Women* have been produced for American television, including a 1958 musical starring Florence Henderson and a ballet version in 1976 with Joanne Woodward. There has also been one adaptation in Canada and four in Britain. The BBC produced two miniseries in the 1950s, in addition to a 1956 movie, *A Girl Called Jo*, and a nine-part series in 1970. The last is still available on VHS tape. As a production of the BBC, it features British actors who apparently weren't able to manage American accents, although the servant Hannah, curiously, sounds like a southern mammy. It's also full of other kinds of nonsense, such as

Amy refusing to say the word *breast* as she is about to thrust a dagger into hers while rehearsing the lines of Jo's play. At the end, during his less-than-romantic proposal, Professor Bhaer tells Jo that it is a German woman's duty to obey her husband. (Needless to say, neither of these moments occurs in the book.)

In the United States, Universal Television produced a two-part, four-hour miniseries shown on NBC in 1978. (It is the only television adaptation currently available on DVD.) Viewed as a kind of American *Masterpiece Theater*, the production was intended to be faithful to the book, even more so than the previous versions. The director, David Lowell Victor, said he particularly attempted to "avoid the Hollywood glossiness" of the 1949 film.[26] The star-studded cast included Susan Dey (of *The Partridge Family* fame) as Jo, Meredith Baxter Birney (later the mom in *Family Ties*) as Meg, Eve Plumb (Jan from *The Brady Bunch*) as Beth, renowned British actor Greer Garson as Aunt March, Robert Young (star of *Father Knows Best*) as Mr. Laurence, and William Shatner of the *Star Trek* TV series as Professor Bhaer.

Dey was twenty-five at the time of shooting and originally thought "too pretty" to play Jo. But she succeeded in playing Jo with naïve simplicity more suited to the role than the overstated tomboyishness of her predecessors. Perhaps by the late 1970s Jo could begin to be simply herself without having to perform an exaggerated masculinity. The scriptwriter, Susan Clauser, said that she set out to portray a new kind of Jo, not just a tomboy but a "woman who wanted to follow her own muse."[27] Thus Jo's writing career gets more screen time than in the previous versions. The miniseries' longer length also allowed Clauser to portray Meg's difficulties with entering into high society and adjusting to marriage, neither of which were touched on by the earlier adaptations. As a result, this adaptation is much more about sisters with distinct personalities and problems than about Jo with her sisters in the background.

Given when it was made, this should be the feminist version of *Little Women*, but it falls short of even Alcott's prefeminist-movement progressiveness. Clauser claimed that she tried to give Jo "an open ending [that would] not clos[e] off her ambitions and her desire," but it's not clear how she did that. Near the end, Bhaer proposes, as in the other adaptations. But Professor Bhaer, who is otherwise rather adorably played by Shatner, unexpectedly asserts his authority over Jo. In the book Jo is clear that she will contribute to their income, saying, "I'm to carry my share, Friedrich, and help to earn the home" (something none of the screenwriters have dared have her say).[28] But here he insists, "The decision is mine. I will take care of you as I see fit," to which Jo meekly responds, "Yes, Friedrich." I don't think there is a greater betrayal of Jo and Alcott in any of the various adaptations than in those two lines.

Reviewers were mixed in their reactions to this *Little Women*. UPI television writer Joan Hanauer summed up the general opinion, calling it "so sweet the flies may stick to your home screen." Another critic dubbed it "the 'Waltons' of an earlier era" and believed it would live long after the era's most popular shows, such as *Laverne and Shirley* and *Charlie's Angels*, went into syndicated reruns.[29] A short-lived television series was spun off, in hopes of capturing the *Little House on the Prairie* demographic, but it lasted only one month.

*Little Women* was also adapted in various languages for television outside of the United States and Britain. In the 1950s, it was made in Italian, Mandarin, Portuguese (in Brazil), and Cantonese. In the 1960s, TV series under the title *Mujercitas* appeared in Mexico, Argentina, and Spain. New television movies based on the novel were also produced in 1973 in Mexico, in 1990 in Italy, and in 1999 in Venezuela. In 2008, a twenty-six-episode series that set Alcott's story in the present day was filmed in Turkish and shown in Turkey, Bulgaria, and Ukraine. Three Japanese anime studios put their twist on the novel, the first being Toei Studio's one-hour special that aired on Fuji TV in 1980. Based on its success, Movie International made a twenty-six-episode series in 1981 with Toei animation. This version, with a blonde Jo, was dubbed into Tagalog, French, and Italian and broadcast in English on CBN, the forerunner to ABC's The Family Channel. The most well-known anime adaptation is *Tales of Little Women*, a forty-eight-episode series produced by Nippon Animation that ran in 1987 on Fuji TV in Japan and across Asia on Animax satellite television. The first half of the series diverges greatly from the novel, emphasizing its Civil War setting. The Marches live near Gettysburg, hide a runaway slave, and endure occupation by Confederate troops until their home is destroyed in the famous battle. They then head to the made-up town of Newcord, where they are taken in by a reluctant Aunt March. At Christmastime the Marches move into a new home, and from there the series begins to mirror the plot of the book. *Tales of Little Women* was shown in English on HBO in 1988 and dubbed into at least twelve other languages, including Korean, Tagalog, German, Portuguese, Russian, Arabic, and Farsi.[30]

ALTHOUGH NO MAJOR motion picture was made for over four decades, the appetite for *Little Women* remained strong. When, in 1994, a fifty-seven-year-old Margaret O'Brien was asked if she thought *Little Women* was too old-fashioned, she responded, "I don't think it ever was. I still get fan mail about it. People want that kind of film even today." That year a new film of *Little Women* was released by Columbia Pictures. It had been the pet project of Executive Vice President of Production Amy Pascal since 1982. Her male producer colleagues had dismissed the idea of making a film of the classic girls' book, just as William A. Brady had in the 1910s.[31]

What finally made the difference was that in the early 1990s, "it girl" Winona Ryder became attached to the project and a kind of rebranding of the film took place. Denise Di Novi (whose credits included *Edward Scissorhands* and *The Nightmare Before Christmas*) was taken on early as producer, with relative newcomer Robin Swicord as screenwriter. Australian Gillian Armstrong (known for *My Brilliant Friend* and *Mrs. Soffel*) was slated to direct. Despite the film's all-female production crew, they were adamant that this was not a film for women only. As Armstrong puts it in the Director's Commentary, Pascal pitched it as a family film for Christmas. When the heads of Columbia saw the final version, they were moved to tears, according to Armstrong. They realized it was "a film for more than little girls and mothers," calling it a touching "epic family story."[32] To prove it, they increased the film's publicity budget. Their gambit paid off. The film far outstripped the studio's expectations, earning $50

The story that has lived in our hearts for generations.

WINONA RYDER

LITTLE WOMEN

Publicity for Gillian Armstrong's 1994 film of *Little Women* played up the novel's association with Christmas. (Moviestore Collection Ltd/Alamy Stock Photo)

million, even as it competed with *Dumb and Dumber*. It would also be distributed to at least twenty-two foreign countries.

The movie's hip young cast certainly helped draw in younger audiences. Ryder was at the peak of her popularity. She starred earlier that year in *Reality Bites* and earned a Golden Globe and an Oscar nomination for her performance the previous year in *Age of Innocence*. Claire Danes, who played Beth, was known for her starring role in the angsty teen television drama *My So-Called Life*, and Kirsten

Dunst, who played Amy, had just wowed audiences in *Interview with a Vampire*. Trini Alvarado, who played Meg, had appeared in Armstrong's *Mrs. Soffel*. The role of Laurie was given to the British Christian Bale, who had made his Hollywood debut in the 1987 Steven Spielberg film *The Empire of the Sun*. Susan Sarandon, costar in the landmark feminist film *Thelma and Louise* in 1991, played Marmee, while the Irishman Gabriel Byrne, who had appeared in a string of modestly successful movies such as *Miller's Crossing*, was chosen to play Professor Bhaer.

Armstrong's film is *the* adaptation of the novel for most *Little Women* fans under fifty. It came out shortly after I read the novel for the first time in my twenties, and I have very fond memories of it. I was thrown by the liberties it took with the book, but I still loved it. The warm hues and candlelight, so different from LeRoy's garish Technicolor production, evoke a time when families gathered around the piano and produced their own theatricals. One of my favorite moments comes after Amy falls through the ice and the sisters, back

The March sisters cuddle with kittens in a scene typical of Armstrong's film's cozy evocation of home. (AF archive/Alamy Stock Photo)

at home, are nestled in bed with a bunch of kittens. This is what home feels like, or, more accurately, this is your image of a home you never knew but wish you had.

Armstrong's film catered to a nostalgia for home and family that was particularly potent in the 1990s, when the idealized domesticity of nineteenth-century novels seemed an admonishment to the "broken homes" then becoming the norm. A new kind of battle was taking place—not against poverty or fascism but against modern life. These were the so-called culture wars, in which traditionalists and progressives argued over everything from science and the economy to art and women's roles. Christian conservatives promoted "family values" and a 1950s-style, gendered division of labor. Meanwhile, although women had entered the workforce in unprecedented numbers, they felt increasingly uncomfortable calling themselves feminists. Armstrong, a product of the backlash years, created a film that, in the words of the journalist Marshall Fine, "manages to be traditional without being conservative." As the syndicated columnist Sara Eckel put it, the film was "a feminist story even Newt Gingrich could love."[33]

On the road to promote the film, Armstrong was clearly wary of linking the film to feminism, which had received, in her words, "irreparable amounts of bad press." She was eager to show that she was not the man-hating type, nor was her film. She also hoped to overcome the impression that it was "a cute little movie for little girls" and to convince men that "there's something there for them too." She even joked about changing the title, so they wouldn't be scared away.[34]

It is reasonable to view it as a feminist film, however, considering the updates Robin Swicord made to the script. For instance, in one scene Jo makes a case for women's right to vote, something she never does in the book (although she would in the 1886 *Jo's Boys*, when the issue had become a more prominent cultural topic). In the film, when a young man tells Jo she should have been a lawyer, she responds, "I should have been a great many things." Swicord gave Marmee the lion's share of the film's progressive speeches, echoing Alcott's proto-feminist views in favor of women's education and against corsets and double sexual standards. Details from Alcott's life also creep into the film. Jo tells Professor Bhaer, for instance, that her father's school was closed because he admitted a black child. (In the books Mr. March is a minister, whereas in real life, as previously mentioned, Bronson Alcott led a school that failed, in part, because he admitted a black pupil.) Swicord explained that she made such changes because she wanted to make overt the things that Alcott had to suggest "between the lines," lest she dampen the popular appeal of her book. "I tried to write the film as I imagined she would have written it today, freed of the cultural restraints of the time she lived," Swicord said.[35]

The result is a film whose dialogue is nearly all invented. For instance, upon first meeting Laurie, Jo confesses offhandedly, "If I wasn't going to be a writer, I'd move to New York and pursue the stage. Are you shocked?" (Although Alcott harbored such ambition herself, her audience would, indeed, have been quite shocked to learn of it.) Marmee says, "I won't have my girls silly about boys," and Amy reports that her teacher said in class, "It was as useful to educate a woman as it was to educate a female cat." Brooke says to Marmee, "One hopes your girls will be a gentling influence," and to Laurie, "Over the mysteries of female life, there is drawn a veil best left undisturbed." In the book, Brooke is nowhere near as priggish as Swicord makes him (and Eric Stoltz plays all too well). In these instances, Swicord has made the conservativeness of the era more overt than Alcott herself did.

Unfortunately, while Swicord has opted for a kind of spirited nostalgia by both idealizing the past and poking holes in its prejudices and proprieties, she has also dulled the power and emotions of the original work. Here Marmee is the all-wise mother figure who preaches to the girls without ever acknowledging her own difficulties or needs. She doesn't admit to Jo, as she does in the book, that she has struggled to control her own anger and that she needs the girls to give her strength after she learns of her husband's illness. In the book, Marmee has heartfelt conversations with the girls about their futures, whereas here she preaches to them. After Meg comes home from the Moffats, she points out the double standard that condemns a young woman for having fun but lets men do whatever they want. Yet she never tells her girls of her hope that they will find worthy mates, regardless of wealth, or agrees with Jo that it is better to "be happy old maids than unhappy wives."[36] Swicord missed an opportunity to pull out of Alcott's text what was truly original and progressive in it.

Jo is also sadly diminished as a character. We see little of her struggles against herself, and her difficult emotions are limited to sadness at losing her sister. She is granted a burst of anger when Amy burns her manuscript (a scene left out of earlier versions and thankfully restored by Swicord), but Jo never discusses her struggles to control her anger with Marmee, one of the most powerful scenes in the novel. Nor does Swicord show us Jo's guilt over exposing Beth to the Hummels' sick baby while she stayed home to write. Sadly, Beth is also simplified. Although she is not as overly angelic as she is in the earlier versions, her painful shyness is barely mentioned.

On the other hand, Professor Bhaer, as played by Gabriel Byrne, is by far the most believable Bhaer on screen. He is not classically handsome but appealing in a romantic, teddy-bear sort of way. Armstrong indicated that they wanted to make Bhaer their "ideal man": good-looking, supportive of Jo's career, and great with kids, thus updating Alcott's portrait of him (although I would argue this is exactly how Alcott wanted us to see him).[37] Unfortunately, though, as in the other movies, Swicord has him not merely supportive of but instrumental in Jo's literary career. In the novel, she achieves considerable success on her own. Here she sends him her manuscript and he gets it published for her, robbing Jo of her independence as a writer.

Regardless of the changes, this version is clearly a loving tribute to *Little Women*. Many of those tied to the project had personal reasons for making this film. Pascal had loved the novel as a child and was named by her mother for two of the March sisters—her full name is Amy Beth Pascal. Swicord checked the book out of the library every year, beginning when she was eight. Armstrong was given the novel for her eleventh birthday and wanted to make the film for her daughter, as did Sarandon, who took the project despite her agent's advice against playing Ryder's mother in age-conscious Hollywood. Ryder said that she had read the book at twelve, and it left a lasting impression for its portrayal of the obstacles women faced in the nineteenth century.[38]

Even as the filmmakers updated *Little Women*, they wanted to remain faithful to it, at least visually. Orchard House again served as the model for the Marches' home, which is re-created with subtle, muted hues. The makeup-free March sisters look more like real girls and less like dolls or fashion plates. Dresses worn by the older sisters reappear in later scenes on the younger ones, handed down as they would have been in real life. Ryder was twenty-three when she portrayed Jo, but she looked much younger. Alvarado was twenty-seven during filming but she resembled the late adolescent Meg, while Danes was only fifteen, nearly the same age as Beth. At twenty, Bale was a much more suitable Laurie than his predecessors—much less Hollywood and possessing more of the awkwardness of being a European in an American setting. One of the most striking differences of this version is that Amy is finally played by a young actress—Dunst, who was twelve—but halfway through the film, she is suddenly replaced by an older actress, Samantha Mathis. Unfortunately, Mathis's prim Amy contrasts too markedly with Dunst's much more playful one.

The real problem, however, was casting the stunning Winona Ryder as Jo. Ryder's petite, fawn-like beauty conveyed none of Jo's coltish awkwardness. Although Ryder's performance won her an Academy Award nomination for Best Actress, she, like Hepburn, was incapable of disappearing into the role. The line that Ryder's Jo lost her "one beauty" when she cut off her hair rings false, as does Jo's declaration that "I am ugly and awkward and always say the wrong thing." Ryder simply can't help being beautiful and, apparently, she can't help knowing it. The way Ryder smiles for the camera or her male costars betrays her consciousness of her own beauty. She is the object of our gaze, whereas Jo is supposed to be the budding writer, the bumbling tomboy, who looks out at the world and has no interest in being looked at herself. There is simply no boyishness about Ryder, and Swicord never has her say the famous line about how she wishes she had been born a boy. Downplaying Jo's gender ambivalence appears to have been a conscious decision. In an interview, Armstrong indicated that she resented the way ambitious women are stereotyped as unattractive and as seeking compensation for their loveless lives.[39] As a result, unfortunately, Jo's resistance to the gender stereotypes of her own day is virtually absent. The only times Ryder evokes this part of Jo is when she is dressed in drag—wearing

Jo played by Winona Ryder, whose petite beauty clashed with the gawky
tomboyishness of Alcott's character. (RGR Collection/Alamy Stock Photo)

a top hat in the Pickwick Club scene (which none of the other films
include), or a moustache and an admiral's hat in the scene where they
are rehearsing the play. In both cases, she lowers her voice dramatically and adopts a stuffy English accent. Ryder alternately performs
an exaggerated masculinity (very briefly) or a coy femininity, much
like her predecessor Hepburn. Neither suits Jo, who is supposed to be
gawky and free of feminine artifice.

However, it appears that Ryder was so instrumental in getting
the film made that without her, it might not have existed. It was her
clout that helped get the project off the ground. Her commitment
was motivated by not only a love of the book but also a desire to
"inspire young people. . . . Young girls, especially, don't have a lot
of good role models," she said in an interview. "They get underesti-
mated by the film industry," which assumes they only want "movies like 'Pretty Woman,'" when really they . . . have been waiting for
something that doesn't completely insult them."[40] In other words,
Hollywood hadn't progressed much since Mae West's heyday. It still
wanted its actresses to play call girls.

Critics uniformly raved over the film. Roger Ebert wrote, "At first, I was grumpy, thinking it was going to be too sweet and devout. Gradually, I saw that Gillian Armstrong . . . was taking it seriously." Janet Maslin, in the *New York Times*, called it "the loveliest 'Little Women' ever on screen." She thought Ryder portrayed Jo "with enough vigor to dim memories of Katharine Hepburn." The British press agreed. The *Daily Telegraph* thought it a "sweet-tempered, joyous reconciliation of modern female aspirations with traditional female roles." The *Independent* called it the "best screen version yet of *Little Women*" and "the most authentic." An outlier was Stephen Amidon at the *Sunday Times*, who felt that Armstrong had failed "to translate Alcott's resolutely Victorian vision into a modern idiom, leaving the movie caught in a nether-land between historical accuracy and contemporary expectations."[41] He's not wrong, but he fails to consider the power of audiences' nostalgia for a soft-lit past of sisterly affection.

Once again, reviewers enjoyed the film's difference from Hollywood's standard fare. The *Washington Post* imagined the film could "buoy American spirits at this time of spiritual impoverishment much as George Cukor's 1933 adaptation lifted hopes during the Great Depression." The *Daily Mail*'s reviewer thought, "it is a pleasure to attend a picture in which the worst swear word is Blast." Syndicated columnist Donna Britt believed other reviewers' warnings that "nothing much happens" were tantamount to saying that women's lives weren't worth making films about. She praised the film for "honor[ing] life's small wonders" in a culture that is "hypnotized . . . by ever-more-wizardly special effects, stupid sex tricks and the 'thrill' of cringing at yet another creative way to kill."[42]

Audiences were as charmed as the critics, sparking a revival in all things Alcott. Within days of the film's release, Orchard House was inundated with visitors, and a movie edition of the novel was launched onto the bestseller lists. Five other editions tied to the movie also appeared, while some critics complained of the trend to market novels based on the film as versions of the original.[43] How were readers to know whether they had read the real book or not? Alcott's renewed popularity also extended beyond movie tie-ins. Even before the movie came out, Random House paid $1.5 million for the rediscovered manuscript of Alcott's early unpublished novel *A Long Fatal Love Chase*, heralded as a "bodice-ripper" by the author of *Little Women*. When the book was published in October 1995, Stephen King reviewed it positively for the *New York Times*, and it became a bestseller.[44] In 1997, still riding the wave of the 1994 movie's popularity, Alcott's first (unpublished) novel, *The Inheritance*, was published and also made into a television movie by CBS.

THE LATE-TWENTIETH-CENTURY revival also spawned new versions of *Little Women* in other forms, most notably an opera by Mark Adamo, which premiered at the Houston Grand Opera in 1998. There had been an earlier opera, Evelyn Everest Freer's 1920 *Scenes from Little Women*, as well as Geoffrey O'Hara's operetta *Little Women* from the 1930s, yet neither was as successful as Adamo's. It was subsequently shown on PBS in its *Great Performances* series in 2001, released on CD, DVD, and in book form, and performed in over seventy venues across the United States and in Canada, Mexico, Japan, Australia, and Israel.[45]

As he wrote the opera, Adamo at first struggled with the novel's episodic structure, which the film adaptations more or less embraced until collapsing the story into a romantic narrative arc. Adamo, however, was looking for conflict and narrative tension, which he found not in Jo's choice of a mate or struggles against convention, but in her resistance to change. At a key point when he was developing the story, he contacted June Allyson for her insight. She told him, "Jo is about to lose everything—meaning her family is outgrowing her."[46] This gave him the idea to contrast Jo's desire for things to stay the same with her sisters' and Laurie's eagerness to grow up. The result is the most successful adaptation of Alcott's novel, in my view, at least on a narrative level. The story Adamo tells does exactly what an adaptation should do: it opens up the original text and makes you feel like you understand it even more deeply. It's not only a work of art in its own right, but it's also in deep conversation with the original, as if the two are distinct entities existing side by side, each enriching the other. The opera makes you want to go back and read Alcott's work not to compare or check for points of dissimilarity, but to reread with fresh eyes.

Adamo also provides the most satisfying union between Jo and Professor Bhaer. In the end, Jo simply extends her hand to him. No rainbows, no umbrellas, no formal proposal of marriage. But this is not an open ending. Jo has clearly chosen love, which has been extolled throughout as life's greatest gift. Earlier, however, Bhaer made a point of sharing his progressive views on marriage, agreeing with Jo that women often do not benefit from it. Bhaer sings, "Too many men bind a woman in marriage like a groom strapping a horse to a harness. And too many women call that love." Instead, Bhaer says, man and woman "should pull together." In my view, Adamo's Bhaer leaves William Shatner in the dust and even outpaces adorable Gabriel Byrne. When he sings "Kennst Du Das Land" to Jo, for the first time I could see Bhaer, played by Chen-Ye Yuan in the PBS performance, as a romantic figure. His gorgeous baritone voice is truly swoon-worthy, unlike the sentimental mooning of Paul Lukas singing to Katharine Hepburn or of Rossano Brazzi to June Allyson. (Byrne didn't even try to serenade Ryder's Jo.)

Reviews of Adamo's opera were generally positive. Alex Ross in *The New Yorker* and Jon Rockwell in the *New York Times* both compared it at first to other "unadventurous" or "carefully conservative" operas that mix lyric tonality with a dash of modernist dissonance. However, they came to the conclusion that Adamo's opera was, as Ross wrote, "a beautifully crafted work" and, in Rockwell's words, "some sort of masterpiece." For Anthony Tommasini, however, in his review of the *Great Performances* broadcast for the *New York Times*, Adamo had failed to marry the two styles. The modernist moments seemed "forced" and the lyrical passages "cloying" or "saccharine."[47]

Six years after Adamo's opera premiered, another musical version of *Little Women* appeared on Broadway. Earlier musical versions had included *A Girl Called Jo*, staged in London in 1955, and one simply called *Jo*, which played off-Broadway in 1964. Neither was particularly successful. The 2004 production, *Little Women: A Musical*, was written by Allan Knee with music by Jason Howland and lyrics by Mindi Dickstein. Jo was played by Sutton Foster, then the new

Broadway sensation who had won a Tony Award two years earlier for her performance in *Thoroughly Modern Millie*. The other notable performance was Maureen McGovern's as Marmee.

By 2004, audiences had a new reason to appreciate *Little Women*'s evocation of the home front during wartime: the wars in Iraq and Afghanistan. As McGovern put it, "The story is very universal for all ages, but given the day, the war, and all those single families, women raising their kids alone with the soldiers away, and the economy in the state that it's in, everyone is struggling, or juggling two and three jobs just to make ends meet . . . it resonates right now very strongly." But apparently such associations were not what drove audiences to the theater. Instead it was name recognition and mothers wanting their young daughters, who had missed the 1994 film, to fall in love with *Little Women* as they had. The show was dubbed another of the "girl power" musicals (such as *Wicked* and *Mamma Mia!*) then popular on Broadway.[48]

Director Susan H. Shulman said she intended to remain faithful to Alcott's novel, but she had no intention of being "slavish to it."[49] Indeed, while it is another loving homage, the musical introduces some significant changes. Like Adamo's opera, Knee's script rearranges the plot, opening with a later scene and then telescoping backward to the beginning, giving the story a more contemporary feel. It opens in New York with Jo reading aloud to Professor Bhaer a rejection letter from a publisher, telling her to forget writing her sensation stories and to go home and make babies because that's "what women are made for," thus manufacturing a heightened conservatism not in the book, as Swicord's script did. Jo then retells the rejected story (with actors performing it in the background) to Bhaer, who tells her she "could do better." Jo responds with anger, singing, "How dare he make me doubt the way I feel / Doubt that each thrilling page is who I am?" Thus Knee establishes the main theme as Jo's ambitions as a writer and projects the conflict outward onto the editor who rejected her story and onto Bhaer, who objected to its violent themes.

The central moment in Jo's developing ambitions is reflected in the song "Astonishing," which Jo sings after she rejects Laurie's proposal. She must be destined for greater things. "I've got to know if I can be astonishing," she belts out. Yet Knee gives her only a brief taste of successful authorship before turning the story over to the romantic arc that all adaptations (except Adamo's) have privileged. Jo's literary ambitions are subsumed into her dull romance with Bhaer without any of the emotional pull of the novel, the opera, or even the films, which provided a broader canvas of sisterly relations and family rather than focusing narrowly on Jo. Ultimately, this version manages to diminish the story rather than realize it (as the films do) or deepen it (as the opera does), making this the least successful adaptation.

Reviewers were certainly not impressed. *Talkin' Broadway* called it a "bloated, charm-deprived show," and *Variety* faulted its "bland score." The critic for the *New York Daily News* pronounced it "as mechanical as an Erector Set and just as emotionally arid." But the Newark *Star-Ledger*'s reviewer decided it was an "appealing tuner [that] glows with wholesome spirits" and thought it would become "a mother-and-daughter must-see," a rare positive line the show's marketers hyped in their attempt to court a specifically female audience.[50]

Within four months the production ran out of steam, playing for only 137 performances and losing $7 million. McGovern received a Drama Desk Award, and only Foster's performance received a Tony nomination. However, a thirty-three-city tour was quickly scheduled, which allowed the show to recoup its losses.[51] That exposure and the generally more positive reviews on the road made *Little Women: The Musical* a sought-after production. In 2016 it made its way to the U.K., and it has been routinely performed in community and school theaters across the country, making this the version that now introduces *Little Women* to many young people during their school years. The Jo they discover is more ambitious than she was in her previous iterations, but she is not as fully realized as in Alcott's original novel. For the character that inspired generations of young women to pursue their own ambitions, we have to go back to the novel itself.

As the 150th anniversary approaches, *Little Women* is set to appear on-screen again. An independent feature film starring Lea Thompson as Marmee and billed as a modern update will be released in

2018. Amy Pascal, now of Pascal Pictures, has begun a remake of her 1994 film with Di Novi again as producer and Greta Gerwig as screenwriter. As of this writing, the project is in script rewrites and may begin filming in 2018. A sure bet, however, is a new version from the BBC, coproduced with PBS's *Masterpiece* and set to air in 2018. The inclusion of *Little Women* in the august series of mostly British literary adaptations is an indication of the novel's status as a revered classic, but the cast is anything but stodgy. Filmed in Ireland, it features Angela Lansbury as Aunt March, Michael Gambon (most famously Dumbledore in the *Harry Potter* films) as Mr. Laurence, and Emily Watson as Marmee. Known for her "raw and unfettered performances," Watson's last BBC adaptation had her playing a middle-aged mom having a raucous affair.[52] Laurie and the March sisters are played by relative unknowns. Maya Hawke, as Jo, is a newcomer to acting, but is already a high-profile model and the daughter of Ethan Hawke and Uma Thurman. Interestingly, Professor Bhaer is played by thirty-year-old Mark Stanley, making him the youngest of Jo's suitors on-screen. For many, the BBC/*Masterpiece* treatment promises to make this production a *Little Women* for the next generation of fans.

# 5

# "THE MOTHER OF US ALL"

## *Little Women*'s Cultural and Literary Influence

*L*ITTLE *WOMEN* IS arguably the most influential book ever written by an American woman. Its nearest contenders—*Uncle Tom's Cabin* and *Gone with the Wind*—cannot match its persistent impact. It has never gone out of print or fallen out of favor. Yet, like those other books, its literary status has been suspect. "With its overt mix of autobiography and invention," novelist and critic Deborah Weisgall has written, "*Little Women* is an enduring model for women's stories, but it is rarely considered literature itself."[1] I agree with her that it should be, and I would add that it is precisely because of *Little Women*'s status as a model for women's and girls' stories that it has been excluded from the category of literature. More than that, it has challenged our very ideas of what is considered "literature."

In the first few decades after its publication, *Little Women* was accorded critical respect in literary histories where Alcott appeared alongside male luminaries such as Hawthorne and Emerson. But at the turn of the century, as the academic study of American literature professionalized, Alcott largely dropped from view. A 1907 essay by

British critic G. K. Chesterton suggests why. His first instinct when confronted with Alcott's popular novels was to run "screaming" in the other direction, but he persevered and discovered that although "they were extremely good," there was little he could say about them. As a man, "I am the intruder," he admitted, "and I withdraw. I back out hastily, bowing."[2] And that is pretty much what the male critical establishment did with Alcott for most of the twentieth century.

She wasn't the only significant writer ignored. The American literary canon became increasingly exclusive until it was limited to male writers. By 1941, when Harvard professor F. O. Matthiessen published his enormously influential *The American Renaissance: Art and Expression in the Age of Emerson and Whitman*, he effectively whittled the nineteenth century down to only five authors: Emerson, Thoreau, Hawthorne, Melville, and Whitman. Alcott is listed in the book's index, but the entry refers to Bronson, not Louisa. By the mid-twentieth century, *Little Women* epitomized the kind of book no longer considered worthy of serious attention, for three reasons: it was popular, it was written for children, and it was written by a woman about women's lives. As a result, critics, when they bothered to notice it at all, could dismiss it as neither requiring nor being conducive to analysis, as Edward Wagenknecht did in his influential book *Cavalcade of the American Novel* in 1952. Noticeably, being a popular book for kids didn't hurt Mark Twain's *Adventures of Huckleberry Finn* much. It still attracted considerable scholarly attention and is often considered a, if not the, "Great American Novel."[3] It would seem that the death knell for *Little Women* was its status as a girl's or woman's book, placing it in another sphere entirely.

That sphere was, frankly, just about everywhere else outside of academia. As we have seen, *Little Women* was frequently onstage and in the movie houses. It was also a core text in elementary through high schools. Henry James called Alcott "the Thackeray, the Trollope, of the nursery and the school-room," and a British critic in 1919 dubbed her "a 'Jane Austen' of the schoolroom." As early as 1893, excerpts were included in a British edition of *Stories for the Classroom*. In the first two decades of the twentieth century, Little, Brown published cheap school editions of Alcott's novel and De Forest's play as well as *The Louisa Alcott Reader: A Supplemental Reader for the Fourth Year of School*. After the novel's copyright expired, other publishers, eager to meet the high demand from teachers, also prepared school editions. In 1925, when the Federal Bureau of Education surveyed teachers and librarians for their recommendations of books to outfit rural, one-room schoolhouses across the country, their top choice was *Little Women*. And in 1933, since, as one commentator put it, *Little Women* "has been a prescribed reading course in the schools of the country," the National Council of Teachers of English distributed study guides for the RKO film to all of the nation's nearly 18,000 high schools.[4]

Children were also reading *Little Women* outside of school in large numbers. Throughout the first half of the century, polls of young readers' preferences consistently placed it at or near the top. In 1909 it was schoolchildren's favorite book, in 1919 and 1926 it ranked first among girls, and in 1927 it was the first choice among teenagers of both sexes who were asked, "What book has interested you the most?" In 1931, girls chose it as the book they would most like to see filmed. At the Carnegie Library in Pittsburgh, it was voted patrons' favorite book from 1919 to 1949. And in 1950, it was the favorite of juvenile readers at public libraries in Chicago and California.[5]

During these years, *Little Women* was understood as much more than a cozy book for girls. This became especially clear in the 1940s and '50s when it was enlisted in the worldwide battle for democracy and was upheld as a quintessentially American text. Whereas scholars were defining classic American themes as man's battle against the wilderness or the individual's resistance to social conformity, for those outside of academia, books about families (even ones made up of girls) also represented the nation. During World War II, although *Little Women* was, understandably, not one of the Armed Services editions sent to U.S. soldiers overseas, it was enlisted for other programs at a time when books were viewed as "weapons in the war of ideas." In 1942, when Nobel Laureate Pearl S. Buck solicited critics' suggestions for books to send overseas that would "tell an Asiatic reader the most about the American people," *Little Women* was among the fifteen chosen. At least one newspaper described these books as epitomizing the "American way" soldiers were fighting for.[6]

After the war, the dissemination of *Little Women* overseas continued. A plan by California schoolchildren to send it and other books
to schools in France and Germany was motivated by their desire to
export their "American childhoods full of meaning to minds blighted
by war and gasping for free air," as one exuberant reporter put it.
In the 1950s *Little Women* was one of the first texts chosen by the
U.S. Information Agency for its Franklin Book Program, which was
designed to translate American books and disseminate them in the
Arab world for, among other purposes, "provid[ing] information and
points of view regarding America, democracy, and the idea of an
open society." Similarly, the 1949 film of *Little Women* was exported
to occupied Japan as part of the campaign by the Central Motion
Picture Exchange to promote American culture and values there. It
was also included in a list of films drawn up by the Motion Picture Service as suitable for showing behind the Iron Curtain, essentially as part of its Cold War propaganda campaign. In 1971, *Little
Women* was one of the nine children's books sent by the Library of
Congress to Romania for the first "American Library" established
by a U.S. embassy in a communist country. And as late as 2003, *Little Women* was once again exported as a quintessentially American
book, this time by First Lady Laura Bush, who brought books "that
reflect 'the values that had to do with living a good life'" to a Russian
book festival.[7]

During the Cold War, *Little Women* had not been welcome in the
Soviet Union. Just as *Little Women* was being promoted as a symbol of American democracy and values, reports of its being banned
in the new Communist Bloc began to appear in the Western press.
One article indicated that *Little Women* was "on the list of 'Marshall
Plan exports designed to dull the minds of the masses.'" It appears
that officials in Russia, Hungary, Germany's Soviet sector, and elsewhere believed that Alcott's novel could be a tool of the West in
the increasingly hostile battles over the hearts and minds of Euro-
peans. According to a *New York Times* columnist in 1948, "British
and American literary spies report that there has been a wholesale
purge of reading material imported from the West" that included
*Little Women*. Another report, under the title "Hungary Bans 'Little

Women' and Strippers Too," credited the banning of *Little Women* to a government's "morality campaign."[8] While the linkage of *Little Women* to explicit sexual material seems ludicrous, presumably it was the representation of a nuclear family's strong ties that made the book immoral in the eyes of communist censors.

In the West, *Little Women*'s cultural influence began to wane at the same time that traditional family structures began to dissolve. As late as 1968, *Little Women* was still one of the two most circulated books in the New York Public Library, and a U.K. survey in 1971 also placed *Little Women* on top. In the following decade, however, its use in schools dropped off, and it was relegated to summer reading lists and eventually to homeschooling courses. By 1988, it had fallen to number twenty-one among American children's favorite books, and it was taught by less than 5 percent of public schools. Competition had much to do with the decline. Books written for children and teens had multiplied exponentially, and the classics that hung on were kept alive by recent movie adaptations. In a survey of 14,000 Cincinnati schoolchildren in 1974, the leader in every grade category was a book that had been recently filmed for television or the big screen. *Little Women* was hanging in there, the professor who conducted the study explained, but had suffered due to students' attraction to television and the movies.[9]

While *Little Women*'s popularity with children and educators declined, however, it soared among academics. Suddenly, with the rise of feminism in the 1970s and '80s, Alcott's novel was considered a rich text worthy of close attention. New meanings could be pulled out of the text—or more accurately, new tools could be used to analyze it—and that made it appealing to the new crop of feminist literary critics that came out of the 1960s and '70s. With its themes of relationships between women, the development of women's identities, women's suppression of anger, domestic rebellion, women's literary ambitions, and how gender roles are constructed, *Little Women* was a core text in the development of feminist literary criticism. Most of the prominent American feminist critics analyzed *Little Women*, including Nina Auerbach, Ann Douglas, Carolyn Heilbrun, Patricia Meyer Spacks, Elaine Showalter, Judith Fetterley, and Sandra

Gilbert and Susan Gubar.[10] When antiquarian book dealers Madeleine Stern and Leona Rostenberg discovered the thrillers Alcott had written under a pseudonym and published them in *Behind a Mask: The Unknown Thrillers of Louisa May Alcott* (1975) and other books, they also provided new opportunities to consider what Alcott had left out of *Little Women*. Though Jo and Marmee must learn to suppress their anger, Alcott's sensational heroines are allowed to enact revenge and manipulate the men who would oppress them.

New editions of *Little Women* also positioned it as a book for adults rather than children, featuring introductions by scholars and texts devoid of illustrations. In 2005 it was "inducted," as critic Deborah Friedell put it, into the Library of America series, which bills itself as the "definitive collection of American literature." By that time, *Little Women* could be embraced as both a children's classic and an important contribution to American literature. The rise of children's literature as a field of study also helped to enhance *Little Women*'s status, as did the shift toward viewing popularity and cultural significance as markers of a text's value. As Friedell wrote in her *New Republic* review of the Library of America volume, "The adoration that the books [the *Little Women* trilogy] have inspired from readers is, in fact, the principal claim for their canonization. Alcott's novels reside in the artistic category of relics that have been of such enormous influence that the question of their quality seems almost beside the point."[11] In fact, the idea of strictly "literary" value had become too nebulous, and feminist critics argued it was laden with male bias.

Yet, in spite of *Little Women*'s elevation to canonical status, scholars still do not sufficiently acknowledge how key *Little Women* has been to the development of women's literary traditions in the United States and abroad. It has been a foundational text not only in the history of women's literature but also in individual writers' very conception of themselves as writers and artists. During the many decades that academics snubbed the book, while schoolteachers embraced it and critics and diplomats enlisted it in a worldwide ideological war, girls were quietly retreating into the nooks and crannies of their homes to pore over the pages they felt Alcott had written just for them. When they were done reading, many didn't simply lay the book aside and pick up another; they went back to page one and started all over again. They couldn't get enough of this novel that illuminated a path to a newly imagined future, one in which they could, like Jo March, spend their hours alone honing their craft and becoming that hallowed, mystical thing: "an author." In short, *Little Women* is *the* book, more than any other, to which American women writers' ambitions can be traced.

*Little Women* has been called "the mother of all girls' books." It is also, arguably, the most beloved book of American women writers (and near the top for women writers around the globe) and has exerted more influence on women writers as a group than any other single book. So ubiquitous has it been that one writer, Lucinda Rosenfeld, felt compelled to confess, "I must be one of a handful of female novelists in America who, as a child, didn't devour this American classic . . . and identify with aspiring writer and tomboy Jo March." A few women writers over the years have outright rejected its influence—Edith Wharton was "exasperated by the laxities [in language] of the great Louisa," Camille Paglia has called it "a kind of horror story," and Hilary Mantel hated Jo March "like poison."[12] They have been in the minority, however, and they still clearly read it.

As female readers discovering their ambitions gravitated toward the book, Jo March was the main draw. She has been called by Carolyn Heilbrun "the mother of us all," and by Elaine Showalter "the dearly cherished sister of us all." Just as Hemingway claimed that all of American literature (by men) came from *Huck Finn*, we can also say that much of American women's literature has come from *Little Women*. Yet women writers were not simply taken with the novel's style and language, as male writers apparently were with *Huck Finn*. *Little Women* gave them the idea to write in the first place, historically something very few young women have been encouraged to do. More than that, it taught them that their lives mattered and showed them an alternative to the feminine ideal that placed babies far above books. Ultimately, *Little Women* validated the very idea of a girl developing her own opinions, earning a living, and deciding to become a writer. As Ursula K. Le Guin describes it, Jo March was the original image of women writing, an image that Alcott made accessible to ordinary girls, "close as a sister and common as grass." "It may not seem much," she admits, "but I don't know where else I or many other girls like me, in my generation or my mother's or my daughter's, were to find this model, this validation." As poet Sonja Sanchez has put it, "Jo broke the mold."[13]

For poet Gail Mazur and novelist Lynne Sharon Schwartz, who were both born in the late 1930s, the image of Jo in her garret instilled in each of them the desire to one day have a room of their own in which to write. "Jo was the model for my own aspirations," writes Mazur. Jo's example led her to request her own attic bedroom when she was fifteen. "It was Jo I was following, alone, snug in her garret, where she could write stories and poems in peace, and no sisters could intrude. Nights, awake with Jo above the slumbering suburban household, I re-read and wept, and wrote fervently in my incoherent journals, and fell asleep in the first room of my own." For Schwartz, reading and rereading *Little Women* was not enough; she wanted to "possess [it] even more intimately" and so began "copying it into a notebook. With the first few pages I felt delirious, but the project quickly palled." Writing the same words she knew so well did not "bring me closer to possession. Only later did I understand that I wanted to have written *Little Women*, conceived and gestated it and felt its words delivered from my own pen."[14]

For many, the identification with Jo was so strong they felt as if she had materialized within them or as if they had inhabited the text with her. "I, personally, am Jo March," Barbara Kingsolver has written, "and if . . . Alcott had a whole new life to live for the sole pursuit of talking me out of it, she could not." Maureen Corrigan not only identified with Jo but felt as if their lives had followed the same path, beginning with their "love of books [which] gloriously screwed us both up." The Ephron sisters Nora and Delia both thought they were Jo. Nora, the oldest, wrote, "[My mother] would tell me how she identified with Jo in *Little Women* and I would go off and read *Little Women* and identify with Jo." Meanwhile, Delia, the second sister, felt she "technically . . . was Jo." Even though Nora had the ambition, Delia was "a tomboy and a rebel" like Jo.[15]

The "common as grass" figure of literary Jo also spoke to girls from a wide variety of backgrounds, including African American novelist Ann Petry, who declared, "I felt as though I was part of Jo and she was part of me." In *Bone Black: Memories of Girlhood*, bell hooks writes that she felt "a little less alone in the world" after finding "remnants of myself in Jo, the serious sister, the one who is punished." Poet Elizabeth Alexander, who claimed to have read the novel 9 million times, found Alcott's novel "formative to me in thinking about what it meant to be an independent woman who loved your family, but defined yourself away from your family." Vietnamese American writer Bich Minh Nguyen was similarly "inspired to be like Jo," and Candy Gourlay, a children's author from the Philippines who now lives in England, recalls her reading experience of *Little Women* as purely emotional, "an aligning of my desires with Jo's. How I wanted to be Jo." Jewish writer Cynthia Ozick has also described the sensation of discovering who she was, or who she would become, through Jo: "I am Jo in her 'vortex'; not Jo exactly, but some Jo-of-the-future. I am under an enchantment: Who I truly am must be deferred, waited for and waited for." She has also expressed the conviction that her identification with Jo was far from unique: "Not so much the male writers, let's admit it, but every writer who grows up has wanted to be Jo." Mazur described how she and her friend, "second-generation Jewish daughters of the 'feminine mystique' fifties," both thought they were Jo.[16]

Judith Martin (also known as Miss Manners) summed up what *Little Women* meant to many girls in the 1950s: "That's where I learned that although it's very nice to have two clean gloves, it's even more important to have a little ink on your fingers." While the other March sisters tried so hard to be ladylike, Jo was only trying to be a great writer. "It was the great revelation to women for generations," Martin has written, "especially in the prefeminist days—that we admire the ladies, the domestic ones, but it's the woman of spirit, the spunky one, we want to be." A very different kind of writer, Erica Jong, born four years after Martin, describes *Little Women*'s powerful image of the woman writer a bit more radically. *Little Women* "told me women could be writers, intellects—and still have rich personal lives. We need to feel that we are more than our looks, more than our wombs. We yearn to use all our gifts—and this has never been easy for women. The books we treasure, and the books that last, proclaim this: Let us be whole, let us be complete."[17] For Jong and so many others, Jo was both writer and woman, a powerful combination so rarely found on the page.

Women writers who grew up in the 1970s and '80s continued to find inspiration in Jo, even as *Little Women* began to lose its dominance in the world of girls' books. Perri Klass and Stacy Schiff both named their daughters after Jo. Anne Lamott was grateful for Jo's example—"thank you, God, for Jo," she writes—because she too wanted to "grow up and tell stories like hers, about girls who kicked *butt*." Stephenie Meyer of *Twilight* fame first read *Little Women* when she was seven, "and it became nearly as real to me as the rest of my life." She "always identified with Jo," particularly with her tomboy and bookworm characteristics. Novelist and journalist Deborah Weisgall, who read the novel eighteen times between the ages of nine and twelve, claimed, "I—along with most readers—was Jo, the tomboy with literary ambition. Like me, Jo was a girl of action and ambition in a culture (and a family) that did not encourage those qualities in a daughter." Peruvian American novelist Natalia Sylvester claims that *Little Women* "had an immeasurable influence on me. I wanted to be Jo, with her ink-stained hands and big dreams. I wanted to be the rebel storyteller."[18] In Jo these women found a model of ambition for girls that was scarcely visible elsewhere in their lives.

As a measure of their affection, authors Jane Smiley, Anna Quindlen, Susan Cheever, Elaine Showalter, Louise Rennison, and Paula Danziger have all written introductions to the novel. "I can see how profoundly the book influenced me as a writer," wrote Cheever, who is known primarily as a memoirist. "Without intending to, Louisa May Alcott found a new way to write about the ordinary lives of women, and to tell stories that are usually heard in kitchens or bedrooms." As a book that celebrated the events in young girls' lives and made them as interesting as any adventures on the high seas, *Little Women* made literature accessible and gave girls the idea that their lives were worth writing about. "In many ways it is the precursor of the modern memoir," Cheever continues. "It is the book that gives voice to people who had traditionally been silent." For Jane Smiley, *Little Women* is a book that shows us how to navigate our lives. She calls it "an essential American novel, perhaps the essential American novel for girls," helping them to shape "their sense of identity, work, friendship, and, eventually, love and marriage." Anna Quindlen writes more personally, declaring that "*Little Women* changed my life." The March sisters were the first characters she had read about who seemed like real people, and more than that, "*Little Women* offered the first glimpse of a life defined by talent and inclination, not simply marriage."[19] In short, Jo's ambitions charted a path for many girls who weren't even aware such a path existed.

Many other influential American women writers—poets, novelists, memoirists, and essayists—have pointed to their intense devotion to *Little Women* in their youths. Amy Lowell looked up to Jo and wanted only Webster's dictionary and *Little Women* with her on a desert island. Mary Gordon received the book from her mother, read it at least fifty times, and then read it again as an adult with her own daughter. Anne Tyler claimed to have "devoured [it] at least a dozen times." For Gloria Steinem, who read it every year until she was twelve, the Marches became a kind of replacement family during her peripatetic childhood. "It was my ritual and my rescue," she has said. "Amy, Beth, Meg and Jo—who was probably why I became a writer—were my family and friends." Sara Paretsky similarly describes *Little Women* as "the staple of my childhood," having first read it when she was eight and then revisited it dozens of times thereafter. Amy Bloom learned from *Little Women* how to think like a writer. When reading it at the age of eight, she first realized "that other people also thought it was interesting to observe other people." Jo's daring in donning her writing cap and announcing that "genius burns" also left a lasting impression.[20] Patricia Henley got tears in her eyes as she explained what Jo had meant to her. "If Jo could grow up to be a writer, then so could I," she told me.

I could go on. In the United States there are at least forty other women writers—from Carson McCullers and Maxine Hong Kingston to Susan Sontag and Jhumpa Lahiri—who have referred to *Little Women*'s influence on them as they were growing up. Canadian authors Margaret Atwood and Shaena Lambert have also named *Little Women* as one of their favorite books, as has Irish Canadian

Emma Donoghue. And it's not just in North America. Many Argentinian women writers have also been influenced by *Little Women*.[21]

Although *Jane Eyre* and *Pride and Prejudice* have been more widely influential in Britain, *Little Women*'s impact on girls there has been profound as well. J. K. Rowling met someone like herself in a book for the first time when she read *Little Women*. "It is hard to overstate what she meant to a small, plain girl called Jo, who had a hot temper and a burning ambition to be a writer," Joanna Rowling has written. Jo March's bad temper and desire to be a writer represented a "lifeline" for the plain, bookish girl who found relatable heroines in literature "pretty slim pickings." In *How to Build a Girl* (2014), Caitlin Moran's heroine Johanna Morrigan, obviously named after Jo March, is described on the cover as determined to "save her poverty stricken Bohemian family by becoming a writer—like Jo in *Little Women*." It is no wonder, considering Moran's claim that "I owe everything I am to Jo March in *Little Women* and Anne Shirley in *Anne of Green Gables*." Young adult author Holly Smale has called *Little Women* "the book that really cemented my desire to write because I wanted to be just like Jo." She made her mother buy apples for her to eat while she scribbled on scraps of paper and piled them up to look like a manuscript. Gabrielle Donnelly, who grew up in London in the 1960s, first discovered *Little Women* when she was nine and felt lost in a rough-and-tumble household full of boys. At night she would retreat to her room to read, and "for the long and glorious hours till bedtime I would become a March sister." Kate Mosse remembers *Little Women* as a "defining novel" of her youth. "Like every girl, I wanted to be like Jo," she writes, "fearless, clever, independent, but capable of loving fiercely and inspiring devotion, a girl who turns down marriage to be a writer. A thoroughly modern miss."[22] Mosse may not have read the second part of the novel, *Good Wives* in Britain, where Jo marries Professor Bhaer. Indeed, for most girls, it was the Jo of the first part of *Little Women* who inspired emulation.

And it wasn't only the novelists, poets, and memoirists who wanted to be like Jo. She inspired women to all kinds of writing careers. British scholar Patricia Pulham suspects that she wouldn't have become a writer or an academic without *Little Women*. "When I read about

Jo March I found someone I could identify with," she has written. "I felt it was a kind of freedom I wanted in my own existence. She made me feel writing was the thing for me." Journalist and novelist Carol Clewlow has called *Little Women* "one of those . . . handbooks of life, almost, handed down by the hopeful to daughters and nieces, and read by most women, certainly of my fortysomething generation, at one time or another." Children's authors of two different eras, Enid Blyton and Jacqueline Wilson, were also heavily influenced by the novel. Blyton fell in love with *Little Women* because here were "real children." She thought, "When I grow up *I* will write books about real children. . . . That's the kind of book I like best. That's the kind of book I would know how to write." Wilson was also struck by the novel's realism. She has tried to get girls to read *Little Women* "because those four sisters are so real." Children's author Francesca Simon has also said that Jo is the literary heroine she most resembles; she identified with her "passion, her keenness and her sense of not fitting in." Other British women writers influenced by *Little Women* include Doris Lessing, A. S. Byatt, Zadie Smith, Helen Oyeyemi, and many others.[23]

Jo's power to inspire young women to become writers has also extended even farther abroad. French feminist philosopher and novelist Simone de Beauvoir read it when she was ten and invented games to play in which she claimed the role of Jo. In the words of her biographer, the novel "gave form to her childhood." Feeling as if she were glimpsing "her future self" (as Ozick had), de Beauvoir "identified passionately with Jo, the intellectual." Not only that, but Jo helped her, she wrote, "find comfort in myself. . . . I was able to tell myself that I too was like her, and therefore it did not matter if society was cruel, because I too would be superior and find my place." The girls in Elena Ferrante's Neapolitan Quartet feel similarly. The young Lila and Lenù, growing up in 1950s Naples at a time when *Little Women* was very popular in Italy, are obsessed with the book and dream, like Jo, of writing a novel to escape their life of poverty. But their paths diverge drastically. Lila, despite her early promise, marries and becomes a more traditional woman, like Meg, while Lenù eventually realizes the dream of becoming a famous author, like Jo.

Furthermore, Italian scholar and writer Marisa Bulgheroni, Indian author Neera Kuckreja Sohoni, and Turkish novelist Elif Bilgin Shafak have all been inspired by Jo March. So was New Zealand author Emily Perkins, who named Jo March as the literary figure she most related to when she was younger.[24]

Nowhere is *Little Women*'s deep influence more apparent than in the large numbers of novels by women—for children and adults— whose genealogy can be traced to Alcott's seminal work. Given how many women writers hoped to emulate Jo, it is not surprising that quite a few chose to rewrite or update *Little Women*, while others simply couldn't help letting the most influential book of their childhoods seep into the characters and plots they created. Children's books that owe an obvious debt to Alcott's pathbreaking portrayal of a spunky young heroine with a literary bent, many of them now classics themselves, include Kate Douglas Wiggin's *Rebecca of Sunnybrook Farm* (1903), L. M. Montgomery's *Anne of Green Gables* (1908) and *Emily of New Moon* (1923), Jean Webster's *Daddy-Long-Legs* (1912), Laura Ingalls Wilder's *Little House on the Prairie* books (1932–43), Betty Smith's *A Tree Grows in Brooklyn* (1943), Madeleine L'Engle's *A Wrinkle in Time* (1963), Louise Fitzhugh's *Harriet the Spy* (1964), Eleanor Cameron's Julia Redfern series (1971–88), J. K. Rowling's Harry Potter series (1997–2007) with the bookish Hermione, and Jeanne Birdsall's *The Penderwicks: A Summer Tale of Four Sisters, Two Rabbits, and a Very Interesting Boy* (2005).

There are also over fifty spin-offs, sequels, prequels, updates, and retellings of *Little Women*. Interestingly, most were produced after 1980, attesting to the novel's continued influence despite the apparent lower number of readers. Among children's books, Susan Beth Pfeffer's *Portraits of Little Women* series (1997–2001) and Charlotte Emerson's *Little Women Journals* series (1998) are direct spin-offs. *Judy Moody* author Megan McDonald's middle-grade series *The Sisters Club* features three sisters, the middle one named Joey. In the second book, *Rule of Three* (2009), they read *Little Women* and are inspired by it to cut off their hair. *The Mother-Daughter Book Club* series, by Heather Vogel Frederick, began in 2007 with a volume focused on *Little Women*, in which four girls read the novel with their mothers and discover how much they have in common with the March sisters. Lauren Baratz-Logsted's *Little Women and Me* (2011) may be the most inventive retelling for children. In the novel, a girl named Emily March has a school assignment to rewrite a classic, for which she chooses *Little Women*. When she is mysteriously transported to 1860s Concord and becomes one of the March sisters, Emily tries to change the outcome of the story, primarily Amy and Laurie's marriage, and discovers along the way that Amy is a time-traveler like herself. Another recent series, Candy Harper's *The Strawberry Sisters*, begun in 2015, is billed by its publisher as "*Little Women* meets Jacqueline Wilson." And although popular children's author Lois Lowry has never written a spin-off or retelling of *Little Women*, her books are peppered with references to it.[25]

Women writing for adults have also been keen to rewrite *Little Women*, updating it or altering its setting, usually referring to the theme of four sisters (or three—sometimes Beth is left out so that no one has to die) who share qualities similar to those of the March girls. In 1990 Judith Rossner, most known for her novel *Looking for Mr. Goodbar*, published *His Little Women* about a man's four daughters, one of whom is a writer named Louisa who has written a novel about them all. Katharine Weber's *The Little Women* (2003) also picks up on the theme of one of the sisters, named Jo, writing about her family. Weber's novel, narrated by Jo and punctuated with commentary by her sisters, depicts the fracturing of the girls' home as the two younger sisters (Jo and Amy—there is no Beth), still adolescents, reject their parents and move in with older sister (Meg), who is away at Yale and sharing an apartment with a boy named Teddy. Shading at times into parody, the novel provides a contemporary commentary on fractured ideals and the ethics of writing about one's relatives.

Donnelly's *The Little Women Letters* (2011), on the other hand, pays much more homage to the original. Set in contemporary London, this book portrays the great-great-granddaughters of Jo March: Emma, who, like Meg, readily pleases others and is about to get married; Lulu, who, like Jo, doesn't fit in and is having a hard time growing up; and Sophie, the Amy character, who is an aspiring actress and a favorite with men. When Lulu finds "Grandma Jo's" letters in the attic, she takes solace from her ancestor's trials and finds in them a guide for her own life. Although their mother is a product of 1970s feminism and wants her daughters to chart new territory, they are happy to be "falling in love and promising to be together forever," as their foremothers did.[26] However, in Grandma Jo's final letter, written to an imagined great-great-granddaughter, she advises finding work you can be passionate about.

Some retellings of *Little Women* are set in Victorian America, among them Joyce Carol Oates's satirical gothic novel, *A Bloodsmoor Romance* (1982). This novel draws on both Hawthorne's *Blithedale Romance* and *Little Women* but reads more like a spoof of popular nineteenth-century thrillers. It features five sisters: a bookish tomboy, a bed-hopping actress, a kidnapped spiritualist, a transsexual, and a wife whose husband's predilection for asphyxia during sex leads to his death. The book is a disorienting mix of feminine piety, perversion, drug abuse, and murder. Oates is perhaps referencing Alcott's thrillers more than *Little Women*, which becomes a source of mockery rather than reverence.

The most successful spin-off from Alcott's novel, ironically, barely mentions the little women. Geraldine Brooks's Pulitzer Prize–winning *March* (2005) envisions Mr. March's wartime experiences as a Union chaplain and gives him a slew of moral quandaries, including an infatuation with a former slave. He writes letters home to his wife, sending his love to his daughters, and Mrs. March appears near the end at the Washington hospital where he lies ill; but otherwise the book concerns itself with the cruelty and injustices of war and slavery. *March*'s relationship to *Little Women* is tangential at best, but perhaps this is what gives Brooks the leeway to tell a compelling story we don't feel obliged to compare to the original.

A number of foreign language reworkings stick closer to the *Little Women* story, or something approximating it, but move it to another time and place entirely. Korean Pak Kyongni's *Daughters of Pharmacist Kim* (1962) became a film in 1963 and a television series in 2005. Italian Lidia Ravera's *Bagna i fiori e aspettami* ("Water the flowers and wait for me," 1986) was about four Roman sisters named Margherita, Giovanna (Gio), Bettina, and Amelia. Ravera followed it up with a sequel, *Se lo dico perdo l'America* ("If I say I miss America," 1988), in which Gio becomes a writer of mystery novels. Popular Spanish-language author Marcela Serrano published *Hasta Siempre, Mujercitas* ("So long, little women") in 2004, and it was translated into Finnish, Italian, and Korean, but not English. The novel, set in contemporary Chile, announces the book's relationship with *Little Women* by featuring an image of Alcott's book (called *Mujercitas* in Spanish) on its cover, and each of its chapters begins with a quote from *Little Women*. Another Italian writer, Letizia Muratori, also adapted Alcott's classic in her novel *Come se niente fosse* ("As if nothing happened," 2012), about a group of women reading *Little Women* and a writer whose life appears to mimic Jo's.

Foreign-set adaptations also include versions written in English, such as Kingsolver's best-selling novel *The Poisonwood Bible* (1998), set in 1960s Congo. Although she wrote it with *Little Women* in mind, she admits "the parallels don't go too far."[27] It is the story of a fanatic American missionary father, his wife, and their four daughters, who each resemble the March girls in cursory ways: the oldest hates housework and is worried about her looks; the twins, who come next, are a tomboy with wanderlust and a girl who is physically damaged; and the youngest, the innocent beloved by all, dies tragically from a snakebite. Kingsolver's novel most resembles *Little Women*, however, in its focus on the women in the family. While almost all stories about colonizers have been told from the male point of view (reviewers were fond of pointing out the parallels with *The Heart of Darkness*), this one is told by the women who are dragged along and try to make a new home in an inhospitable environment. Another novel that imagines the March sisters as part of the colonial project is Jane Nardin's *Little Women in India* (2012), written for teens and set in nineteenth-century India. Nardin follows the fortunes of the four English May daughters, whose privileged lives of parties and husband hunting are disrupted by the 1857 uprising that forces them to take refuge in a remote village where they begin to question colonial rule.

English Pakistani author Sarvat Hasin's *This Wide Night* (2016) positions the March sisters among the colonized subjects, although after the end of British rule. Published in India and set in 1970s Karachi during the India–Bangladesh War, *This Wide Night* features the four Malik sisters—Maria, Ayesha, Leila, and Beena. This novel not only moves Alcott's story to a new time and place but also makes the bold move of altering its point of view. *The Wide Night* is told entirely in the voice of the girls' neighbor, Jimmy, thus essentially imagining how *Little Women* would have been different if told from Laurie's perspective. No wonder the publisher describes the book on its jacket as "*Virgin Suicides* meets *Little Women* in Pakistan."

Comparing a new novel to *Little Women* is, in fact, a familiar marketing strategy. Julia Alvarez's *How the Garcia Girls Lost Their Accents* (1991) has been promoted on its cover as "a kind of Dominican American '*Little Women*.'" The book jacket of Kate Saunders's *The Marrying Game* (2004) begins, "Like Louisa May Alcott's classic *Little Women*, *The Marrying Game* opens on Christmas Eve, with four sisters at home worrying about money." And Saunders herself called her first novel, *The Prodigal Father* (1987), "a sort of punk *Little Women*." Nadiya Hussain's *The Secret Lives of the Amir Sisters* (2016) is described as "a moving and heart-warming modern British Muslim take on *Little Women*." In the case of Alice Hoffman's *The Story Sisters* (2009), one reviewer called this book about three hyper-imaginative sisters who believe that mortals have stolen them from their fairy family "'Little Women' on mushrooms."[28]

Over the years, critics have identified a significant number of women's novels that appear to nod toward *Little Women* in various, if less obvious, ways: in the United States, Lucille Fletcher's *The Daughters of Jasper Clay* (1958), Jamaica Kincaid's *Lucy* (1990), Jane Smiley's *Moo* (1995); in Britain, Diane Tutton's *Guard Your Daughters* (1953), Fay Weldon's *Big Women* (1997), and Sherry Jones's *Four Sisters, All Queens* (2010).[29] In fact, a number of novels (not to mention television shows from *The Golden Girls* and *The Facts of Life* to *Sex and the City* and *Girls*) celebrate sisterhood (real or created) by featuring four or sometimes three female friends or sisters with distinct personalities. They are not exactly direct descendants of Alcott's novel, but there is no denying that *Little Women* originated the four-sister theme and paved the way for many followers. Besides those already mentioned, we can add Emma Dunham Kelley's *Megda* (1891), Sydney

Taylor's *All-Of-A-Kind Family* (1951), Amy Tan's *The Joy Luck Club* (1989), Terry McMillan's *Waiting to Exhale* (1992), Ana Castillo's *So Far From God* (1993), Ann Brashares's *The Sisterhood of the Traveling Pants* (2001), Eloisa James's *Much Ado About You* (2005; includes "A Love Letter to Louisa May Alcott" at the end), Shirley Geok-lin Lim's *Sister Swing* (2006), Danielle Steel's *Sisters* (2007), and Joy Callaway's *The Fifth Avenue Artists Society* (2016).

Other works in which the heroines read (and often reread) *Little Women* include Ellen Glasgow's *The Sheltered Life* (1932), Dorothy West's *The Living Is Easy* (1948), Perri Klass's *Other Women's Children* (1990), and Kate Atkinson's *Behind the Scenes at the Museum* (1995). For her story "The Garden Party" (1922), also a portrait of girls growing into women, Katherine Mansfield likely borrowed the names of sisters Jose and Meg and their brother Laurie from *Little Women*. In Alison Lurie's Pulitzer Prize–winning *Foreign Affairs* (1984), one of the characters gives herself the surname "March" after her favorite childhood heroine, Jo. In Edwidge Danticat's *Untwine* (2015), twin sisters watch the movie versions of *Little Women* and say the characters' lines with them. Girls act out their "own version of *Little Women*, in which Beth didn't die" in Amy Bloom's *Lucky Us* (2014). In A. S. Byatt's novel *The Game* (2012), when one of the characters gets her first story published, she comes "running from the post . . . like a character from *Little Women*, crying, 'Look, look what I've done.'" And Jennifer Weiner's novels also contain many references to *Little Women*.[30]

The extent to which *Little Women* has echoed throughout literary culture should make it a core text in college classrooms, the kind of text students must know if they want to understand the roots of American and women's literary traditions. Instead, the novel is not taught much at all. When it is taught, it is usually in children's literature courses. A database of texts in all genres used in college and university courses ranks *Little Women* at 431 overall.[31] For comparison, *Walden* ranks 31 and *Adventures of Huckleberry Finn* 47. Perhaps a more interesting comparison, however, is two women's texts rediscovered and promoted by feminist critics in the 1970s and '80s: Charlotte Perkins Gilman's short story "The Yellow Wallpaper" (1892) ranks at 50, and Kate Chopin's novel *The Awakening* (1899) at 55. Both of these are considerably shorter than *Little Women*—always an attractive feature for college teachers—yet neither has had the cultural or literary impact of Alcott's novel. However, academics remain uncomfortable with books written for children and, perhaps even more so, books for girls. What educators seem to be missing is that *Little Women* operates on many levels and deals complexly with cultural prescriptions of femininity. It is not as simple as it may at first appear. As I have found in my own courses, Alcott's novel sparks discussions and debates not easily resolved. While *The Awakening* and "The Yellow Wallpaper" had to bide their time until the culture had reached a certain level of feminist consciousness for readers to appreciate them, *Little Women* has always been read because its contradictions and complexities have allowed us to read it differently over time. It has grown with us, and we with it. But that process has not been easy.

# 6

# "A DIVIDED HOUSE OF A BOOK"

## Reading *Little Women*

For a literary work to have cultural longevity it must contain themes and characters about whom people care deeply, inspiring debates as if what happens on the page is real life. Reading such a book is a rewarding if sometimes unsettling experience. We may find that the person next to us in a class or book club feels so differently about it that we wonder if we read the same text. Or we may read it again as adults and wonder what we were thinking as kids. What we thought was thrilling now seems preachy, or what appeared a light frolic now has dark undercurrents. As a result, we may turn against our childhood favorite or appreciate it more deeply than ever. *Little Women* is just that kind of rich, complex, often contradictory book that can inspire such intense reactions.

There has never been much agreement about how to read or what to think about *Little Women*. Is it a realistic tale of a New England family during the years of the Civil War or a nostalgic, even sentimental portrait of a family life that never really existed? Is it a rebellious tale of one young woman's resistance to the restrictions of her era, or a dispiriting portrait of her capitulation to the status quo? Despite 150 years of discussion, the debates over these questions remain unresolved. The one constant has been that while the possibilities for women's lives have expanded and shrunk over the generations, young women continued to read themselves into the book, mapping it onto their lives as they grew into adulthood and then looked back on their formative years. *Little Women* has been enjoyed, discussed, and picked apart by early-twentieth-century new women and flappers, midcentury baby boomers, and late-twentieth-century feminists, never losing its power to delight and provoke.

The critic Margo Jefferson has called it "a divided house of a book [that] still stands, ramshackle[,] worn and full of life." *Little Women* has a split personality, simultaneously looking backward and forward, inward and outward. It points backward to a simpler time of family cohesion *and* looks forward to a complicated time when women would find work away from home and family. It also turns inward toward the family gathered around the hearth *and* faces outward toward a world of adventure and possibility. As a result, *Little Women* has been read as conservative *and* progressive, such that reviewers of the 1994 film noted its ability to appeal to feminists as well as proponents of family values. However, the tension between those two visions has been there since the beginning. Critics and scholars have disagreed about how traditional or modern the book and its various adaptations really are—whether it is essentially wholesome family fare or a deeply radical book, a didactic sermon or a novel that brings its characters to life. Such "critical commotion is one mark of a masterpiece," as the critic Alice Kaplan has written about a very different book, Albert Camus's *The Stranger*.[1] Books that we disagree about simply last longer, particularly if the debates they generate still matter to us. That is certainly the case with *Little Women*.

FOR THE BOOK's first hundred years of life, the discussion about *Little Women* focused on whether it was a realistic or a sentimental, idealized portrait of life. To those for whom the book still lives, *Little Women* is a work of realism. Alcott promoted realistic writing within the novel itself: Jo declares, "I like good, strong words, that mean something," and Professor Bhaer encourages her to avoid the types of sensational literature and "study simple, true, and lovely characters, wherever she found them, as good training for a writer." Throughout the novel the characters speak naturally, moving the dialogue along with an energy that reminds us of how real people talk. Take, for instance, the girls' bickering in the opening pages of the book:

> "Jo does use such slang words," observed Amy with a reproving look. . . . [Jo] began to whistle.
> "Don't Jo; it's so boyish."
> "That's why I do it."
> "I detest rude, unlady-like girls."
> "I hate affected, niminy piminy chits."[2]

As readers we can almost see and hear Jo and Amy, as if they are real girls before us.

The book's initial reviewers repeatedly pointed to the book's resemblance to real life. They were surprised that a novel in which so little happens could sustain readers' interest but attributed the book's charm to its realism. "Everything about the story is 'as natural as life,'" stated one reviewer. Another compared the novel's incidents to photographs, a technology then in its infancy but already changing audiences' expectations about art's relationship to reality.[3] *Little Women* is very much concerned with the happenings of everyday life, so much so that at times little seems to be happening. But audiences found this quiet sort of book refreshing. They were used to gothic literature with mysteries to decipher and the supernatural to contend with, romantic literature's alternate reality of dreams and extreme psychological states, sensational literature's plot twists occasioned by kidnappings or mistaken identity, or sentimental literature, which stirred up the feelings against social injustice, such as *Uncle Tom's Cabin* (1852). *Little Women* represented a rather new style of literature.

In the United States, the so-called rise of realism is associated with the Civil War and developments in technology and science, as well as with male writers such as Mark Twain and Henry James.

However, women were writing realistically long before the war. In the 1840s and '50s, writers like Caroline Kirkland and Rose Terry Cooke had begun to write fiction based on their experiences, which meant staying close to home. So when Louisa May Alcott wrote *Little Women* out of her own life, she wasn't exactly a pioneer, but she was making a significant contribution to a new way of writing that would never entirely go out of style. Her innovation was that she portrayed such fully realized characters that readers then and now have instantly felt as if they were real people, wholly unlike the idealized characters most common at the time. Each of the March sisters has a flaw she cannot easily overcome. Marmee admits her failings. Laurie struggles to do the right thing. Even Professor Bhaer is afraid to propose to Jo and proves himself to be, like all the other characters, only human. The plot moves along much like real life, with small trials and triumphs. The great crises in the novel are death and loss—again, as in real life.

Some critics over the years acknowledged Alcott's contribution to the literary movement of realism. As early as 1907, G. K. Chesterton declared that *Little Women* "anticipated realism by twenty or thirty years; just as Jane Austen anticipated it by at least a hundred years." He pointed in particular to the scene in which Professor Bhaer proposes to Jo. Alcott makes a point of presenting what should be an idealized scene as full of imperfections. Jo is anything but a typical romantic heroine. "She looked far from lovely," the narrator tells us, "with her skirts in a deplorable state, her rubber boots splashed to the ankle, and her bonnet a ruin." Bhaer, for his part, is also rather battered by the rain: "his hat-brim was quite limp with the little rills trickling then upon his shoulders . . . , and every finger of his gloves needed mending."[4] The unkempt, middle-aged professor was hardly the romantic hero readers were used to.

Yet, while the novel's realism continues to strike readers profoundly, many over the years have insisted that its portrait of family life and romance is idealized and sentimentalized. The word *sentimental* has evolved over the past two centuries to signify exaggerated emotionalism or nostalgia. There is no denying that *Little Women* tugs at the heartstrings. The question is whether it does so excessively.

Early reviewers almost unanimously viewed the emotions evoked by the novel as ordinary and natural. There was nothing "over-wrought" about it, claimed one reviewer. Another declared, "There is just enough sadness in it to make it true to life." Yet skepticism toward literature that evoked emotions was starting to creep into critical commentary. The *Galaxy* reviewer admitted that "it isn't *à la mode* now to be moved over stories," but he thought the "few tears [and] many hearty laughs" the novel elicited would do readers good.[5] Literature was expected to have a beneficial effect on readers, and proponents of realism believed that romantic and sentimental fiction could overwork readers' emotions, deluding particularly young female readers about what they could expect in life. (The most famous literary depiction of this theme, Gustave Flaubert's *Madame Bovary*, was published in France in 1856, twelve years before *Little Women*.) Realism, by contrast, was supposed to be the more ethical literary mode. Alcott, it could be said, agreed. Although she enjoyed writing sensation stories, in which the emotions are decidedly overwrought, she staked her literary reputation on her realistic writing.

As realism and then modernism became the dominant literary aesthetics in the twentieth century and literary texts capable of draw-ing out readers' emotions were deemed sub- or even nonliterary, *Lit-tle Women* came under attack for being too sentimental. When the Broadway play was produced in 1912, the shift away from sentiment was in full swing, yet most reviewers did not fault the play or the novel it was based on for mawkishness. Probably the term most often used to describe the play was *wholesome*, crediting *Little Women* with doing good and countering the more deleterious effects of most pop-ular entertainment. Even one critic who thought "the sentimental-ity was occasionally laid on with a trowel," concluded that the play "never cloys because it is so genuine in its sweetness." A much later stage adaptation, in 2004 on London's West End, was again noted for its ability to wring a few tears out of "sardonic, anti-sentimentalist" theatergoers. The play made for an evening "as warm and wholesome as hot milk," the reviewer concluded.[6]

*Little Women* has always walked the fine line between *genuine* realism and *sweet* sentimentality. Consider again the scene in which

Professor Bhaer proposes to Jo. While Jo and Bhaer are anything but a romantic hero and heroine, their humble love is elevated above commonplace emotion. In what must be the novel's most sentimental line, Bhaer's "rapture" is described as "glorify[ing] his face to such a degree that there actually seemed to be little rainbows in the drops that sparkled on his beard." Most readers could not help groaning at that. Yet the narrator also undercuts the idealization by noting how passersby must mistake them for "a pair of harmless lunatics."[7] Throughout the novel, in fact, Alcott makes sure her readers keep their feet on the ground by reminding them that Beth is no angel but a very human girl, that Marmee is not perfect, and that Jo has to learn to manage her destructive temper. The tug-of-war between realism and sentiment works for most readers, but for some sentiment wins out, to the novel's detriment.

After World War I, literary critics uniformly employed the term *sentiment* pejoratively and were fond of using the synonyms *sweet* or *treacly*. In the 1920s, Ernest Hemingway, that archenemy of emotion in literature, had not actually read the novel but still associated it with an innocence that was incompatible with modern life. He mocked the budding writer Lavinia Russ by telling her she should be carrying *Little Women* instead of a play by Ibsen because she was "so full of young sweetness and light."[8] For the rest of the century, *Little Women* would be associated with cheap, easy, outmoded emotions.

At the heart of the literary war against sentimentalism was, to be frank, a distaste of the feminine. The expression of emotion was associated with the world of women, namely the home. This association becomes explicit in a story like Hemingway's "Soldier's Home" (1925), which I regularly teach in my American literature survey. Coming a few weeks after *Little Women* on the syllabus, it throws into relief how much literature had changed after World War I. For a soldier returning home, like Hemingway's Harold Krebs, women and the homes they inhabit are full of complicated emotions he wants nothing to do with. He can only stare at the bacon fat hardening on his plate as his mother cries and tells him she loves him.

Even in 1868, Alcott understood the association of emotion with the feminine. Jo prefers the more masculine version of her name because Josephine is "so sentimental." She refuses to cry when Amy burns her manuscript because "tears were an unmanly weakness." In the end, however, when she challenges Professor Bhaer for being so sentimental as to want her to call him "thou," the form of address common in romantic poetry, he tells her that he is proud to "believe in sentiment" with the rest of his German brethren.[9] Thus Alcott turns the tables by privileging sentiment through a male character. But that wouldn't matter in the coming decades. She had written a book for girls that covered the full spectrum of their emotions, from anger to grief, and worse than that, she made readers cry. Critics would find it hard to forgive her for that.

When the RKO film came out in 1933, some reviewers took the opportunity to take a pot shot at Alcott's original novel. *The Nation*'s critic alluded to the custom of referring to the novel "as the classic expression of a certain kind of American sentimentalism," and another critic admitted he never could stand Alcott's "sugared sentimentality," although he loved the film. Katharine Hepburn, it seems, had redeemed the sentimental story with her exaggeratedly masculine performance as Jo. But in the period after World War II, *Little Women* became inseparable from sentimentality and nostalgia. The MGM film in 1949 was attacked for being "sweet and cloying," "a sentimental Technicolored Valentine."[10]

That same year, *Little Women* was indicted in James Baldwin's famous attack on sentimentality. His excoriation of *Uncle Tom's Cabin* in "Everybody's Protest Novel" used *Little Women* as a point of reference, apparently assuming that readers would know it better than Stowe's novel. "*Uncle Tom's Cabin* is a very bad novel," he wrote, "having, in its self-righteous, virtuous sentimentality, much in common with *Little Women*." He went on to explain, "Sentimentality, the ostentatious parading of excessive and spurious emotion, is the mark of dishonesty, the inability to feel; the wet eyes of the sentimentalist betray his aversion to experience, his fear of life, his arid heart; and it is always, therefore, the signal of secret and violent inhumanity, the mask of cruelty."[11] He goes on, but that is enough, I think, to suggest how virulently anti-sentiment mid-twentieth-century American writers and critics were. I find it hard to believe, however, that Baldwin actually read *Little Women*. He seems to be using it as a shorthand, as Hemingway did, relying on the cultural associations it carried to help bring down his more immediate prey, *Uncle Tom's Cabin*.

In 1965, the British critic Brigid Brophy would address the issue of *Little Women*'s sentimentalism head on, writing a long article that ran both in the London *Times* and on the cover of the *New York Times Book Review*. Her essay about sentimentality in art, titled "A Masterpiece, and Dreadful," was occasioned by the recent airing of the 1933 film of *Little Women* on BBC television and her subsequent rereading of the novel. Alcott was, she supposed, "of all writers the one whose name *means* sentimentality." Brophy set out to rescue the novel from such condemnation. Its ability to evoke tears was not a sign of its excessive emotionalism; in fact, crying over literature was a legitimate response to a book so skilled in the "gentler and less immoral sort" of sentiment. "Having . . . dried my eyes and blown my nose," she writes, "I resolved that the only honorable course was to come out into the open and admit that the dreadful books [*Little Women* and *Good Wives*] are masterpieces," although she is careful to qualify her praise. Sentiment should be applied conservatively, and it is in Alcott's "artistic honesty" and restraint that she finds the novel's merit.[12]

When the novel turned one hundred years old in 1968, the many reassessments that appeared again highlighted how impossible it was to pin down *Little Women*. The *New York Times Book Review* ran another lengthy essay, this one by American novelist and critic Elizabeth Janeway, who called the book "dated and sentimental" yet "as compulsively readable as it was a century ago." It commits the "literary sin of sentimentality which falsifies emotion and manipulates the process of life," but it succeeds still because "it is *about* life, and life that is recognizable in human terms today." Children's author Lavinia Russ, writing for the children's *Horn Book Magazine*, found it strange to be going back to *Little Women* in a year that had witnessed the assassinations of Martin Luther King Jr. and Robert Kennedy. "To think, let alone write, about a book remembered as the story of a loving New England family in the nineteenth century seems about as timely as a history of antimacassars" (the cloths used to protect the backs of chairs). But Russ ultimately realized how timely the novel was with its belief in striving to be good and make the world a better place. If young people would follow Alcott's lead, then there was still hope for the nation to emerge from the darkness of that terrible year.[13]

In another centennial reassessment, the Irish writer Sean O'Faolain wrote "This Is Your Life . . . Louisa May Alcott" for *Holiday*, a travel magazine in which many famous authors appeared. O'Faolain's delightful essay, which deserves to be read in its entirety, again touched on the sentimentalism debate: "I will not quarrel with any reader's right to lay [Alcott's] book aside because there is too much sweetness and light in it," he writes, "but I do feel that the balance she strikes between the dark and bright sides of life is more true to common experience than the opposite imbalance of our so-called realists."[14] In other words, *Little Women* is neither a realist nor a sentimental text, as they have become defined by their extremes of "dark and bright." Rather, it is a novel that has lasted precisely because it manages to place itself in the middle, where most of us live.

Disagreement continues about whether *Little Women* tips toward realism or sentimentalism. For some, the novel's emphasis on goodness makes it patently unreal. The writer Mary Gaitskill resented the book's "impossibly sweet view of life" when she was growing up and was not convinced by the March sisters' avowals of contentment as they happily shouldered their burdens. This was nothing like the "real life" she knew. London journalist Miranda Kiek is afraid to tell people how much she loves the novel because she invariably gets the response, "Isn't it just a load of schmaltz, only fit for Christmas?" For critic Laura Miller, *Little Women* is the epitome of the type of children's book that is "populated by snivelers and goody-two-shoes, the most saintly of whom were sure to die in some tediously drawn-out scene."[15]

For others, however, the story and characters remain genuine. Sutton Foster, who played Jo in the 2004 Broadway musical, regrets that people think it is "precious and Hallmarky and tender." For her, the story has "passion and heart and determination and heartbreak and desire and absolute devastation." Anna Quindlen always felt as if the March sisters must have "roots in real life simply because they were so alive, so patently real." The director of a recent stage production, Danielle Howard, likewise insists, "The characters, they're not just storybook. They're real people, confronting real day-to-day problems, their own flaws."[16]

As for the novel's virtuousness, it is important to recognize that the March sisters aren't good already but are trying to be good. The girls never attain some pinnacle of perfect virtue (except for Beth, who admittedly doesn't have to work much at it). Even after Beth's death, Jo struggles to be the dutiful daughter. Alcott shows us Meg's failures as much as her successes as a new wife and mother. Amy is rewarded with Laurie and with wealth in the end not because she is good, Alcott seems to suggest, but because she is charmed. Those who see the novel as sickeningly sweet don't seem to remember how the girls grumble and resist as they shoulder their burdens. One of my favorite chapters is "Experiments," in which Marmee, tired of listening to her daughters complain about their burdens, allows them to take a week off from their responsibilities in order to show them that "all play, and no work, is as bad as all work, and no play."[17] At the end of the week, she takes the day off herself so they will see what it is like to take care of everything themselves, an experiment that results in domestic chaos and unhappy girls. While most novels and sermons of the era preached self-sacrifice as the height of virtue, Alcott's characters slowly learn that being "good" benefits themselves as much as others.

Perhaps it's *Little Women*'s association with Christmas that has made it inescapably sentimental for some. The story opens with the girls at home preparing for Christmas, and many of the subsequent films, plays, radio dramas, and television specials opened or aired at Christmastime, capitalizing on the holiday's associations with a nostalgic idealization of home. The nineteenth-century cult of the home still has strong appeal, even outside of the holiday season. We bemoan the fact that families don't sit down to dinner together and are all on their devices instead of interacting with each other. Alcott's portrait of home as a haven from the outside world pulls at our deepest longings. She has an uncanny ability to make it seem not only ideal but also possible. In Perri Klass's novel *Other Women's Children*, a female pediatrician reads *Little Women* at night to help her fall asleep, reminding her of "all the cozy domesticity of my fantasies, the *Little Women* mix of loving family, hard work, and moral uplift." For Gloria Steinem, the novel was so attractive precisely because her family never stayed put. It represented the kind of house "with a picket fence and a school I could walk to" that seemed like home to her.[18] *Little Women* plays on such urges despite—or perhaps because of—the modern family's fragmentation. Seen from another view, the March home might be so appealing precisely because it is not entirely traditional. It has no patriarch, and everyone has her role to play. No one is on top, unless it is Marmee, who is a gentle guide rather than a boss. So while the novel's image of home may seem essentially conservative, there is something rather subversive about it as well. It is this tug-of-war between traditionalism and modernity that continues to make *Little Women* such a vital, living text.

BEGINNING ABOUT THE TIME of the novel's centennial, questions about *Little Women*'s progressiveness or lack of it came to the fore in discussions of Alcott's book. By the 1970s, it was impossible not to read *Little Women* through the tense debates over women's rights. There had been almost no notice of the novel's defiance of cultural norms before that time. One exception is a 1913 review of the Marion de Forest play that identifies Jo as "something of a Pankhurst sort of person," referring to the English militant suffragist Emmeline Pankhurst. Jo's "forceful, untamed nature" was deemed relatively harmless, however, considering that it was only her own family she "sets afire . . . instead of ducal palaces."[19] The critic was right in saying that Jo would like to upend social conventions, but neither she nor her creator would have advocated militant methods.

Alcott herself was a staunch defender of women's right to vote, a cause that had stalled in the years leading up to and during the Civil War. She was the first woman to register to vote in Concord, in 1879, and she held three meetings at her home to rouse up the women of the town to join her. She signed a letter to the *Woman's*

*Journal* about her suffrage activities, "Yours for reforms of all kinds." Although suffrage and women's rights are not mentioned directly in *Little Women*, they would become a prominent theme in the sequel *Jo's Boys*, published in 1886. By that time it seemed very much as if the tide was beginning to turn (although it would be another thirty-four years before the Nineteenth Amendment finally gave women the franchise). In one scene, Nan, the tomboyish girl in whom Mrs. Jo sees much of her former self, declares, "The women of England can vote, and we can't. I'm ashamed of America that she isn't ahead in *all* good things." Nan, we are informed, "held advanced views on all reforms," like her creator.[20]

As a young woman, Jo was even more ahead of her time and even more alone in her views. In *Little Women* there is no community of women who are discussing the larger social issues and women's place in them, as there is in *Jo's Boys*. Instead, Jo goes through life "with [her] elbows out," Alcott's way of describing her resistance to convention. Jo's difference from her sisters is most noticeable in her relationship with Amy, which comes to a head in the chapter "Calls" in part two. Jo refuses to behave appropriately on their visits to their so-called social betters, while Amy wants to adhere to social norms. Jo calls Amy's insistence on women's agreeableness even in the face of bad behavior "a nice sort of morality." "I only know that it's the way of the world," Amy responds, "and people who set themselves against it, only get laughed at for their pains. I don't like reformers, and I hope you will never try to be one." To which Jo retorts, "I do like them, and I shall be one if I can; for in spite of the laughing, the world would never get on without them. We can't agree about that, for you belong to the old set, and I to the new."

Neither this conversation nor the scene in which it occurs is included in any of the novel's adaptations on film or stage. All of them tend to reduce Jo's "love of liberty and hate of conventionalities," as Alcott puts it, to her boyish ways, love of writing, and burning of her dresses by standing too near the fire.[21] While telling, these traits are hardly threatening to the social order. Perhaps this is why commentators didn't pay much attention to Jo or recognize how iconoclastic she was before the second wave of feminism.

Even the rebellious 1920s overlooked Jo. In an article titled "Subversive Miss Alcott," which ran in *The New Republic* in 1925, the author, Elizabeth Vincent, couldn't understand why "every little girl in America" still read such an old-fashioned book. It wasn't the novel that was subversive, ultimately, but girls' insistence on reading it despite "our insurgent age." In Vincent's examination, Jo is nothing more than a tomboy, and Meg's belief that a woman's highest duty is in the home is "a fine popular doctrine for the age of equality and economic independence." The flapper Marjorie Harvey in F. Scott Fitzgerald's story "Bernice Bobs Her Hair" (1920) similarly thought there was nothing progressive about *Little Women*. "What modern girl could live like those inane females?" she quips.[22]

By 1968, however, *Little Women* no longer seemed so innocent. Janeway took the lead in her *New York Times Book Review* essay. Although she thought the novel overall "dated and sentimental," she declared that Jo was the original feminist, fulfilling "the dream of growing up into full humanity with all its potentialities instead of into limited femininity: of looking after oneself and paying one's way and doing effective work in the real world instead of learning how to please a man who will look after you, as Meg and Amy both do." Although Jo marries in the end, she is "not a sweet little wife but a matriarch," Janeway argued, making the woman who created her a "secret rebel against the order of the world and woman's place in it."[23]

In the letters responding to Janeway's piece, *Little Women* became, not for the last time, a lightning rod for debate about the virtues of feminism. Janeway sounded like Betty Friedan or "some other militant feminist," complained one woman, who took exception to Janeway's privileging of work outside the home and felt personally attacked as a stay-at-home mom. If some women "want the 'child-raising off their backs,'" she protested, "then let them hire their children out to nannies, and get on downtown to the office, for God's sake. Get *them* off our backs. We have work to do."[24] Janeway had clearly touched a nerve, one that would be at the heart of discussions of *Little Women* from then on. Reading *Little Women* was no longer a nostalgic activity or something only girls did. Alcott seemed to be commenting on the turbulent transition women's lives were undergoing in the late twentieth century.

Some journalists, including Gerald Nachman, saw the linkage of the novel to feminism as a comic opportunity. Writing for the *New York Times*, he imagined a film adaptation called "Little Women '70" that would star Betty Friedan as Jo and have Beth die in a botched abortion. His fictional director described the concept as *Little Women* "seen now in ironic perspective against the background of the Women's Liberation Front, an inevitable outgrowth of the activities of the girls in the novel."[25] But feminists were beginning to directly challenge the notion, on which Nachman's satire rests, that Alcott could be associated only with the education of prim little girls.

At the same time that Nachman was poking fun, the first national publication of second-wave feminism, *Women: A Journal of Liberation*, published an essay titled "Louisa May Alcott: The Author of *Little Women* as Feminist." Although she was typically "a prime example of everything hip culture scorns, literati ignore, and feminists detest," journalist Karen Lindsay wrote, Alcott should instead be viewed as a humanist and a feminist, although admittedly not a radical one. Alcott never directly criticized the institution of marriage, for example, although she challenged its romanticization by having Jo choose Professor Bhaer instead of Laurie. Given the current state of children's literature and television, Lindsay argued, girls of 1970 could do much worse than to read *Little Women* and Alcott's other books.[26]

Stephanie Harrington struck a similar note in a 1973 *New York Times* article titled "Does *Little Women* Belittle Women?" It was a review of the BBC's nine-part miniseries adaptation, which had just aired in the United States. Compared to most television fare, such as "the weekly humiliation" of Edith Bunker on *All in the Family*, the BBC production "takes on the force of a feminist tract." But that wasn't saying much, Harrington claimed. The novel *Little Women* was still "a perfectly disgusting, banal, and craven service to male supremacy," given its celebration of marriage and motherhood as the pinnacle of a woman's life. Even Jo eventually succumbs to the feminine mystique of selflessness. Yet, amid the sea of female caricatures on large and small screens, the March sisters stood out because they were still allowed to be themselves. "They at least think. They at least, in their own terms, grow," Harrington argued. Most impressively, they were given the respect of being called women, a considerable step ahead of Marlo Thomas's "That Girl." Playing on the Virginia Slims slogan that used feminism to sell cigarettes, Harrington concluded, "No, we have not come a long way, baby. Nobody ever called Jo March baby."[27]

When feminist scholars emerged within academia in the 1970s, they were particularly drawn to *Little Women*, but they weren't much interested in favorably comparing the novel to current fare and celebrating its incipient feminism. In various ways, they set out to demonstrate what Nachman's fictional director had identified as his theme: "Just why these women were so little [and] how male chauvinism made them feel so small."[28] For many early feminist critics, *Little Women* was a prime example of the internalized patriarchal viewpoint that had compromised and thwarted women writers, who simply couldn't help but portray their female characters as limited, submissive, and powerless.

One of the first feminist critical texts to focus on literature by women was *The Female Imagination* (1975), by Wellesley English professor Patricia Meyer Spacks. She analyzed how *Little Women* focused on the "glorification of altruism" for women. Saintly Beth is "rewarded by dying young," Spacks argued, while rebellious Jo, who yearns for the freedom granted men, is punished by marrying "a man who can control her." Three years later, in *Communities of Women: An Idea in Fiction*, Nina Auerbach, professor of English at the University of Pennsylvania, provided the first extended feminist analysis of *Little Women* and found that while it celebrated female community in the first part, Alcott had betrayed her "deepest fantasies" by denying the possibility of "permanent sisterhood" in the last part of the book.[29]

But it was Judith Fetterley's 1979 analysis of *Little Women* as "Alcott's Civil War" that has been most influential on subsequent readings of the novel. Inspired by the reprinting of some of Alcott's sensationalist stories, which often portrayed marriage as a prison for women, Fetterley saw darker undercurrents in Alcott's most famous children's novel, a text that now seemed to be at war with itself. The novel's overt messages favor female submission and self-sacrifice, including Amy and Jo's seemingly carefree renunciation of their artistic and literary ambitions. Yet the novel also contains subtler messages, Fetterley argued, about the limitations imposed on women and the lack of alternatives to marriage. The great paradox of the book is that "the figure who most resists the pressure to become a little woman is the most attractive and the figure who most succumbs to it dies." Although Fetterley ultimately regretted Alcott's capitulation to traditional notions of womanhood, her analysis opened up new ways of talking about the tensions in *Little Women*.[30] In other words, while Alcott herself came to be seen as a more complex figure—someone who could write about drugs, madness, and suicide as well as benevolent virtues for children—her masterpiece, *Little Women*, also began to appear more multidimensional.

Ever since, readings of *Little Women* have addressed the question of whether it is a subversive or submissive text, whether it is a product of its time or pushes against nineteenth-century cultural mores, particularly as they concern women. There have been many important analyses of the novel's historical and biographical contexts, but the main points of contention focus on whether we can read *Little Women* as a feminist text, and what it means to read it through the lens of our contemporary expectations concerning gender.

As feminist criticism entered the scholarly mainstream, the number of academic articles on the novel exploded from only five in the 1970s to over twenty in the 1980s and more than thirty-five in the 1990s. Three currents in literary criticism made it possible for scholars to take *Little Women* more seriously. First, the idea of a novel's "cultural work," or its effect on readers and even the social order, became as significant a measure of its worth as traditional measures of aesthetic value. Second, the practice of literary analysis began to move away from unifying interpretations and toward indeterminacy and the recognition of competing themes, which *Little Women* had in spades. Third, the rise of gender studies initiated a turn away from thinking of men and women as simply distinct biological entities and toward considering gender as something learned and performed, not fixed but mutable. *Little Women*, more than perhaps any other novel written before the second wave of feminism, is fundamentally about how girls learn to become women or perform gender as it was constructed in the second half of the nineteenth century (and as it more or less continued to be through the 1960s). As scholar Gregory Eiselein has written, "Before Simone de Beauvoir (a devoted reader of *Little Women*), Alcott understood that one is not born, but rather becomes, a little woman."[31] The novel also shows how men are educated into their gender, as Laurie must give up his music and prepare to take over his grandfather's business.

All of this has led to intense debates about how much *Little Women* participated in or pushed against the dominant ideologies of its day. In the 1980s, critics were largely unwilling to forgive Alcott for marrying Jo to Professor Bhaer instead of making her a writer. Carolyn Heilbrun, while acknowledging that "Jo was a miracle," also concluded that Alcott "betrayed Jo" by robbing her of her autonomy. Scholars Angela Estes and Kathleen Lant, picking up the theme of hidden violence from James Baldwin, stressed the "horror" of Alcott's "dismemberment of the text," particularly in the way she destroys "fiery, angry, assertive" Jo and the female utopia to which she belongs. They describe the ways Jo gradually loses power until she finally takes on the self-effacing personality of her dead sister, Beth, becoming a "zombielike Jo." For children's literature specialist Beverly Lyon Clark, Alcott stifled Jo in *Little Women*, and was above all "ambivalent—about writing, about self-expression, about gender roles."[32] All of these critics focus on the transformation of Jo from part one to part two, which has been the most troubling aspect of *Little Women* for feminist critics.

Such debates spilled over into the popular press when Gillian Armstrong's film came out in December 1994. Feminist writers and critics outside of academia wondered whether *Little Women* was still a book worth reading and talking about, and, predictably, they did not agree. One view, represented by Gaitskill in her article for *Vogue*—titled, like Harrington's, "Does *Little Women* Belittle Women?"—was that *Little Women* should still be read. Although she had rejected the book as a child, Gaitskill realized now that it could help women move toward "a new, more fully dimensional feminism that includes both gentleness and strength" and away from the image of powerful, gun-wielding babes that often passed for feminism in popular culture. *Little Women* could also provide a useful model for today's writers, she decided, because it was emotionally honest, not sentimental, as she remembered it. Critic Caryn James disagreed. In an article for the *New York Times*, she set out to counter the "cult of Jo [that] has conspired to make her a proto-feminist saint." The novel was much more ambiguous than that, she felt. Her own reading as a girl had been that Amy was the sister to envy: she had golden curls, went to Europe, and got the cute rich boy next door. But upon rereading the book, she decides that it hasn't held up all that well thanks to the prevalence of "preachy, do-good lessons from Marmee."[33] For her, *Little Women* was simply not the feminist tract the film suggested it was.

When the film made its way across the Atlantic, British writers and professional women who were asked for their opinions were largely critical, and some were downright caustic. The journalist and biographer Brenda Maddox, an American expat, was the first to chime in for the *Times*. She didn't need to reread the book, she said, because its lessons on womanhood had already been etched on her psyche, and she wasn't happy about it. "*J'accuse* Miss Alcott of making little women of us all," she wrote. "For all its ostensible preaching about women's self-sufficiency, *Little Women* is as politically incorrect as *Penthouse*. Its message is that woman's role is to stand and wait, place her husband above her children, and never let her learning or quick tongue get ahead of her duty to be gentle, subdued and nurturing." The *Observer* interviewed a number of women about the book and film, including author Michele Roberts, who felt that the novel promoted an unattainable and damaging model of self-sacrificial womanhood. "Come the end of the novel, [Jo's] been tamed into submission by horrid Marmee," she complained. There was simply nothing feminist about Alcott's story. Novelist and journalist Linda Grant agreed, calling *Little Women* "a sickening book." Having read it again as an adult, she thought that "it reveals its grisly agenda," namely the preaching of feminine, wifely virtues. Liz Forgan, managing director of BBC Radio, went so far as to call *Little Women* "profoundly unfeminist, truly dangerous stuff for little girls."

The *Independent* also wanted to know what British women thought of *Little Women* and drew this opinion from novelist and self-proclaimed "militant feminist" Julie Burchill: she liked the first part but thought *Good Wives* "pretty disgusting. If Louisa May Alcott had been really sound," she contended, she would have written a third volume and called it "Divorced Lesbian Sluts."[34]

Some staunch feminists, however, were less willing to throw their childhood favorite to the wolves. Germaine Greer said that the book still moved her deeply. On rereading it forty-five years after first having it imprinted on her imagination, she wrote, "The tears run down my face like rain; tears of mirth, tears of sympathy, and tears of I-don't-know-what." Steinem admitted that her view of the novel had changed, but not for the worse: "I'm now old enough to identify with Marmee, and to appreciate this rare literary model of a hard-working single mother." Although she wished Alcott had been able "to tell more of the truth," she wondered, "where else in popular culture can young readers find an all-female group discussing work, art, and all the Great Questions? . . . Most of all, where can they find girls who want to be women—instead of vice versa?"[35] In Steinem's mind, cultural images of young womanhood had still not caught up to the iconic portrait of a feisty Jo March as first envisioned in 1868.

In 2005, when the Library of America published the *Little Women* trilogy (including *Little Men* and *Jo's Boys*), the debates geared up once again. Rereading the novels brought some surprises for critics. Whereas the three film versions ended with Jo getting married and getting published, the novel does not end so patly. As Deborah Friedell read it, Jo gave up her writing and burned her sensation stories (forgetting that Jo writes again after Beth's death and is rewarded with success). "She learns to cook and to keep house. She marries the professor, starts a school, has children. . . . This is not exactly the woman's fate that has edified generations of Jo's readers." Stacy Schiff agreed in her op-ed "Our Little Women Problem" for the *New York Times*. To her great disappointment, especially since she had named her daughter after Jo, she said the novel turned out to be more Rapunzel than the proto-feminist tale of her recollection. In response, Elaine Showalter, who had edited the new edition, wrote to the *New York Times* to encourage Schiff to read the books again and see that Jo is "the great feminist heroine" who does not renounce her career in favor of family life. "Jo does not stop working or pick up the feather duster when she marries," Showalter explained. She not only codirects a boarding school with her husband but makes sure the boys are taught to respect women's rights and even puts them to work as babysitters.[36]

The widely varying readings seem to depend on which parts of *Little Women*—and its sequels—one focuses on. I'm inclined, with Steinem and Showalter, to see *Little Women*'s glass as half full rather than half empty. I don't entirely disagree with those readings that see the novel as not particularly feminist, but to me they tell only part of the story. Does the Jo of part two cancel out the Jo of part one? Scholar Barbara Sicherman found that early female readers did not view Jo as having failed to realize her potential, as contemporary critics have done. Having so few models of unconventional womanhood in their own lives, readers from the 1860s to the 1960s gravitated toward Jo "as an intellectual and a writer, the liberated woman they wanted to become. No matter that Jo marries and raises a family; such readers remember the young Jo . . . and her dreams of glory." One critic has argued that readers are drawn to *Little Women* precisely because they can pick and choose which parts matter to them, and for most readers it is "the far naughtier beginning and middle."[37] Even if we can't agree on how to read the book, we can find in its various parts those elements that most speak to us.

Maybe it's not such a bad thing that *Little Women* is such an ambiguous novel. In its competing narratives of quest and romance, rebellion and resignation, rejection and adjustment, *Little Women* offers its readers multiple options, none of which is *the* one message of the text. Jo is both writer and family member, revolutionary role model and little woman, male-identified tomboy and feminine nurturer. *Little Women* therefore provides a wonderful opportunity to tease out the relationships between these identities and consider how women have inhabited multiple selves. In Jo we can see how these competing identities create internal conflicts, making not only for a fractured text but a fractured heroine. Her great desires, as Alcott identifies them—"to be independent, and earn the praise of those she loved"—are rather contradictory. How can Jo hope to achieve independence, which implies separating from her family, and earn their praise, which implies a submission to their wishes or at minimum a compromise? As one critic has pointed out, Jo's dreams of a career are coded masculine while her dreams of connection are coded feminine. She wants to be an independent writer *and* a member of a loving family, a pairing not traditionally available to women. Ultimately she makes a compromise between the two that is "the result of a genuine maturation" rather than a capitulation to conventionality.[38]

My students tend to understand this and roundly reject the equation of Jo's marriage with her subjugation. A woman can marry and still be independent, they tell me, and they like to review the passage where Jo explains that she hasn't given up her career altogether. At the end of *Little Women*, when Jo is in her thirties and married with two boys of her own as well as many others at the Plumfield School that she and Bhaer manage together, she is reminded of her earlier dreams to be a famous author. She begins, "Yes, I remember; but the life I wanted then seems selfish, lonely and cold to me now." This line is often cited by critical feminist scholars and writers, who rarely continue to the next sentence, where Jo says, "I haven't given up the hope that I may write a good book yet, but I can wait, and I'm sure it will be all the better for such experiences and illustrations as these," meaning her family and her work at the school.[39] What has seemed like a defeat to feminist critics seems to my students a reasonable response to life. They reject the dichotomy between writing/career and family/love. I felt the same way when I first read the novel in my early twenties. That line jumped out at me and gave me hope that Jo would write her great book yet, a book enriched by her family life rather than crushed by it.

Another passage almost entirely neglected by critics explains why Jo's dreams of fame seem cold to her now. Beth's death initiates a great change in Jo that could seem as if feelings of guilt have led her to try to replace Beth. But there is more to Jo's transformation. Beth may say to Jo on her deathbed, "You must take my place, Jo, and be everything to father and mother when I am gone," but she also tells her, "you'll be happier in doing that, than writing splendid books, or seeing all the world; for love is the only thing that we can carry with us when we go, and it makes the end so easy." Then and there, "Jo renounced her old ambition" and felt "the blessed solace of a belief in the immortality of love."[40] This is not mere sophistry or conventional romantic thinking to which Jo succumbs. Love isn't the thing to which she must sacrifice her ambitions to become a true woman or to be accepted by her society. Instead, Alcott says that it is the one thing in life that really matters, in the end. Anyone who has sat at the bedside of a dying loved one knows the truth of Beth's words. It is the people they love who are on their minds.

If *Little Women* has one major theme, it is learning to live with and for others. Meg, Jo, and Amy all start out rather myopically, wanting things for themselves. As they each learn to let others' needs take precedence at times, they discover that doing things for others makes them happy as well. It's not always easy, however. After her sister's death, Jo, in particular, struggles to be as self-sacrificial as Beth. In fact, Jo isn't capable of it. At the prospect of living the rest of her life at home, in service to her aging parents, she thinks, "I can't do it. I wasn't meant for a life like this." And Alcott doesn't make her. In her view, women didn't fulfill their true natures by living solely for others. The kind of life she promoted was one of cooperation, in which each does his or her share to make life more comfortable for each other. Marmee teaches this lesson early on, in the "Experiments" chapter, where she tells them that "the comfort of all depends on each doing her share faithfully."[41] In the end, Jo and Professor Bhaer share the running of Plumfield School, which, as we see in *Little Men*, is itself a kind of cooperative community. Each pupil has a role to play in the school's success. While not always recognized as a key tenet of feminism (although it should be), the idea of sharing life's burdens, regardless of gender, remains a radical prospect for many.

I sometimes get impatient with readings of *Little Women* that take a hard line on Alcott's betrayal of Jo. I agree with my students who want Jo (and themselves) to have a family *and* a career. We can talk about how difficult that is, trying to keep the writer or artist or intellectual part of yourself alive when the baby wakes up early from her nap or starts refusing to nap altogether, and how unfair it is that men have not had to choose between family and career. But let's not say that Alcott robbed Jo of her individuality by giving her a husband and children. In the chapter "All Alone," where Jo realizes after Beth's death that she can't live at home forever, we see how lonely she is and how much she wishes she could love someone. Alcott wanted Jo to be a literary spinster like herself, largely because the idea of women combining love and art seemed wholly impossible in the 1860s. Jo's belief that she may one day write even better works from the experiences she is having was pretty revolutionary. Not only that, but in 1886, Alcott had Jo pick up her career again in *Jo's Boys*, writing a book like *Little Women* that touches the hearts of her readers and makes her a celebrity. Alcott also gave careers to three young women in that book: two who marry (Amy's daughter, Bess, an artist, and Meg's daughter Josie, an actress) and one who does not (Nan, a doctor with no interest in marrying).

In recent years, as the idea of feminism has broadened and deepened, readers have been able to more fully recognize the novel's key tensions as inherent to women's lives and even the human condition. Complementing Alcott's realistic portrait of the way women have had to accommodate their dreams in order to have families, she also shows that men like Laurie and Professor Bhaer have to make compromises. Bhaer gives up his true vocation—teaching at a college out West—to instruct little boys at Plumfield so that he can have a home with Jo. And Laurie gives up his dream of a being a musician so he can work in his grandfather's business and have a stable home with Amy.

In many other ways, as well, the novel extends the boundaries of conventional womanhood in the nineteenth century. Each of the girls is given a different personality and a unique talent that she is encouraged to cultivate. Jo and Amy leave home as part of their development into adult women. Alcott allows Jo to reject a perfectly lovable and wealthy suitor and to contemplate life without marriage (virtually unprecedented in nineteenth-century literature). And the novel allows female characters a wide range of emotions, including unfeminine anger, frustration, moodiness, willfulness, and self-centeredness, not to mention masculine ambition.

Alcott's portrait of marriage is especially progressive. For starters, marriage is not presented as the end point of a woman's development; we see in Meg's storyline that it requires new adjustments. Alcott also promotes a non-patriarchal, companionate view of marriage: Marmee encourages Meg to invite John into the nursery, and to talk with him about politics, and Jo and Bhaer share the same sphere, working together at Plumfield instead of each toiling away at home or at work. In this way, Alcott introduced to a wide audience the notion that to be partners in life, men and women must be allowed to come together as fully formed individuals. Her parents' friend the transcendentalist Margaret Fuller had written about this concept in her feminist treatise *Woman in the Nineteenth Century* (1845), and it was a principle Abigail Alcott promoted to her daughters. Too many women, they thought, entered marriage as incomplete selves and simply became their husband's appendages or dependents. Not so the March sisters.

Whether *Little Women* is propaganda for the patriarchy, cautionary tale, or radical argument for women's equality wrapped up in a book for children—or all of these things at once—it seems our readings of it will continue to multiply as we decide which parts of it matter to us most. Nonetheless, the question of who should read *Little Women* and why remains. Is it a book that should be read in schools? Is it worthy of continued attention? Should boys be encouraged to read it? And does it still matter to girls today? Again, there are no easy answers.

# PART III

## A CLASSIC FOR TODAY

# 7

## "A PRIVATE BOOK FOR GIRLS"

### Can Boys Read *Little Women*?

When I began teaching *Little Women* in my American literature survey courses, I wondered how many of my students had read the book before. In that first class, only one said she had read it in high school. A few of the women had been given the book to read as girls. None of the men had read it. This was a small sample, admittedly, but I wondered if it was being taught in middle and high schools. Surely if books such as *The Adventures of Tom Sawyer* and *Adventures of Huckleberry Finn* were being taught, their near-contemporary and, shall we say, feminine counterpart, *Little Women*, was as well. It didn't take much digging to find out how wrong I was and why Alcott's classic had not endured as a book for schools while Twain's tales of boyhood had.

*Little Women*, it turns out, is barely on teachers' and students' radars. Its educational heyday in the first half of the twentieth century is a distant memory. Surveys of teachers' favorite or recommended texts conducted by the National Education Association ranked *Little Women* at 47 in 1999 and 73 in 2007. A 2010 survey of four hundred English teachers indicated that none were teaching anything by Alcott. The same year, the annual *What Kids Are Reading* survey, based on 6.2 million students' reading records, listed the forty most frequently read books by grade. *Little Women* was not mentioned in the report.[1]

Also in 2010, however, *Little Women* received a potential boost from the new Common Core Standards Initiative. Along with benchmarks students should reach in each grade came lists of "exemplar texts" having sufficient quality and appropriate complexity for each level. *Little Women* made the list for grades 6–8 (as did *The Adventures of Tom Sawyer*). It hasn't much benefited from the recommendation, however. According to the 2012 *What Kids Are Reading* report, which includes a focus on the Common Core exemplar texts, only 0.08 percent of the 7.6 million American students surveyed had read *Little Women* the previous school year. By 2014, while some texts on the Common Core exemplar list had received a nice boost since the initiative began—Franz Kafka's *The Metamorphosis*, for instance, was read by ten times as many students as before, and *Tom Sawyer* by four times as many—*Little Women*'s increase was only two hundredths of a percentage point, meaning it was read by 0.1 percent of students. In the 2016 surveys, conducted in the U.K. as well as the United States, Alcott was not mentioned in either report, which represented the reading habits of 9.8 million students in the United States and 750,000 in the U.K.[2]

Most educators and parents have been less than thrilled with the Common Core, which many states have challenged. The list of "exemplar texts" has been particularly controversial among education specialists, raising concerns about creating a new literary canon. Classics in general were deemed to be overrepresented on the list, but *Little Women* was the target of a specific kind of criticism. For instance, one education blogger complains,

> I yowled when *Little Women* first appeared on the Common Core
> list of exemplary texts for 8th graders. And I'm still yowling. The
> point is not whether you or I loved this book eons ago. The point
> is whether it is appropriate for today's 8th graders. . . . If someone

polled 500,000 8th-grade teachers, asking them for book recommendations, what are the chances that *Little Women* would appear on anyone's list?[3]

In other words, *Little Women* is presumed to be hardly worthy of rescue from the educational oblivion into which it has fallen.

Another blog post takes a different approach to the subject, but its title pretty much says it all: "Please, Do Not Teach Little Women!" The author, who chairs the English Department at a middle/high school in Connecticut, thinks that *Little Women* is appropriate as an independent reading choice but nothing more. She has "a great fear that some educators will consider the novel a 'teachable text.'" She regrets that girls will not "linger over every page," as she did when a child, and that they will be forced to take multiple choice tests about it rather than be allowed to develop a personal relationship with the March girls. Her regret that the novel could cease to be a private pleasure, read alone with a flashlight under the covers, is understandable. But then she claims, "Although I am not gender-biased with literature, I would not assign this novel to pre-teen boys." She pleads instead for teachers to choose *Tom Sawyer* and to leave *Little Women* alone. Her claim to a lack of bias notwithstanding, her comment that she would not assign this novel to teenage boys perfectly reflects the clear gender bias that she and many teachers have about using what are deemed to be girls' books in their classes. Another educator, a library media specialist, reacted to the Common Core list by asking, "How many 12 year old boys will be engaged by *Little Women*?"[4] As far as I can tell, no one is concerned about whether twelve-year-old girls are engaged by *Tom Sawyer*. But their reaction is not what concerns educators. It's the boys' responses they are worried about.

Still assuming there must be some elementary and middle-school teachers out there using *Little Women* in their classes, I naïvely posted a query on a very active listserv that includes academics in education and children's literature as well as education professionals working in schools. I simply asked who was teaching the novel, hoping I could follow up with interviews about their experiences. I received only a handful of responses. They were not encouraging. They mostly explained in various ways that teachers don't teach *Little Women* because it's a book for girls and they fear turning off the boys, whom they perceive as unwilling to read books about girls. One educator admitted how unfair this was, considering that the girls are made to read books focusing on boys. Another was more vehement, stating simply that the boys would loathe it. The surest way to teach them how to hate reading would be to make them suffer through *Little Women*, she said. It is "a private book for girls," not one to read "publicly, in a classroom." Yet another respondent explained that it was not well suited to classroom discussion in a mixed-sex school and that it was more appropriate for girls to read at home.

This is the real issue. A book that is about girls, whose very title seems to announce its gender exclusivity, is to be kept at home, not brought into the glaring light of the schoolroom. As we have seen, this wasn't always the case. *Little Women* was initially a wildly popular book devoured by children and adults of both sexes. It gradually became, however, "more of a women's novel, then an adolescent girls' book, and finally . . . a notable piece of children's literature, specifically perhaps, a work for seventh and eighth grade girls," as one teacher wrote on its centenary.[5] Since then, I think it's fair to say, the book has migrated further down the age scale, to fifth and sixth grade. As a book for young girls, then, *Little Women* seems to warrant little if any attention in the schools. I searched in vain for a local school where I live, in New Orleans, that was teaching it. Even at a progressive K–12 private girls' school, where I knew a couple of the English teachers, not only was no one teaching it, but my attempts to interest them in the idea fell flat. As one of them showed me the way out after one of our meetings, she admitted that they teach *Adventures of Huckleberry Finn* and wondered, "If we don't teach *Little Women*, who will?"


THE STORY OF how *Little Women* has migrated from the classroom to optional summer reading lists and homeschooling text lists (another way it stays at home) has at least three strands that relate to feminism, the preference for contemporary texts, and concerns about a crisis in boys' reading. In the first instance, I can't help but wonder whether

*Little Women* fell out of favor with educators because of its association with feminism. At about the same moment (the 1970s and '80s) that it became a hot topic of conversation among feminists, *Little Women* went underground and under the covers, where it could safely remain a book for girls without wider cultural significance. As we have seen, *Little Women* became less of an innocuous family tale and more the kind of book that could ignite uncomfortable discussions. Teachers were likely wary of addressing feminist issues with their students and found boys' books less potentially controversial.

Of course, the erasure of *Little Women* is part of a larger silencing of women's voices in literature classrooms, which has only become more profound as issues relating to women's lives have become more socially volatile. As just one documented example, the *New Yorker* critic David Denby describes, in his recent book on how literature is taught in American schools, one supposedly exemplary tenth-grade English class that spent the year exploring the theme of the Individual and Society. How many of the assigned texts were written by women? Only a few poems by Sylvia Plath, over an entire year, while they read books such as George Orwell's *1984*, Aldous Huxley's *Brave New World*, Paulo Coelho's *The Alchemist*, Hermann Hesse's *Siddhartha*, Kurt Vonnegut's *Slaughterhouse Five*, and Nathaniel Hawthorne's *The Scarlet Letter* (the only book they read *about* a woman). The female students were visibly frustrated, so Denby asked the teacher to explain and learned that "intensity mattered more [to the teacher] than inclusiveness." I couldn't help thinking that *Little Women* (or a host of other novels by and about women) would have contributed valuable, and surely "intense," perspectives on what it means to be a female individual growing up in America. Instead, the "individual" remains male. In fact, the only two books about girls that routinely appear on middle- and high-school reading lists are *The Diary of a Young Girl* by Anne Frank and *To Kill a Mockingbird* by Harper Lee.[6] As was the case in my daughter's own sixth- and seventh-grade English classes, I suspect these books are used to teach issues related to the Holocaust and civil rights rather than the experiences of girls growing up.

The second strand of the story is about a push, beginning in the

1980s as part of the canon wars, to teach contemporary books instead of the classics. Although *Little Women* never had a secure position in the canon, it got lumped together with other "old" books then under fire for neglecting the perspectives of minorities and purporting to be universal. While teachers have made more room for contemporary young adult literature in their classrooms, some of the core classics, like *Adventures of Huckleberry Finn*, *The Scarlet Letter*, *Lord of the Flies*, and *To Kill a Mockingbird* remain the most frequently taught.[7] With less and less room for such texts, however, those on the fringes, such as *Little Women*, have been dropped altogether.

The third and perhaps most important strand of the story of how *Little Women* disappeared from the classroom is the widespread concern about boys' reading habits—or lack thereof—which purportedly reached "crisis" proportions in the early 2000s but is still very much with us. Whereas research in the previous decade had focused on a gender gap in education that disadvantaged girls, a turn toward focusing on the ways boys were left behind in seemingly feminized educational environments dominated research and the mainstream media. Departments of education in the United States, Australia, Canada, and the U.K. began initiatives to encourage boys to read. In the United States, *Newsweek* ran a cover story in 2006 that sparked a conversation on op-ed pages, websites, and morning news shows. While some have argued that the crisis is a manufactured one, part of the backlash against feminism's gains, articles continue to appear about how boys are failing to thrive as well as girls are, particularly in regard to reading.[8]

Teachers and school librarians, who are overwhelmingly female, were more or less admonished for letting their own (feminine) reading preferences govern their text choices and recommendations. One librarian explained the problem this way: "Boys are interested in reading about video games and sharks, but they're being handed books like *Little Women* and *Anne of Green Gables*." Library director Michael Sullivan was equally blunt in his essay "Why Johnny Won't Read": "We insist that all children read books that foster internal reflection, that emphasize the emotional rather than the physical. We define good books as those that conform to the way girls think. . . . The main reason why librarians and teachers often have so little respect for what boys like is that most of them are women—and guys' tastes [for gross humor and scary things] don't appeal to them." In response to the criticism directed at them, educators have quite understandably bent over backward to entice boys to read, but not only by providing more options. Instead, they have flattened the options so that texts about boys predominate—the more male focused and the more contemporary, the better. And to be sure, plenty of anecdotal evidence shows that teachers and librarians are not handing *Little Women* to boys; on the contrary, they, along with parents and peers, are actively discouraging boys from picking up or checking out so-called girls' books at all.[9]

The belief in a fundamental difference between boys and girls is stronger than ever. As one recent article on the subject explained, boys' brains are simply wired to prefer action and adventure stories, and it is the teacher's job to "provide boys with topics and genres that are of specific interest to them." Girls won't be left behind, the logic goes, because girls don't mind reading books about boys, whereas boys won't read books about girls. For that reason, one expert argued, the schoolroom library should contain twice as many "boy books" as "girl books." Teacher education textbooks include multiple variations on the theme that "the English teacher must choose common reading that will appeal to boys," as one textbook explicitly states. "The assumption has become a truism," a scholar of gender and reading concluded, "one to which most teachers and librarians active today subscribe." No wonder then that education professors often stress in their courses what boys like to read, directing their students—future teachers, most of them women—away from the books they had loved reading when they were young. Although today's educators and researchers don't specifically rule out stories about girls, that has been the net effect. The male-dominated classics have been joined by male-dominated contemporary literature, creating a national reading curriculum in which girls appear as sisters and sidekicks but almost never as protagonists.[10]

Boys' distaste for girls' books, a product of the gender distinctions in everything from toys to books that children pick up on very early, seems to arise as they discover that girls and everything associated with them are viewed as inferior.[11] Boys are teased by their peers, or steered by their parents or other adults away from books with girls on the covers. This bias has spilled over into the publishing world as well. It is widely known that gender accommodations in the marketing of two of the most popular series in recent decades significantly contributed to their popularity with male readers. The author of the Harry Potter series had to hide her gender behind the initials J. K., and the *Hunger Games* books featured gender-neutral covers with mockingjay symbols instead of the heroine, Katniss Everdeen.

THE GENDERING OF children's books has a long history, in which *Little Women* plays a prominent role.[12] In the early nineteenth century there was little differentiation between books for boys or books for girls. By midcentury, though, we start to see a split. Publishers began to produce adventure stories about boys escaping from the domestic world ruled by women as well as books specifically designed to convince girls of the rewards of staying at home and taking care of others. Previous children's literature had stressed obedience to authority for both sexes, but the new boys' books no longer did, while girls' books continued to do so. Thus boys were encouraged to develop into young men who were enterprising, autonomous, and adventurous. Girls, on the other hand, were encouraged to develop into young women who were content to huddle by the hearth and happily obey (male) authorities on whom they were utterly dependent.

The narrative tension of these girls' books derived from the pressures on liberty-loving girls to give up their individuality and independence to conform to a repressive ideal of womanhood—a pattern that many readers see in *Little Women*. The publisher Thomas Niles had asked Alcott to write a book for girls precisely because a new crop of boys' books had emerged without corresponding books specifically for girls. We know that Alcott initially rejected the idea, perhaps in part because of the underlying assumption that a book for girls must of necessity lack adventure and confine itself to home life.

Yet Alcott didn't want to write a conventional narrative. By sending Amy off to Europe and Jo to New York, she didn't exactly conform to expectations.

Just because books had become differentiated by gender, however, does not mean that actual boys and girls followed their precepts, nor does it mean that they read only the books designed for them. Girls frequently read their brothers' books. If they had to remain at home in life, they didn't always want to do so in their reading. It was assumed, in fact, that girls would benefit from understanding the world their brothers imaginatively lived in, but the opposite view was almost never considered. It was widely supposed that boys had no interest in reading girls' books, at least those portraying a dispiriting, restrictive domesticity with little action or excitement.

Nonetheless, some men later admitted having crossed the divide to read what has since become known as *the* book for girls—*Little Women*. President Theodore Roosevelt, literary scholar William Lyon Phelps, author Rudyard Kipling, and *New Yorker* critic Alexander Woollcott all had fond memories of reading the novel as children in the late nineteenth century. At the turn of the century, *Little Women* was still recognized as "one of the few 'girls' books' that all boys will read, even if they do it on the sly or in a corner." In 1897, Willa Cather was concerned about the way children's literature had split along gender lines. In a column for the *Home Monthly* she argued, "It isn't wise to make that hateful distinction [between boys' and girls' books] too early; avoid it while you can." She recommended in particular the books of Louisa May Alcott, which readers of both sexes continued to love into adulthood.[13]

Fast-forward to the second half of the twentieth century, and we see that assumptions about what books boys and girls will read had solidified to the extent that books written for boys dominated the publishing industry and school curricula. Although the women's movement had a positive impact on the publishing world, and many more books with active female protagonists have been published, the progress has benefited girl readers but not boys. Today the publishing and reading worlds remain largely segregated by gender. What is considered a book for girls is simply any book featuring a female protagonist, even though most such books today have little to do with indoctrinating appropriately submissive, so-called feminine behavior.

The issue of privileging books featuring male protagonists, from picture books on up, has been a hot topic in recent years, particularly as it relates to the publishing industry. In 2011, the *Guardian* ran a story with the headline "Study Finds Huge Gender Imbalance in Children's Literature: New Research Reveals Male Characters Far Outnumber Females, Pointing to 'symbolic annihilation of women and girls.'" The dominance of white protagonists is also being vigorously addressed, as is the issue of gender stereotyping books for children. In the U.K., the "Let Books Be Books" campaign has been widely publicized and highly successful at getting publishers to stop labeling books as for boys or for girls and getting newspapers to stop reviewing them if they are. The problem starts with gendered baby books and goes all the way up to adult books, the covers of which tend to feature highly feminine designs for fiction by female authors.[14]

Yet researchers continue to stress the need for male-oriented texts in the classroom. One recent study concluded that "boys in particular will benefit from having access to books predominately aimed at males, as they are less likely [than girls] to transcend gender boundaries" in their choices of reading material. Thus the study's authors recommend same-sex, small-group work rather than whole-class discussions of the same text, so that boys can read about boys and girls can read about girls.[15] The primary concern of such studies is motivating boys to read. The effects of sex-segregated reading on students' attitudes toward the opposite sex are not considered in any of the literature, so far as I can tell.

The issue of whether boys' reading preferences are due to biological differences or socialization continues to be debated, but it is surely some combination of the two.[16] While the argument for brain chemistry presumes there is something natural and therefore right about it, the extent to which boys develop prejudices against not just girls' books but also anything having to do with girls deserves serious discussion. It is human nature to seek out stories about people like ourselves. But is it not equally natural to be curious about people unlike ourselves? Why would anyone want to discourage boys from developing that curiosity? And if boys enjoy books about aliens, which they certainly do, why not also books about girls?

Many thoughtful commentators have acknowledged the harm done by our culture's hypermasculinization of boys. Perhaps most usefully, one researcher has challenged the many opinion pieces and studies on boys' reading preferences for the way they perpetuate a narrow view of masculinity. Their "attempts to build literary curriculum on received notions of what is appropriately masculine" tend to alienate many boys who have broader views of what it means to be a boy than do the adults so eager to cater to their presumed tastes. In fact, such efforts can only reinforce essentialist notions of gender that lead to homophobia, heterosexism, and sexism, which in turn can lead to bullying and violence.[17]

The crux of the problem is that by condoning intolerance of the female and the feminine, in reading preferences or otherwise, we do a disservice to both girls and boys. Shannon Hale, author of *Austenland* and the *Princess Academy* series, has forcefully raised the issue on her blog and on Twitter, touching a nerve with many librarians and children's authors. In a piece called "No Boys Allowed: School Visits as a Woman Writer," she describes how sometimes boys are not invited to her presentations because her books are about girls. She is outraged at "the belief that boys won't like books with female protagonists" and "the shaming that happens (from peers, parents, teachers, often right in front of me) when they do." She goes even further, suggesting that the resulting gender bias and shame can have long-lasting, harmful effects on boys' psyches:

> . . . the idea that girls should read about and understand boys but that boys don't have to read about girls, that boys aren't expected to understand and empathize with the female population of the world . . . this belief directly leads to rape culture. To a culture that tells boys and men, it doesn't matter how the girl feels, what she wants. You don't have to wonder. She is here to please you. She is here to do what you want. No one expects you to have to empathize with girls and women. As far as you need be concerned, they have no interior life.

After Hale went public, other female authors of children's books featuring girl protagonists reported having faced similar gender prejudices at schools.[18]

While some may think that Hale's linkage between rape culture and boys being told not to read books about girls is a stretch, I think it is fair to connect the dots between the dismissal of girls' voices and perspectives and the lack of empathy toward females in our culture that can result in abuse. There is plenty of evidence that far too many boys grow up with little regard for the humanity of the female half of the population. The high rates of sexual harassment in the workplace and rapes on college campuses provide ample evidence. Researchers are noting how masculine identities require the repression of empathy. Psychologists are also beginning to recognize the important function that reading fiction can play in developing it.[19] At a minimum, we should be able to agree that it would be good for boys to read some books from a female perspective. And what better book than *Little Women*, with its gender-bending protagonist, Jo, and her best friend, Laurie, both of whom challenge the rigid gender boundaries that persist? Its title notwithstanding, *Little Women* is a book that both boys and girls can benefit from reading.

There is some evidence that boys can respond positively when encouraged to read *Little Women*. One school librarian likes to tell the anecdote (presumably because it is an aberration) of a "typically masculine" boy who one day settled down to read *Little Women*, "inarguably the most femininely titled book in literary history," and brushed off the teasing of his classmates. "You're missing a great book," he told them, and he continued reading.[20] My own experiences with attempting to interest boys and men in *Little Women* have been largely positive. In my American literature survey courses, I regularly teach Alcott's novel to a diverse group of traditional and so-called nontraditional (i.e., older) students. I will never forget the response of one online student who saw in the March sisters' struggles his own difficult journey toward adulthood. "Despite being a 30 year old man," he wrote, "I'm very sad to be done with this novel, and very happy to have read it." Nor will I forget the day an African American male student, who listened to the novel at nights while he worked as a security guard, came to class quite upset because Jo had turned down Laurie's marriage proposal. For these and many other (although not all) of my male students, *Little Women* was a revelation. They didn't expect to become so absorbed by it, but they were.

I have also found that young boys can be enticed to read *Little Women* as well. When invited to speak to my daughter's sixth-grade English class, I took the opportunity to encourage the students to choose *Little Women* for their book clubs. I told them about the novel's popularity and influence, the March sisters and who they were based on, and the career of the woman who wrote it. Before leaving, I asked them if *Little Women* was a book only for girls, and the students were very vocal in their answer. "Noooo," they chorused. We talked about how they had just read a book about a boy, Tom Sawyer, and how *Little Women* was from more or the less the same time period and showed not only what it was like to grow up as a girl but also what it was like for their friend, Laurie (a boy, despite his name), to grow up as a boy. They seemed to agree that it was useful for girls to read about boys and for boys to read about girls. During our discussion, the boys in the class asked as many questions as the girls; I didn't notice them tuning out or acting as if this discussion was not for them.

Later that week, the teacher told me that three groups had chosen to read *Little Women* for their book clubs—two groups of girls and one group of boys. When I went back to talk to the three groups, they unfortunately hadn't read much of the novel yet, but we did discuss which of the sisters they liked best so far and how they were handling some of the slang and archaic language (in some cases, not well). The three boys who had chosen the book seemed to be as interested as the girls were. One in particular impressed me. He liked Jo and was curious to know more about Laurie, who had just been introduced. When he came to write his book review, he was quite persuasive in his recommendation of *Little Women*, arguing that it gave the reader a better understanding of life in the 1860s, when young men had to go to war and young women had to follow rules about how to dress and how to behave.

This experience convinced me that there was much to be gained by asking or encouraging boys to read *Little Women* and not much to be lost. None of the three boys exhibited any discomfort about reading the book, nor did any of their classmates make comments about their choice, their teacher later told me. Even though the other boys in the class didn't read it, they were at least exposed to the idea that boys can read books that are supposedly for girls, and the sky wouldn't fall. I came away thinking that it can be done, no matter what teachers and parents say. (The biggest hurdle, frankly, was not the book's title or the gender of the protagonists, but the length of the novel. I encouraged them to treat it as two books in one, thus giving them permission to read only the first part, which does stand alone as a book in its own right. This is something teachers could easily do if they are concerned about how long the book is.)

ONE REASON THAT so many male readers have been uncomfortable with *Little Women*—and perhaps the most important reason they should read it—is that it flips the perspective between boys and girls in a way few other literary texts have done. In the words of Carolyn Heilbrun, it is "perhaps the one fictional world where young women, complete unto themselves, are watched with envy by a lonely boy." Girls are for once at the center, and boys and men are on the margins. The March sisters have lots of conversations that have nothing to do with boys, so *Little Women* passes the Bechdel test with flying colors. One man said that he read *Little Women* when he was young precisely to get an inside view of how the opposite sex thought and acted, and he strongly believed that all boys should do the same.[21]

When Laurie tells Jo that he is essentially a voyeur, peeping into the Marches' windows—"it's like looking at a picture to see the fire, and you all round the table with your mother"—we are supposed to feel sorry for him. "I haven't got any mother, you know," he says quite pathetically, and Jo instantly resolves to make him an honorary member of the family. For male readers, though, Laurie's position vis-à-vis his female neighbors can be unsettling. The scholar Jan Susina believes that boys feel left out of the text, as he did, because the male characters (including Laurie, John Brooke, Mr. March, and Mr.

Laurence) inhabit the place that female characters have always occupied in men's literature: on the margins, looking in. "Alcott situates the male reader," he argues, "in the role of Laurie, the fortunate outsider, who is simply allowed to observe the actions of women without speaking." Ultimately, Susina believes that "Alcott infantilizes her male characters." I think what he really means is that she emasculates them, at least according to conventional notions of masculinity. He appears to have felt the same way himself in his graduate course on children's literature when *Little Women* was introduced and "the balance of power shifted" because all of the female students knew the book but none of the men did. "The women in the class became the voices of authority," he says. "The male students were effectively silenced."[22] Susina realizes that the experience was a valuable one to him, as someone who would become a professor of children's literature and have primarily female students in his classes. Yet I can't help thinking that it was also a useful lesson for all of the male students in the class to feel for once as if they were the outsiders. Most female students have felt this way in their literature classes, reading primarily books about men and rarely having the "authority" to speak about what makes the male protagonists tick.

Not all male readers feel excluded by *Little Women* as Susina assumes they do, however. For library director Philip Charles Crawford, *Little Women* was fundamental to his childhood; it was the first book in which he saw himself reflected. Unlike Susina, Crawford did identify with Laurie because he also didn't enjoy sports and preferred playing with girls. Jo and Laurie were "a revelation" to him. "They were everything society told me I shouldn't be. They were gender nonconformists, a tomboy and a sissy who were able to express their gender identities nontraditionally and get away with it." In the characters of Jo and Laurie, Alcott portrays gender as fluid, something that must be learned but that can also be modified and even rejected to some extent. Jo is adamant about her desire to be a boy, while Laurie has been teased at school (the boys called him Dora) and is now affectionately called Laurie and Teddy by Jo, who seems determined to make him one of the sisters. Throughout, we see Laurie struggling to conform to conventional expectations for young men because he yearns to be a musician while his grandfather wants him to take over the family business. *Little Women* is the perfect text for examining with students how gender is constructed and how it is often imposed from without, not from within (something they already know innately but are quickly being taught to ignore). Crawford also sees similar acceptance of alternative femininities and masculinities in books such as *The Secret Garden* and *The Penderwicks*, yet he regrets that none of them helps children learn to deal with the bullying that inevitably results from gender nonconformity.[23]

Sadly, such bullying can also result when boys read *Little Women*, and not only from their peers. The writer Luis Negrón has recounted his painful experience of having been discovered reading it when he was a boy. It was the first book he checked out from the library, and like so many readers before him, he spent hours completely absorbed in the story. When his father made an unexpected return home, he proudly showed him the book, but his father became enraged. "You raising a fag?" he shouted at Luis's mother. After a stormy argument, his father drove off again, leaving his mother to turn her anger on her son. She screamed at him, "Queer! Little woman!" snatched the book from him, and tore it up. Another gay man who openly declared his love for *Little Women*, thankfully without retribution, was Leo Lerman, a son of Jewish immigrants and an editor for Condé Nast. He wrote of his deep affection for the book in 1973 for *Mademoiselle* magazine, under the title "Little Women: Who's in Love with Louisa May Alcott? I Am." According to one film critic, *Little Women* has been "universally popular" with gay boys and men, particularly since Katharine Hepburn's portrayal of Jo in the 1933 film.[24]

Perhaps this is why other men who admit to having read *Little Women* thought of it as so taboo that they could liken it only to sneaking illicit sexual material. Author Tracy Kidder was fourteen when he fell in love with *Little Women* and found it "absolutely captivating," but he was afraid of anyone knowing, so he "kept it secret like a piece of pornography." Editor and critic Charles McGrath also tried to hide the book when he read it in fourth grade. He had been "enthralled" by *Little Men* so went back to *Little Women*, but "because the title made it sound like a girls' book, I covered my copy with a brown wrapper, not realizing that this probably made 'Little Women' seem even more embarrassing. I could have been carrying around 'Lashed by Lust' or 'Bondage Boarding School.'" As adults, at least, men can perhaps give themselves more latitude. The Irish writer Sean O'Faolain thought that if he were caught in his study reading *Little Women*, "I could hold it up with, at most, a self-deprecatory smile or an At-My-Age shrug and go on escaping, unabashed."[25]

There are also plenty of boys and men who have felt much less conflicted about their interest in *Little Women*. Two annotated editions of *Little Women* currently available, for instance, were edited by men, John Matteson and Daniel Shealy, two of the most prominent Alcott scholars. Both men first read the book, as Susina did, when they were adults; but some men report having read it as children, including film critic Roger Ebert, actor Gabriel Byrne (whose mother read it to him), and former Supreme Court Justice John Paul Stevens. George Orwell recalled how much of his early perceptions of America were colored by his childhood reading, which included *Little Women* and *Good Wives*, both of which he loved. The Australian critic Peter Craven vividly remembers how, at age eight or nine, "my best friend came up to me at primary school and told me he had read a really great book," *Little Men*, to which Craven "crushingly" replied, "That's a girls' book." His friend disagreed, and although he was still dubious, they read it "with great exhilaration" and then proceeded "at great speed, through the whole Louisa May Alcott corpus of classics," including *Little Women*. He still believes, "If ever in the history of the world there was a girls' book, it's *Little Women* and its sisters," but he isn't afraid to admit having enjoyed them. BBC broadcaster Melvyn Bragg similarly picked up *Jo's Boys* first and then got the courage to read *Little Women*. Later he found that many men admitted to having read it, "although most of them would qualify the admission by muttering on about sisters or cousins leaving it lying around . . . or the teacher 'forcing' them to read it at school." The political operative James Carville, also known as the Ragin' Cajun, read *Little Women* at school but doesn't qualify his experience at all. He calls the book one of his childhood favorites. When his fourth-grade class read it aloud, it made him cry.[26]

Other men who have read *Little Women* at some point in their lives include the novelist Michael Dorris, who cited Professor Bhaer's advice to Jo to "write what you know" when describing his own literary practice; Stephen King, who referred to it throughout his *New York Times* review of *A Long Fatal Love Chase*, including quotations and describing scenes; and Julian Fellowes, who, when accused of borrowing a scene from it for *Downton Abbey*, admitted to having read it years earlier. Best-selling author John Green goes farther than most, counting *Little Women* as one of his literary influences and saying he "didn't understand why boys weren't supposed to read [it]."[27]

In the popular imagination, the idea of a boy or man reading *Little Women* is laughable, as demonstrated by comic references to the novel on television. In the popular 1970s BBC sitcom *Porridge*, set in a prison, Fletcher sells another inmate a copy of *Little Women* by convincing him it is an "erotic classic" about "the sex-starved lady pygmies of" South Malaysia. In a 1997 episode of *Friends*, Joey reads it on a dare. After Rachel opens the freezer and discovers *The Shining*, Joey's favorite book, which he hides there when he gets scared, Rachel says she will read it if he will also read her favorite book, *Little Women*. The episode ends with Rachel putting *Little Women* in the freezer for Joey, who is scared that Beth is going to die. Bart Simpson also reads *Little Women*, having been drafted to read a bedtime story to Lisa one night in a 2011 episode of *The Simpsons*. When he stumbles over every word, Lisa teaches him to read. Later, absorbed in the book, he is confronted by some bullies at school. "Are you aware that 'little women' is another word for girls?" one of them asks Bart snidely. They force him to read it aloud and then eventually get caught up in the story themselves. Finally, in a 2013 episode of *Girls*, Ray, a character known for his lack of (manly) ambition, is trying to get back from Hannah his copy of *Little Women*. He received it from his godmother, who had written in the back of the book some advice to him he desperately needs. Ironically, Hannah left the book in the apartment of her hyper-masculine boyfriend.[28]

All jokes aside, if we agree that it is important for boys at least occasionally to read books about girls, particularly those in which girls appear as individuals rather than as extensions of boys' lives, then *Little Women* is an ideal text. Jane Roland Martin, in her book *The Schoolhome: Rethinking Schools for Changing Families*, recommends that boys read *Little Women*, arguing, "Given that the ability to take the point of view of another is a basic element of morality itself, it is unconscionable—I would say positively immoral—to deprive them of the opportunity of identifying with the other half of humanity. . . . How can boys respect girls if they are never encouraged to see the world as girls do?" Maybe boys will even recognize that the March sisters aren't that much different from them after all. That is how Mark Adamo felt when he read *Little Women* and identified with Jo's feelings about losing her older sister to marriage. He had felt the same way when his sister, with whom he was very close, became engaged. Ultimately he understood the book to be about balancing our fear of vulnerability with our need for love. "It is very much about adult emotions," he said in the composer's commentary to his opera. His capacity to see Jo not as a "girl" but as a person like himself enabled him to write a critically acclaimed opera about her.[29]

If we keep *Little Women* private, almost as if it is a rite of passage for girls to keep secret along with their books about puberty and their changing bodies, are we not saying that it's exclusively about female identity and thus not about "American" identity? Perhaps that is why it is rarely mentioned as a candidate for The Great American Novel and has never been a part of the National Endowment for the Arts' Big Read program, which has sponsored 1,225 one-month programs in cities across the country. (*Tom Sawyer*, of course, has been a Big Read book.) More than that, are we not also saying that female experience should be kept private? That it has no place in public discourse, meaning that men shouldn't know about it? When we relegate *Little Women* to home reading and to girls only, we miss the opportunity to engage in the larger debates the book raises about gender and what it means to grow up. *Little Women* is one of the most valuable texts we have for helping readers young and old, male and female, to think about the complex issues of identity formation and maturation, and what role gender plays in them. Why then would we tell boys that it's not a book for them?

# 8

# "BEING SOMEONE"

## Growing Up Female with *Little Women*

MUCH OF THE discomfort with including *Little Women* in public discourse has to do with its depictions not only of girls, but of girls turning into women. Our culture prefers girls to stay small, young, and full of potential. The recent resurgence of book titles with the word *girl*—*Gone Girl*, *Rise of the Rocket Girls*, *Lab Girl*—speaks to our preference for the young person still looking ahead over the woman who looks wistfully behind her. We regret, in Robin Wasserman's words, "the transition from girlhood to womanhood, from being someone to being someone's wife, someone's mother."[1] Even more than that, I would say, our culture is threatened by the grown woman's possibilities: sexually, politically, and otherwise.

Girls have been told in myriad ways to stay girls as long as they can. Many have cooperated, some even starving themselves in an effort to do so; others have flat out refused to participate in girldom (like Jo). Meanwhile, others have been eager to leave girlhood's diminished status behind and appropriate the power of womanhood (like Amy). Clearly, however, the transition is anything but simple, and few maps have been available to help guide girls through it. The fairytales we all grew up with, which depict adolescent girls falling asleep until they are awakened by a prince, were less than helpful. *Little Women*, however, provided a detailed map of sorts through the ups and downs of growing up female—perhaps the most important one ever created, judging by its impact on countless women's perceptions of themselves. For generations, girls and young women have come to understand themselves through Alcott's portraits of four very different sisters.

The personalities of Meg, Jo, Beth, and Amy have become a kind of shorthand that girls could use to make sense of their own identities. For 150 years, girls have wondered, which March sister am I? Which one do I want to become? My mother told me that her parents thought she was a Meg, but secretly she was a Jo, an identity that took her many years to finally reveal. Margo Jefferson recalled that after her older sister, who got to read *Little Women* first, claimed Jo as her alter ego, she was determined not to be "left with Meg," the dutiful daughter. So instead she chose Beth, the sister who "makes no effort to win love: she is loved because she is loving." But as an adult, she decided that she "should have wanted to be Amy." Another reader remembered, "Of course, I identified with Jo, but sometimes wondered if I couldn't also be the pretty one, Amy, or the mature one, Meg. I pondered this question deeply—who am I really?"[2] Others have adopted the girls' names, so strong was their identification. In short, reading *Little Women* has been more than a literary experience; it has also been a deeply personal one, helping to shape readers' understanding of themselves.

Jo, in particular, has been a touchstone for so many girls who felt they could not or did not want to measure up to conventional (white) norms of womanhood—which must be a very large number, considering how widespread her appeal is. It is ironic, really, that the girl who didn't want to be a girl has been one of the most popular literary heroines of all time. Her popularity speaks volumes about the deeply unsettled feelings that girls of all backgrounds have felt as they approached the restrictions of womanhood. For many young lesbians, Jo was particularly important. "It's a complete cliché for a lesbian to claim Louisa May Alcott's *Little Women* as a key text in her self-understanding and relationship to the world," writes scholar Elizabeth Freeman. "After all, who was Jo but our tomboy self, our 'behind the mask' self, our struggle against normative femininity?"[3]

It is interesting that when asked to write a book for girls, Alcott chose to focus on what Henry James called "the awkward age," those years when a girl is not yet a woman but is also no longer a little girl. In other words, she captured her female characters in the throes of change, a highly unusual choice. Mary Wollstonecraft had noted seventy years earlier that while heroes were allowed to "become wise and virtuous as well as happy" over the course of their stories, heroines were "to act like goddesses of wisdom, just come forth highly finished Minervas from the head of Jove." From the outset they were supposed to be fully formed icons of femininity, incapable or unneedful of growth. When Margaret Fuller wrote *Woman in the Nineteenth Century* twenty-three years before *Little Women*, she despaired over how girls were discouraged from growing into their own natures when they conflicted with traditional notions of the feminine. The result? "Now there is no woman," she wrote, "only an overgrown child."[4] By the time Alcott wrote her novel of the March sisters, not much had changed.

By examining how each girl evolves over the six or more years covered in the two parts of the novel (excluding the final flash forward), Alcott wrote one of the earliest and most influential female *Bildungsromane*, or novels of development. She adapted a highly male genre and thereby granted girls the opportunity to imagine themselves as works in progress, as human beings without a set destiny but one they could make for themselves. While the male *Bildungsroman* charted a trajectory from innocence to maturity, or dependence to autonomy, the typical story of the female child coming of age was one of containment and restraint. More about "growing down," than growing up, it tended to show the heroine learning to conform to feminine norms rather than discovering herself as an individual. Even if it contained a rebellious middle, portraying girls who run and play like boys and yearn for achievement or fame, they generally ended rather depressingly with marriage, subservience, and renunciation of earlier dreams. Many critics have, in fact, viewed *Little Women* as another example of the failed female *Bildungsroman*, leading one to claim that it owes its enduring relevance to its central theme of "tam[ing] girls into women." I would argue that *Little Women* is more complicated than that, and it still lives because we continue to wrestle with what it means to grow up female and how to write women's lives outside of the conventional romance plot.[5]

BY FOCUSING HER NOVEL on the process of growing up, Alcott made a clear break with other children's literature, writing what we would today call young adult (YA) literature. The popular boys' books of the time celebrated the period of irresponsible youth before dutiful adulthood and didn't bother looking beyond their heroes' boyish pranks. (Twain would continue the trend with Tom Sawyer and Huck Finn, who refuse to grow up and actively resist any attempts to domesticate or tame them.) Yet Alcott perceptively understood the transition into womanhood as the most difficult time in a girl's life. It was the moment when life was still full of possibilities—but Alcott wasn't content simply to walk her heroines up to the altar. She made sure to show us the messy parts along the way and took us beyond the point when a girl's life ends and a woman's begins. In other words, she complicated readers' understanding of what it meant to grow up female.

Adolescence did not exist conceptually when Alcott wrote *Little Women*. Girls and boys were supposed to simply morph into young women and men, or "little" women and men. As the terminology suggests, this stage of life was viewed as a training ground for sex-differentiated roles as adults. Largely agricultural communities created an environment in which children were trained from an early age to replicate their parents essentially, to become farmers or preachers or shoemakers, or the wives of such men. A period of transition into a new identity was therefore hardly required.

In the final decades of the nineteenth century, when psychologists first named and identified adolescence, it became known as a uniquely turbulent period, distinct from all others, when the old child-self was falling away and a new sense of oneself as an individual was being born. It could last from about the age of fourteen into the midtwenties, during which time the adolescent was likely to experience fluctuating and sometimes extreme emotions. The end result was supposed to be a more advanced, adult self. As education became more widely accessible and city life became the norm, children's destinies could vary widely from their parents. The so-called crisis of adolescence therefore came when one's future differed from the past or was somehow undetermined.[6] This history of adolescence, however, generally presupposes a male child embarking on his future. The history of girls' maturation is different.

During the Victorian era, girls were expected to grow up to adopt a role, or two roles, really: wife and mother, precisely in that order. There was not supposed to be an adolescent crisis; there were simply one's duties to learn. In the meantime, they were expected to stay close to home and family until they were turned over to husbands, thus remaining dependents first in their family of origin and then in their husband's home. Yet as the century wore on, even girls experienced new educational opportunities while marriage rates declined (largely as fallout from the Civil War). As a result, many young women felt the pull toward independence and left home on their own, as Jo does when she goes to New York. Meg, who is sixteen when the story begins, seems to be most comfortable with her new status as a "little woman," apprenticing herself to Marmee and learning how to be a proper woman and future wife. Jo, on the other hand, seems to point toward a more modern form of adolescence, torn as she is between familial ties and a desire for independent selfhood. She also is developing a less gender-specific concept of her future role. She calls herself the "man of the family" in her father's absence, and she expects to be the family's breadwinner, a role she assumes in the second part of the novel, even after her father has returned.[7]

For girls, maturation has also always been closely tied to sexuality and the loss of purity or innocence. Girls who were sexualized early, such as slaves or workers who were preyed upon by their masters or bosses, were denied their adolescence. Yet even middle- and upper-class white girls could be sexualized early. There were famous examples of Victorian men attracted to prepubescent girls. Edgar Allen Poe married his thirteen-year-old cousin. A friend of Poe's, best-selling Scots Irish American novelist Captain Mayne Reid, married his wife when she was fifteen and he was thirty-five. Wilkie Collins is known to have carried on an extensive flirtation via correspondence with a twelve-year-old girl. The actresses Anna Cora Mowatt and Ellen Terry both married older men when they were quite young—Mowatt at fifteen and Terry at sixteen. Two famous English clergymen—future Archbishop of Canterbury Edward White Benson and the prime minister's son Stephen Gladstone—became engaged to young girls they later married. And the popular art historian John Ruskin fell in love with a series of young girls. His wife, Effie Gray, first drew his amorous attention when she was twelve years old, and they married when she was nineteen. After that marriage dissolved, purportedly because she was "already too old to be truly desirable," according to Effie's biographer, he fell in love with a ten-year-old but waited until she was eighteen to propose. (She turned him down.)[8]

Victorian literature is full of girls who marry much older men. In 1868 Captain Mayne Reid published an autobiographical novel titled *The Child Wife* in *Frank Leslie's Illustrated Newspaper*, where many of Alcott's works also appeared. Alcott's sensation fiction also offers many examples. In her novel *A Long Fatal Love Chase*, written in 1866 but unpublished in her lifetime, the heroine, who is relentlessly pursued by an older man ("past thirty"), is described as a "girl" and a "child." The man first falls in love with her "graceful girlish figure" and thinks she is fifteen, although she is really eighteen.[9] In "A Whisper in the Dark," first published in 1863, Sybil is seventeen when her forty-five-year-old uncle whisks her away from the only home she has known and imprisons her when she refuses to marry him. And in "Love and Self-Love," published in 1860, the heroine is only sixteen when her guardian, twice her age, becomes her husband.

Marriage at the age of sixteen or seventeen was not uncommon, even in the Northeastern United States, where child marriage rates were much lower than elsewhere in the country. In Massachusetts, where *Little Women* takes place, 23.5 percent of the women who married in 1861 were under the age of twenty (compared to 1.9 percent of the men). Of those, 302 were seventeen years old and 137 were only sixteen. When the United States began collecting such data in 1880, 11.7 percent of girls between fifteen and nineteen years of age were married.[10] (Parental consent was required for girls under eighteen.)

The picture of when exactly a girl was deemed capable of becoming a woman gets even murkier when we consider the legal age of consent, or the age at which a girl was deemed competent to declare her consent to a sexual act. In 1868, it was twelve in England and only ten in the United States. In 1885, the age was raised to sixteen in England, in response to a public outcry against childhood prostitution.[11] (Today in the United States, U.K., Canada, Ireland, and Australia, the age is between sixteen and eighteen.)

Victorian confusion and discomfort about the girl on the cusp of becoming a sexual being is perhaps nowhere more apparent than in Lewis Carroll's *Alice in Wonderland*, first published in 1865, three years before *Little Women*. Alice's body morphs in monstrous ways, literally outgrowing the small house that cannot contain her. Carroll (Oxford don Charles Dodgson) was no less uncomfortable with the maturation of the real Alice Liddell, who was ten years old when Dodgson made up his story about Alice's adventures for her. He feared the time when she and the many other girls he befriended and photographed would outgrow the frame he placed around them, once writing to a girl, "*Please* don't grow any taller, if you can help it, till I've had time to photograph you again." Next to his words he drew a girl's body without a head, as it now extended beyond the edges of the photograph. When he met Alice Liddell again at age thirteen (after a two-year separation from her family, imposed by her mother), he was struck by how much she had changed. "And hardly for the better," he wrote in his diary, indicating the she was "probably going through the usual awkward state of transition," a euphemism for puberty.[12]

In the 1860s, menarche occurred at about fifteen, Jo's age at the beginning of *Little Women*. (Today the average age is closer to eleven or twelve.) Although Alcott never mentions menstruation, budding breasts, or other physical changes, that is precisely what is happening to the March sisters. And all the discussions of gloves, hair, and dresses have everything to do with these changes. Decorum and convention were ways of outwardly marking what wasn't discussed openly. Once a girl started wearing her hair up, covering her hands with gloves, wearing long skirts, and refraining from running or talking openly to boys, she was assumed to have advanced to the stage of sexual being. The March girls don't participate in the more formal coming-out ceremonies, which signified a young woman's readiness for marriage (and thus sex) among the upper classes, so these other signifiers took their place. As historian Deborah Gorham has written, "After puberty, a Victorian girl was expected to give up both vigorous physical activity, and play. When she put up her hair and donned long skirts, she was to begin to prepare herself with adult seriousness for adult femininity."[13]

When we are first introduced to Jo, we see an awkward girl with long limbs and large hands and feet. She possesses "the uncomfortable appearance of a girl who was rapidly shooting up into a woman and didn't like it." Meg soon reprimands her for whistling like a boy, saying, "You are so tall, and turn up your hair, you should remember that you are a young lady," to which Jo responds, "I ain't! and if turning up my hair makes me one, I'll wear it in two tails until I'm twenty." She also hates the thought of having to "wear long gowns, and look as prim as a China-aster." When she later decides to cut her hair, she does so not only to get money for her mother's trip to Washington where her father lies ill (her mother says it wasn't necessary), but also as a way of resisting the new forms of adult femininity. Jo likes the idea that she will have a "curly crop" that looks "boyish." Yet she cries that night over the loss of her "one beauty," suggesting how confusing the transition to womanhood is for her.[14]

New forms of dress were central to that transition. Jo burns her dresses by standing too close to the fire, a sign not simply of her carelessness but also of her further rebellion against the idea that she has to start wearing long, full skirts. When Meg goes to the Moffats', or Vanity Fair, she is given a "coming out" of sorts as the French maid dresses her up like a doll, covering her neck and arms with powder, reddening her lips, and lacing her plump figure into a low-necked dress so tightly that she has trouble breathing. High-heeled boots and a coquettish fan complete the effect. Alcott subtly ridicules the whole scene and makes Meg come home and repent for her night of frivolity. However, in part two of the novel, Alcott allows Amy, now sixteen, to take the production of femininity to new heights. Amy, ever the artist, paints her clothes to imitate the more expensive versions her friends wear. In the "Calls" chapter, Amy tries to make Jo in her own image, while Jo enjoys exaggerating the performance for comic effect and then divulges the secret of Amy's "brilliant performances," such as painting a pair of soiled white boots to look like blue satin for one of Sallie's parties.[15] Amy is mortified by the exposure of her fraud. The last laugh is on Jo, however, who loses out on the trip to Europe while Amy is rewarded for her ability to play the part of the lovely, pleasing woman. By this point in the novel, Jo is learning that rejecting that role comes at a cost.

THE OUTWARD SIGNS of approaching womanhood altered over the decades as the March sisters, with their concerns about gloves and dresses, faded into icons of Victorian young womanhood. Flappers cut their hair short (a move prefigured by Jo, although they wouldn't admit it) and shortened their skirts, essentially claiming the freedom of girlhood. But in my mother's generation of the 1950s and '60s, young women wore longer skirts and gloves again and put a premium on prim, decorous behavior, not to mention sexual purity. The March girls would have felt pretty much at home, if it wasn't for Hollywood promoting a feminine ideal that mixed girlishness and sexuality, à la Marilyn Monroe. My generation of the 1980s (post–Title IX) played school sports, almost never wore skirts, and wore gloves only to keep warm in winter. But I wouldn't say that the outward tensions about what it meant to become a woman had disappeared. In a way, they only intensified. The ideal was an amalgam of the three Charlie's Angels: smart, sexy, *and* sporty. The most admired girl in my high school was a straight-A student, star volleyball player, and perfect blonde beauty (other students called her "Barbie").

The year I graduated from college, 1991, the development of girls became a matter of widespread public concern with the publication of the American Association of University Women's *Shortchanging Girls, Shortchanging America*. The report concluded that girls suffered a significant loss of self-esteem during their teen years and were routinely deterred from male-dominated fields such as math and science.[16] In response, conferences, programs, documentaries, and a flurry of books by psychologists, social scientists, and education experts tried to identify and remedy what was seen as a widespread problem of girls failing to thrive in a hostile culture that devalues their abilities and sexually objectifies them.

Meanwhile, girlhood was also increasingly viewed as a physically vulnerable time. Who can forget the nonstop media coverage of the (still unsolved) murder of six-year-old JonBenét Ramsey in 1996? Her face, all dolled up for the beauty pageants in which her mother had entered her, was splashed across magazine covers across the nation. When twelve-year-old Polly Klaas went missing from a slumber party in Petaluma, California, in 1993, the search for her was national news until her body was found two months later. Winona Ryder, who grew up in Petaluma, was deeply moved by Klaas's story, offering a $200,000 reward for her discovery. When Ryder learned that *Little Women* was Klaas's favorite book, she became even more determined to get a film of the book made. At the end of the film is a dedication to Klaas.[17] *Little Women*, as a symbol of girlhood innocence, had become an important corrective to the hypersexualization of girls, which could lead to their destruction.

In 1994, the same year Ryder starred in *Little Women*, the most influential book about the girl crisis was published: Mary Pipher's *Reviving Ophelia: Saving the Selves of Adolescent Girls*. It was an instant success and remained on the *New York Times* bestseller list for an astonishing three years. As audiences and reviewers celebrated the wholesomeness of Gillian Armstrong's portrait of the March family, with a strong mother figure and girls relatively easily navigating the path to womanhood, Pipher was signaling the alarm about contemporary adolescent girls' loss of self-worth. As the second wave of the women's movement was beginning to wane, it was reenergized as a movement to rescue girls from a poisonous culture, making the 1990s, as one commentator put it, "the Decade of the Girl."[18]

Some have questioned whether the crisis really existed, at least on the scale Pipher and other authors alleged, while others have regretted the messages about girls' victimhood it spawned. For instance, media scholar Kathleen Sweeney points out that "girls continue to be perceived as the gender in need of 'correction'—better math scores, more science, better self-esteem." It is also important not to generalize about all girls, and to recognize that girls' experiences are affected not only by gender but also by race, class, ethnicity, sexuality, and other factors. African American girls, for instance, have been found to be more resilient, more adept at resisting the limiting gender stereotypes imposed on them, while white middle-class girls seem to be most affected by those pressures.[19]

The basic message of *Reviving Ophelia* is that girls suffer psychologically from the way our culture reduces their value to their physical attributes. Girls' reactions to what Pipher calls "lookism" vary, and some are able to effectively resist it without long-term negative effects. Yet I think we can agree that to be female in our society is to realize, usually at puberty, that our bodies are judged as much more important than any other attributes we possess, and that this is often a disturbing discovery. Pipher observed self-directed girls who in elementary school dreamed of becoming doctors or authors but then realized in middle school that the media, boys, their friends, and even their own parents were observing their bodies and wanting them to look and to act in certain ways. Pipher argues that "girls are expected to sacrifice the parts of themselves that are masculine on the altar of social acceptability and to shrink their souls down to a petite size."[20] The alarming increase in anorexia and other eating disorders, depression, self-harm, substance abuse, and overly risky behavior in girls all pointed back to the psychic crisis they experienced as they hit puberty and lost their sense of control and identity.

The damaging effects of the sexualization of girls (on themselves and on boys) have not waned since Pipher's book became a bestseller; they have only gotten worse. The American Psychological Association's 2007 *Report of the APA's Task Force on the Sexualization of Girls* provides a wealth of evidence for how girls and women suffer when their worth is reduced to how sexually attractive they appear to men. The report calls for further study of, among other things, "issues of age compression ('adultification' of young girls and 'youthification' of adult women)."[21] Sexy clothing and high heels are manufactured for and marketed to girls as young as preschool age while social media and the Internet, which girls often embrace in their early teens, exponentially reinforce the "lookism" Pipher described.

When Pipher outlined what girls need to counter the damaging effects of our gender-stereotyping, even misogynistic, culture—safe, nurturing homes; "identities based on talents or interests rather than appearance, popularity or sexuality"; "a sense of purpose"; and "quiet places and times"—she provided a pretty fair description of what the March sisters, Jo in particular, have. This is what girls respond to when they read *Little Women*. Jo has been for generations a prime example of the girl who is "defined not by how she looks or who she dances with, but by what she does," Anna Quindlen has written. "[She] spoke of possibilities outside the circuit of feminine wiles and fashion consciousness."[22] In other words, Jo represented all of us who ever wanted to be something other than the quiet, submissive young lady or the alluring sexual object. There was another way, she taught us, a way to be in the world that was genuinely ourselves. It's not always easy for Jo, and she gets a lot of flak for her difference, especially from Meg and Amy, but she manages to assert her right to reject ladyhood and retain her family's love.

Girls have four ways to react to the pressure they experience to adapt to stifling standards of femininity, Pipher observed: "They can conform, withdraw, be depressed or get angry."[23] Meg and Amy to varying degrees conform, Beth withdraws, and Jo gets angry and for a while becomes depressed. What Alcott portrayed are four different responses to growing up that still reflect the ways girls navigate the path toward maturity. Meg, as the oldest, has it more or less thrust upon her and has to be the pioneer, venturing out to balls and into an engagement (at the ripe age of seventeen) with only her mother's guidance. Amy, as the youngest, is eager to show how grown up she is; she practices her adult vocabulary and feminine wiles until, in the second part, we see that she has learned them to a tee. Jo resists, with every fiber of her being, the pressure to be ladylike—that is, grown up—while Beth doesn't actually grow up at all, wasting away instead of becoming an adult woman.

MEG IS THE MOST conventional of the four, thanks to her temperament as well as her good looks. She is the one beauty of the four and thus appears to have her path laid out for her. When the sisters and Laurie discuss their "castles in the air," Meg's dream is to be rich and loved for her good deeds, Jo's is to be a rich and famous author, Amy's is to be a famous artist, and Laurie's is to be a famous musician. (Beth only longs for things to stay as they are.) Each of them has the tools to make their dream a reality—Jo her pen, Amy her pencils, and Laurie his music—except for Meg, or so she believes. Laurie corrects her by explaining that her face is her key to happiness. In other words, he suggests, she will be loved for her looks, not for her talents or virtues. While the others can and will work actively to accomplish their goals, Meg has only to be pretty and wait for the right man to come along.

Meg is no fully formed Minerva, however. She still has some growing and learning to do. Her temper is modest compared to Jo's, but she does threaten, when cross, to drown Beth's "horrid cats." Later, when Brooke proposes, she toys with his affection, enjoying the power she has over him (a ploy my students have not admired in her). Even after Meg's marriage, Alcott makes a point of showing us that she still has a lot to learn. Despite her efforts to be the perfect woman, she has a catastrophe with the currant jelly that won't gel and proceeds to have a terrible row with Brooke when he brings a friend home for dinner, expecting her to be the perfect wife. Later she spends an exorbitant amount on silk for a new dress, blurting out to him, "I'm tired of being poor."[24] It's a crushing blow for him, but she later makes up for it by selling the silk to Sallie and giving him the money to replace his worn old coat.

Meg is only twenty when she marries and, presumably, twenty-one when she gives birth to twins. Not all runs smoothly in the "Dovecote," their idyllic cottage. Alcott shows her girl readers that life after the presumably happy ending isn't all roses. No longer the pretty girl who had prospects, Meg feels "old and ugly" after her twins are born, an inconsequential woman who has been "put upon a shelf." To restore domestic harmony, she has to learn to invite John into the nursery and to leave the care of the children to others occasionally. Not that young readers are likely to notice any of this, however. As scholars Sarah Blackwood and Sarah Mesle point out, "It's hard to understand anything about [Meg's] compromises when you read *Little Women* for the first time, in your girlhood, before you've wrangled with womanly compromises of your own." But if you pick up the novel again after having had your own kids, you will be surprised to read about, among other things, sleep training a child—an experience all parents share but one that is rarely written about. Alcott shows us, through Meg, that adulthood is "a slog," as Blackwood and Mesle write. "And motherhood, especially the sentimentalized version, is particularly brutal because it's a slog you are only meant to enjoy."[25]

While Meg is the book's archetype of domestic femininity, Amy is its model of ornamental femininity. She is the most overtly designing in her attempts to develop her powers of attraction. Her aspirations far exceed Meg's; she hopes to become a great belle and in part two of the novel easily accomplishes her goal. Unlike Jo, Amy embraces her budding womanhood, which she feels empowers rather than diminishes her. At sixteen, "she has the air and bearing of a full-grown woman" and has "learned to use the gift of fascination with which she was endowed." Although not a natural beauty like Meg, the blonde, blue-eyed Amy easily succeeds at making herself into a fashionable work of art, gaining first the attention of Laurie's college friends, then Fred Vaughn, and finally Laurie himself. It is not only with men that she succeeds, however. She wins over her fellow art school students, the mean girls at the fair, and then her aunts, one of whom takes her to Europe. Once abroad, Amy blossoms further. "Always mature for her age," she now becomes "more of a woman of the world." She enjoys her power over men (including Laurie) and tears around Nice in her own carriage, taking the reins herself and yelling out to Laurie in the street, her "free manners" scandalizing a French mother who hurries her young daughter in the opposite direction.[26] Amy was the daring American girl abroad ten years before the publication of Henry James's *Daisy Miller*.

In the end, of course, Amy wins Laurie and decides that she won't be an artist after all (because she possesses talent but not genius, something Laurie also discovers about his music). Readers often forget that Amy wants to become a famous artist because she gives it up so easily. She will become instead, as the wealthy Laurie's wife, "an ornament to society." To many readers, Amy has seemed to be the clear winner among the four March sisters. In her *New York Times* essay "Amy Had Golden Curls; Jo Had a Rat. Who Would You Rather Be?" film and book critic Caryn James wrote that favoring Amy over the other girls was a "no-brainer." Pretty Amy went to Europe, had adventures, and married the dashing boy next door, while Jo lived in a dumpy boardinghouse in New York and married a boring professor.[27]

While Meg and Amy represent two paths toward conventional womanhood, Beth and Jo are in many ways their opposites and, as a result, much more interesting. If Amy sits at one end of the spectrum, expending great effort to grow into a "lady" as quickly as possible, then Beth sits at the other end, unable to even imagine herself as a grown woman. Beth was obviously Alcott's favorite, and she made her Jo's as well. Jo admires her sister's small, seemingly inconsequential life, but critics have not. They have discussed her much less than the other sisters and, when they have noticed her, they have often dismissed her with belittling phrases. She is "the least vital and the least interesting," "the flattest and most immature of the characters," or "doll-like Beth, the permanent little woman," lacking "even sufficient self-reliant impulses to stay alive."[28]

Yet the most remarkable thing about Beth is not simply her angelic goodness but her apparent lack of interest in growing up. If Meg and Amy are eager to grow up, and Jo is reluctant to, then Beth seems to reject the possibility altogether. At the beginning of the book, twelve-year-old Amy insists that she is not a child, but later on, Alcott describes Beth at seventeen as still a child. Beth, not Jo, is the one who most resists moving into adulthood and wants things to stay as they are. She is just less vocal about it. Beth is shy and prefers to stay at home, seemingly afraid of the outside world. She does not go to school and spends her time caring for sick and injured dolls. While her sisters and Laurie have big dreams for their futures, Beth wants only "to stay at home safe with Father and Mother, and help take care of the family." When pressed, she admits that she had wanted a piano, which Mr. Laurence has already given her, but now she only wishes that "we may all keep well and be together, nothing else."[29] A page earlier, she admitted to longing for heaven, wishing she could go there at once rather than wait through a long life. This declaration takes place well before the crisis of her illness. It would seem that contracting scarlet fever was inevitable for one who already had little desire to mature and is already yearning for the afterlife. After nearly dying of the disease, Beth unsurprisingly never fully recovers. While the effects of scarlet fever can linger, it is not clear what is killing her. My students often ask me what is wrong with Beth.

Alcott is not explicit. Many have assumed that she dies ultimately of complications from scarlet fever, which can lead to rheumatic fever and thus heart failure. But Beth is not described as having the typical symptoms of painful, swollen joints or heart pain. In real life, Louisa's sister Lizzie, the prototype of Beth, was also not described as having these symptoms or having rheumatic fever (then a known disease). She was suffering from low spirits and a wasting disease, the cause of which doctors could not identify. They called it simply "hysteria"—in other words, maladies in women with psychological causes that male doctors couldn't explain. Today she might be diagnosed with depression or perhaps even anorexia nervosa. In fact, when Lizzie died, she was nothing but skin and bones. As for Beth, critics have understood her death variously as the result of "a nameless wasting disease," a "prolonged suicide," and even her self-effacing nature.[30]

With no rational explanation for Beth's decline, we might surmise the cause was psychological. What we see in the second part of the book is a young woman who should be on the verge of adulthood but is instead receding into childhood. Although not exactly an invalid, Alcott says, Beth nonetheless stays close to home and is a constant source of concern for her family. Even when her health appears to be stable, her moods are not, and Marmee seems to be worried that she is slipping into a depression. Jo suspects Beth may be in love, perhaps with Laurie, a sign of the volatile adolescent emotions she assumes Beth must be experiencing. "I think she is growing up," Jo tells Marmee, "and so begins to dream dreams, and have hopes and fears and fidgets, without knowing why or being able to explain them. Why, Mother, Beth's eighteen, but we don't realize it, and treat her like a child, forgetting she's a woman."[31] Yet Beth is not becoming a woman. Instead, she is preparing to die.

When Beth finally tells Jo that she is dying, she explains that she was never like the rest of her sisters. "I never made any plans about what I'd do when I grew up. I never thought of being married, as you all did. I couldn't seem to imagine myself anything but stupid little Beth, trotting about at home, of no use anywhere but there. I never wanted to go away, and the hard part now is the leaving you all."[32] This remarkable speech demonstrates Beth's incredibly low self-esteem and inability to envision her future self. Many critics have interpreted her illness as the ultimate expression of self-sacrificial womanhood and her death as its inventible culmination. Noting that Beth first contracted scarlet fever from her selfless service to the Hummels, scholar Ann B. Murphy expresses the common view that Beth's death was a warning about the "ominous dangers of selflessness." She then goes even further, claiming that "Beth, of course, dies from a mysterious disease arising from terminal goodness—from her inability to distinguish between nurturing others and the radical self-denial expected of femininity."[33] Yet what if Beth's illness is something else—a response to and even rejection of the prospect of growing into a woman's body?

Beth's refusal to grow up bears an uncanny resemblance to the modern teenage girl who starves herself as part of an effort to stunt her growth, to maintain the prepubescent body in which she feels comfortable and in control. Beth seems unwilling to visualize a future that would entail the full realization of the capacity of her female body: sex, motherhood, nursing—and the feeling of selflessness that such experiences can create. Anorexics strive not simply for thinness but for purity and cleanliness, feeling disgust at the female functions of their bodies (menstruation, sex, and pregnancy) and starving themselves as a way of suppressing their bodies' capacity for femaleness. Viewing Beth not simply as a too-good-to-be-true paragon of femininity but as a girl who may be rejecting her female self or tragically succumbing to the pressure to be as "little" a woman as possible makes her a much more consequential character than she has been given credit for. Although we can't know for sure what ails Beth, if we consider the possibility of anorexia, which didn't yet have a name but was a phenomenon that had been around for centuries, Beth's inability (or even refusal) to grow up can be read as a serious commentary on the limits of adult female identity as it was then (and to a great degree still is) constructed.[34]

Anorexics are usually submissive, obedient, and self-sacrificial to the point of being unaware of their own desires and needs, traits that also correspond to the feminine ideal. At the beginning of part two of *Little Women*, Beth is described in her fragile state as "an angel in the house," a label that signifies her perfect alignment with domestic femininity and, potentially, the history of religious fasting, both of which prized a supreme capacity for self-denial. Food plays a surprisingly prominent role in *Little Women*, perhaps due to the scarcity of food (particularly the forbidden kinds) in real life. Alcott filled her novel with feasts, but Beth is strangely nonexistent in these scenes—present but never shown as partaking of or enjoying food. In the most poignant of these scenes, Jo prepares an elaborate feast of lobster, asparagus, bread, corn, potatoes, salad, blancmange, and strawberries while Beth mourns her dead canary, who has starved to death from lack of care. When the meal is served, Jo, Meg, Amy, Laurie, and Miss Crocker each try and then reject each ill-prepared item, to great comic effect; Beth is noticeably absent, reappearing only when it is time for the bird's funeral.[35]

As the most enigmatic and, for many, inconsequential character in the book, Beth's function in the novel is not well understood. My students have reacted to her at times with surprising disdain and animosity, rejecting her extreme virtue and even viewing her lingering illness as a possibly manipulative ploy for attention. They tend to share Brigid Brophy's view that Beth's sunny goodness and patience "are a quite monstrous imposition on the rest of the family," inflicting a "blight" of unworthiness on everyone around her. Alcott certainly never intended readers to see Beth as anything but the sweetest and most overlooked of the March sisters. "There are many Beths in the world," the narrator tells us, "shy and quiet, sitting in corners till needed, and living for others so cheerfully, that no one sees the sacrifices till the little cricket on the hearth stops chirping." If there is a stratagem behind her illness, we can best understand it as an attempt to reconnect a fragmented family. Beth is the emotional glue that binds the family together, singing, "Birds in their little nests agree" while Jo and Amy argue in the opening pages of the book.[36] Her initial illness helps unite a family in danger of dissolution when Marmee has gone to care for Father and Amy and Jo are at each other's throats. Beth's lack of recovery coincides with the family's further separation, first with Meg's marriage and then with Amy's trip to Europe and Jo's move to New York. And her death actually becomes a catalyst for the romances between Laurie and Amy, and Professor Bhaer and Jo—romances that enlarge the family and bring it back together, as the final scene demonstrates.

Jo, of course, has always been considered the most important of the March sisters. She is the one girl most readers have always wanted to be, and for good reason. Jo shows us a different path out of the wilderness of female adolescence and into an adult womanhood that is modified to fit her own needs. Rather than conforming to ideals of femininity or succumbing to their destructiveness, as her sisters do, she figures out how to thrive in spite of them. Unlike most unconventional nineteenth-century heroines (such as Edna Pontellier, Emma Bovary, Lily Barth, Daisy Miller, or the unnamed narrator of "The Yellow Wallpaper"), Jo neither dies nor gets carted off to an insane asylum. Instead, she simply, refreshingly, does what is not expected of her. Within the first five pages, Jo announces that she wishes she were a boy, refuses to behave in a ladylike manner, and designates herself "the man of the family" while their father is away. Beth alone seems to understand and accept her desires to avoid becoming a "lady" or a full-grown woman, consoling her over her disappointment in not being able to go to war and encouraging her masculine identification. "Poor Jo; it's too bad! But it can't be helped, so you must try to be contented with making your name boyish and playing brother to us girls," Beth tells her.[37]

Later Jo throws snowballs at Laurie's window, runs with him, spoils her dresses, and cuts her hair. At no point do we sense that her community or her creator will punish her for her missteps. And even though Meg attempts at every turn to tame her (but not Marmee, interestingly), Jo stands her ground. As she explains in a letter to Marmee, "I'm Jo, and never shall be anything else." Nonetheless, when their father returns home and assesses how each of the girls has changed, he sees Jo in a decidedly different light. "In spite of the curly crop, I don't see the 'son Jo' whom I left a year ago," he tells her. "I see a young lady who pins her collar straight, laces her boots neatly, and neither whistles, talks slang, nor lies on the rug, as she used to do. . . . I rather miss my wild girl," he confesses, "but if I get a strong, helpful, tender-hearted woman in her place, I shall feel quite satisfied." It appears that caring for Beth "in a motherly way" during her bout with scarlet fever has effected Jo's transformation. But I suspect that Jo is also on her best behavior for her father's return. Marmee seems more content to let Jo be Jo. In fact, time and again Marmee comes down on the side of letting Jo put off the "little womanhood" her father and Meg push on her. In the case of Jo's friendship with Laurie, Marmee sees nothing improper in it when Meg insinuates that it is not as innocent as Jo imagines. When Meg tells Jo that Laurie has given her a compliment, Jo announces that she doesn't want "any sentimental stuff." Marmee agrees. "I hope Meg will remember that children should be children as long as they can," she says in Meg's hearing.[38]

In the second part, nineteen-year-old Jo continues to behave in unfeminine ways. With Meg now settled into her new home, Amy takes over as Jo's chief disciplinarian, trying in vain to teach her to "be calm, cool, and quiet" because "that's safe and lady-like." Jo makes a mess of it, of course, "as her elbows were decidedly akimbo at this period of her life." She is incapable of flirting, she tells Laurie, or pleasing without effort, as Amy does. He likes that she is "a sensible,

straightforward girl," but he would also like her to be a little sentimental about him. She steadfastly refuses. While he develops feelings for her, "indulg[ing] occasionally in Byronic fits of gloom," she
keeps him at arm's length, continuing to prefer "imaginary heroes to
real ones."[39]

Partially in an effort to disrupt Laurie's growing romantic interest
in her, Jo decides to leave home. Yet she also goes to please herself.
She is restless and wants to spread her wings a bit, a very novel stage
in a young woman's development in the nineteenth century, at least
for the middle classes. Girls of the lower classes might leave home to
work (as in fact the Alcott girls did), but they rarely strayed as far as
Jo does when she moves to New York. Jo's time there, spent working,
writing, socializing, and theatergoing, is as central to her development as it would be for a young man. New York is her college, where
she learns important lessons that will help her become an author.
While still at home, she had begun to advance in her literary career,
winning a prize and publishing a novel (to mixed reviews). Now she
ventures into the male sphere of seedy newspaper offices to sell her
wares and learns how to please the public with thrilling stories. Just
as she worried about Laurie falling into debauchery while he was
away at college, she herself begins to "liv[e] in bad society, . . . imaginary though it was."[40]

When her new friend Professor Bhaer gives her Shakespeare to
take as her model, he advises her "to study simple, true, and lovely
characters, wherever she found them"; in other words, to write from
life. Eventually he rails against the sensation papers she is writing
for, and she hides her writings from him, promptly burning them
and creating such a prodigious blaze the chimney almost catches
fire. Although feminist critics have viewed this scene as the height of
patriarchal belittlement, for Alcott it was a portrait of the developing
writer. For *Little Women* is also a *Künstlerroman*, a genre as decidedly
male as the *Bildungsroman*. The story of the artist's coming of age was
typically not about a woman, and when it was (as with Madame de
Staël's *Corinne*), it invariably ended in death. Jo instead is allowed to
grow as a writer, advancing from writing for hire to writing out of her
life, deciding, as so many young writers have before and since, that

she doesn't have the experience to make a great writer yet, so she'll wait to write until she has something worth saying: "I don't know anything; I'll wait till I do before I try again, and, meantime, 'sweep mud in the street,' if I can't do better—that's honest, any way."[41]

When summer comes and Jo returns home, she finds Laurie as in love with her as ever. Her response to his proposal—simply that she doesn't love him the way he loves her—has crushed the hopes of countless readers. Yet I think Jo is right that Laurie is too rich for her (he likes "elegant society" and she doesn't) and that they are too alike with their "quick tempers and strong wills." Marriage to Laurie would be a gilded cage, perfectly suited to Amy but not to Jo. He needs "a fine mistress for [his] house."[42] By refusing Laurie, Jo allows herself to mature in new directions.

Beth's final decline and death are the crucible through which Jo must pass to discover who she truly wants to be. Although Alcott had wanted to allow Jo to become a "literary spinster" like herself, she felt forced into choosing a mate for her. The "funny match" she came up with was not just a joke, however. With Bhaer, Alcott made an argument for the kind of companionate marriage advocated by Margaret Fuller and that her mother had hoped for with her father: a union of individuals who choose to work together toward a common goal. Husband and wife were to be intellectual as well as romantic partners. Even if the fortyish, rather stout Bhaer is not our romantic ideal, he was much more than simply a practical choice for Jo. But Alcott did not tempt her heroine with the cold life of the mind through a scholar like Casaubon or St. John Rivers, as George Eliot and Charlotte Brontë did for their heroines. Alcott's professor is a warm father figure who loves children and promises Jo a family and home full of love and affection.

A union with Bhaer also promises Jo a vocation. When he proposes, she is adamant that she will "carry my share . . . and help to earn the home."[43] He goes away for a year to teach in the West and earn money to support his nephews while Jo toils away at home. When Aunt March dies and leaves Plumfield to Jo, together she and Friedrich turn it into a home and school for boys, fulfilling Abigail Alcott's dream of working together with her husband in a school.

Abigail had as many ideas about education as Bronson did, but marriage to him precluded their collaboration, and she stayed at home while he hired unmarried women to assist him in the Temple School. Their daughter had a more progressive view.

On the whole, it seems to me that Alcott is addressing a fundamental conflict for women—how to love and be loved without losing one's self. Alcott gave generations of girls like the poet Gail Mazur "permission to try to become what we wished, . . . help[ing] us to recognize—and to live with, knowing we're not alone, the conflict between the writer's need for solitude and self-absorption and the yearning for the warmth of love."[44] All relationships, even those within the family, require great compromises by the individual, especially the self-directed artist. Alcott knew this well. Simply remaining single did not mean freedom. Louisa spent her adult life torn between her own desires and the needs of her family, which included parents, sisters, nephews, and the niece she adopted.

In the end, Jo grows up by learning to accommodate some aspects of the female role that she decides she wants (such as marriage and motherhood) while continuing to resist others, particularly the injunction that women should live only for and through their husbands and children. Jo finds common purpose with her husband in running a school and retains a separate identity. When her children are grown, she can return to the "castles in the air" she once dreamed of, and she becomes a famous author in *Jo's Boys*. Alcott thus gave young female readers a path toward maturity that entailed compromise but not tremendous sacrifice. Jo longs for both independence *and* connection—quest *and* romance—and she manages to have both. Jo more or less "has it all." As one scholar puts it, Jo "consolidates 'masculine' dreams of ambition with 'feminine' ones of connection."[45]

A companionate marriage isn't the only way to get there, but Alcott didn't suggest other alternatives. Although Jo's path does not seem predestined toward marriage and motherhood—she vociferously pronounces her right not to marry on at least two occasions—her family clearly expects her to. When Marmee describes her plans for her daughters' futures, it is clear that their job is to wait and prepare to be worthy for good men to come along and offer them marriage and new homes. If none come, Marmee hopes they will be happy to stay at home, but there appear to be no other options.[46] In the essay "Happy Women," which Alcott wrote at the same time that she was starting to work on *Little Women*, she described a variety of content "old maids," hoping to show young women that all was not lost if they did not find a husband, that in fact a single life was better than making a hasty, unfortunate match. In her next novel, *An Old-Fashioned Girl*, she would hold out the possibility of living and working alongside other women. Two young artists live and work together and refuse ever to be parted. Even though one of them is soon to marry, her friend will join her in their new home. As the century wore on, the cohabitation of women became more common and became known as "Boston marriages." But Alcott never entertained that possibility for Jo. Thus she had to figure out how to have Jo marry without sacrificing herself and so give some readers, if they weren't too mad at her for Jo's rejection of Laurie, hope that they could one day do the same.

For *Little Women*'s initial readers, the question of who the March girls would marry was paramount. But as girls have come to have more options on the path to adulthood, readers have been less focused on that all-important question. I know that my eleven-year-old daughter's attention lagged during the second part of the novel. And girls growing up in the U.K. or other countries where *Little Women* and *Good Wives* are sold separately often just read part one. As one woman told me, "Why would I have wanted to read a book called *Good Wives*?" It would seem that the life choices the March sisters make as they age matter less to girls now. In fact, girls are finding other heroines to help point the way forward for them. Yet Meg, Jo, Beth, and Amy are still very much present in the literature and entertainment girls are consuming today.

# 9

## "WANTING TO BE RORY, BUT BETTER"

### Little Women and Girls' Stories Today

W HEN I GAVE my daughter *Little Women* on her eleventh birthday, I wondered if it would matter to her as it had to so many girls before her. Did her generation still need Jo and the other March sisters as models and guides? They were being told they could accomplish anything they set their minds to. Girl power seemed to be all the rage. Meanwhile, however, girls were telling journalists and researchers that they endure persistent sexist comments from boys at school but don't want to say anything for fear of being labeled "feminist" or "bitchy." And they try not to appear too smart or assertive for fear of alienating boys. As they mature, they learn to attract boys by walking the line between being sexy and being taken for a whore.[1] It would seem that Alcott's fable of growing up female hasn't grown less relevant after all. Jo's example as a nonconformist is as vital as ever.

*Little Women* isn't exactly on girls' radars, though. A survey in the U.K. in 2003 indicated that only 3 percent of children had read the novel and that 66 percent had never even heard of it. But when adults are surveyed, *Little Women* still ranks highly. That same year, the BBC's Big Read ranked *Little Women* at number 18 among British readers' most-loved novels—not just children's novels. In 2007 it was at 11 overall (and number 7 among women) in a list of the "favourite books," and in 2014 the *Guardian* placed it at number 20 on a list of the hundred best novels in English. In the United States, a Harris Poll in 2014 put *Little Women* at number 8 among Americans' "favorite book[s] of all time" and in 2016 at number 9 on a list of Americans' favorite books from childhood. Yet, when kids themselves are asked what they are reading, *Little Women* doesn't even register.[2]

INSTEAD OF GROWING up with Jo March, girls are growing up with a host of new literary heroines who are clearly descended from her. Before the age of ten, girls encounter an awful lot of princesses, most of them created by Disney. Fortunately, they are not nearly as passive and insipid as those my generation grew up with. Belle from *Beauty and the Beast*, created in 1991, was the first Disney princess who did not simply wait around for the prince to come and rescue her. She had her own interests (especially books), rejected a persistent suitor, and tried to rescue her father. Then, of course, she fell in love with the Beast, who turns out to be a handsome prince, but Belle was still a revelation. Her creator, the screenwriter Linda Woolverton, has explained that Jo March was her inspiration for Belle—or, more precisely, Katharine Hepburn's portrayal of her.[3] Subsequent princesses got increasingly bold and unconventional until finally a prince was unnecessary. In 2013's *Frozen*, the first Disney film directed by a woman, the prince turns out to be the villain, and it is sisterly love, not "true love's kiss," that is magical. Elsa's anthem of liberation, "Let It Go," became not only a girl-power anthem but also a rallying cry for young feminists and LGBT teens.[4] Although ostensibly about Elsa's inability to continue hiding her fearful power of freezing everything she touches, the song is really about growing up, breaking away from authority, and accepting yourself.

There are also plenty of spunky heroines in picture and chapter books, if you look for them. But what happens when girls start choosing their own books to read, say in the middle-school years from ages eleven to thirteen? By that point, girls are choosing a lot of fantasy and dystopian literature, particularly *Harry Potter* and *The Hunger Games*, two of the best-selling series in recent years, which also happen to feature direct descendants of Jo March. J. K. Rowling, who, as I mentioned earlier, has identified Jo March as her favorite literary heroine, created a bookish heroine to stand alongside her titular hero. Hermione, who is admired for her smarts, not her looks, uses her brains to rescue the wizarding world from evil— not just her family from poverty, as Jo does. And Hermione's untamed locks are as potent a symbol of her unconventionality as Jo's chopped mane.

Katniss Everdeen bears an even closer resemblance to Alcott's creation. Like Jo, she is primarily concerned with providing for her

Hermione, played in the *Harry Potter* films by Emma Watson, is one of the bookish, unconventional descendants of Jo March. (RGR Collection/Alamy Stock Photo)

family in her father's absence and especially looks out for a younger sister who needs her protection. She also has a close male friend, Gale, whom she thinks of as a brother but who wants to be more than friends. It's also interesting that romance is imposed on Katniss as it was on Jo. In *The Hunger Games* it is the expectations of the fictional audience in the text that force her to pretend to be Peeta's girlfriend, whereas in *Little Women* it was the book's actual audience demanding that Jo fall in love. In both texts, we also see the tomboy heroines make the uneasy transformation into wives and mothers. It's just as jarring to see Katniss as a mom at the end of the series as it is to meet Mrs. Jo in *Little Men*. Whether or not Suzanne Collins felt she had to marry off Katniss, it is true that fans were as obsessed with who Katniss would choose (Gale or Peeta) as Alcott's fans were about who the March sisters would marry. Before the final novel of the trilogy was published, fans joined "Team Peeta" or "Team Gale," and today there are numerous online quizzes you can take to see which team you are on. In the end, Katniss didn't pick her close friend but instead the more steadying influence, Peeta. Not everyone has been happy with her decision. Sounds familiar.

The character of Katniss from *The Hunger Games*, played in the films by Jennifer Lawrence, bears many similarities to Jo March.
(RGR Collection/Alamy Stock Photo)

Perhaps it is Jo's likeness to her more popular successors that has kept her alive in readers' minds. In a poll for World Book Day in 2016, respondents chose as their favorite heroes or heroines Hermione at number 3, Jo at number 6, and Katniss at number 7.[5] (Two other Jo descendants, Anne Shirley of *Anne of Green Gables* and Matilda Wormwood of *Matilda*, were also in the top 10.) Nonetheless, a book like *Little Women* is facing an uphill battle with most young readers today, who struggle with its old-fashioned language and style. The slang of one era, however fresh it was at the time, may not translate well to another. The book's language is much less formal than that found in most nineteenth-century novels, though.

An even greater drawback is the novel's supposed preachiness, the death knell for any work hoping to gain the attention of young readers. As a friend's daughter told her, after reading *Little Women* on her mother's recommendation, "I don't like books that tell me who I should be and what I should do." Lessons have hardly been banished from children's and young adult literature, however. (My personal favorite is when Harry Potter is racked with fear that he will become like Voldemort until Dumbledore teaches him that it's not destiny but the choices he makes that will define him.) Ultimately, I don't think the lessons Marmee teaches her daughters are the problem—things like it's better to marry for love and respect than for money, home is happier when everyone chips in rather than living for themselves, and everyone is better off when both parents participate in raising the children. The problem seems to be that it's the mom who is doing the teaching. Moms of tween girls are quite familiar with the eye roll directed at them whenever they try to provide advice. Today's girls are giving Marmee one big eye roll.

The main obstacle to *Little Women*'s continued popularity, though, is that young readers are interested in a fundamentally different kind of literature. Girls want adventure, not domestic drama, and they are much more interested in fantasy than realism. I learned this from my own daughter and her friends as well as the girls I visited with at the Louise S. McGehee School in New Orleans, an independent school for girls training to be future leaders. The seventh graders I met with were a diverse and well-off group of articulate and well-read girls.

Although a number of hands went up when I asked who had read *Little Women*, only two had read the book all the way through. The others said they had started it but not finished. "Nothing much seems to happen," one girl said. "There's no story," another chimed in. "It just seems like real life." Young readers are used to getting sucked into a story, something today's authors are very good at doing. Most of the girls who had not finished the book admitted that they had given up after only two chapters. Many more never picked it up at all, despite receiving the book as a present or hearing about it from their teachers, because it looked too long. When I told them that it's still published in two volumes in the U.K., they said, "Oh, it should be here too. Maybe then I'd read it."

Most of what the girls at McGehee and elsewhere seem to be reading for pleasure are dystopian, paranormal, and fantasy books that feature girls with magical powers or special gifts—girls as witches, warrior princesses, or hunters. They were interested in extraordinary girls and adventure plots, in which girls are put into extreme circumstances, fighting for their family's survival or trying to save the world. Romance was still a draw, though. Girls want it all in their stories: romance *and* quest plots. Often they are intertwined, as in Veronica Roth's popular *Divergent* series. Sometimes, though, girls are more interested in the romance. *The Fault in Our Stars* and *Twilight* both came up in our discussion. Their teacher told me later that in recent years her girls had all been reading a trilogy by Jenny Han that began with *The Summer I Turned Pretty*. "That's more or less what it's about," she told me, horrified that they were drawn to such vapid stories. The heroine, whose name is Belly (short for Isabel), is just shy of sixteen and beginning to realize that she is pretty. She is enjoying her new power and the way the boys look at her. Belly is much more Amy than Jo. The book centers on her summer at the beach with the boys she has known since childhood, one of whom she has always had a crush on. But now they see her differently and, well, you can imagine the rest. Perhaps I'm not being entirely fair. One reviewer online, a mother, described it as a pretty realistic book about the awkward age for girls: "[Belly] feels a nearly constant conflict between wanting to grow up and be a little reckless, and wanting to stay in her comfort zone and do what she knows is safe." She recommended it for mother-daughter book clubs, to talk about issues like whether to drink at a party and what to do when a boy kisses you.[6] It's true that girls are more likely to encounter these dilemmas than, say, deciding whether to volunteer in their sister's stead for a fight-to-the-death game broadcast on national television.

*The Summer I Turned Pretty* falls into the popular category of what one critic has called "chick lit jr.," or YA novels that adapt the chick lit genre—novels by women, for women, and about women, in a contemporary, realistic setting—for a tween and teen audience. Like its older cousin, chick lit jr. garners little respect and can deal with some pretty superficial issues, such as which lipstick to wear to school, but it also takes on more serious ones, like when to lose one's virginity. Because these novels also address growing up female in a more recognizable world than the most popular YA texts, they may be the true successors of *Little Women*. Books in this category include Megan Cabot's *Princess Diary* series, *The Sisterhood of the Traveling Pants* and its sequels by Ann Brashares, the *Gossip Girl* novels by Cecily von Ziegesar, and the humorous novels by Louise Rennison. Although such novels owe a lot to *Little Women* (a genealogy acknowledged by Rennison, who wrote an introduction to *Little Women* for Puffin Classics), these novels differ from Alcott's in the way they have erased parental role models and familial bonds. Today's heroines look to their inexperienced peers, rather than their parents, for guidance. Perhaps as a result, these novels tend to focus on external appearance, sexual experience as a marker of womanhood, and male validation. A British reader summed up the difference in her online review of *Little Women* when she said that although most contemporary novels for teens were all about "how to Get The Guy," *Little Women* was "really about becoming a person you can respect."[7]

But most troubling to parents and other observers in recent years is the popularity of the so-called "mean girl" books rife with conspicuous consumption, casual sex and drug use, recreational eating disorders, and rampant teenage cruelty. The queen bee of this subgenre of chick lit jr. was the *Gossip Girl* series, which rose to number one on the *New York Times* children's paperback bestseller list in the mid-2000s and ran to thirteen books in all. These were also the most popular books at McGehee in recent years, I was told. Although ostensibly for readers fourteen and up, the *Gossip Girl* series also attracted much younger girls, promising them access to a world of privilege and seemingly adult behavior. The first novel begins, "Welcome to New York's Upper East Side, where my friends and I live and go to school and play and sleep—sometimes with each other. . . . We have unlimited access to money and booze and whatever else we want, and our parents are rarely home, so we have tons of privacy. We're smart, we've inherited classic good looks, we wear fantastic clothes, and we know how to party."[8]

Naomi Wolf identified the way this series and its imitators turned Alcott and Austen on their heads by promoting the idea that a girl's value is determined solely by her wealth and beauty. Even more troubling, she noted, "These novels reproduce the dilemma [girls] experience all the time: they are expected to compete with pornography, but can still be labeled sluts." In the series, girls are shamed when their sexual exploits become public but deemed prudish if they aren't willing to give it up in the dressing room at Bergdorf's. Unlike the ball scene in *Little Women*, where Meg's transformation into a "doll" becomes an opportunity for her to learn what kind of woman she doesn't want to be, these novels have nothing to say about their characters' sexual objectification and exploitation. The series' lack of morality is intentional, according to the author, Cecily von Ziegesar, who said in an interview, "I always resented books that tried to teach a lesson, where the characters are too good: They don't sweat, they tell their mothers everything."[9] Intentionally or not, von Ziegesar wrote an anti–*Little Women* (ironically, published by the same firm as Alcott's novel—Little, Brown) and girls loved it. Fortunately, the world of literature and entertainment for girls is large, and *Gossip Girl* represents only one distressing corner of it.

Another popular early twenty-first-century story of girls growing up is a clearer successor to *Little Women*: the television series *Gilmore Girls*. Although the series ended in 2007, it ran in syndication for many years and was available on DVD. Then *Gilmore Girls* was given new life by Netflix, which began streaming the full series in 2014, igniting the nostalgia of twentysomething women eager to reflect on their adolescence when they were growing up with Rory.[10]

The series has some similarities with the world von Ziegesar was writing about: The main girl character, Rory, attends Chilton Prep School, where the kids, unlike her, have money and want nothing more than to be popular and get into Harvard and Yale. But Rory holds herself apart from that world as much as she can, and the main action takes place in the quaint New England town of Stars Hollow, which has more in common with the setting of *Little Women* than with most of twenty-first-century America. No wonder *Gilmore Girls* has been criticized for being "too precious." Some critics can't believe that "people like this exist." In other words, the characters don't reflect the gritty reality that television (or literature) is supposed to portray. Nonetheless, the show became, in the words of one critic, "a cultural touchstone for millions of women."[11]

*Gilmore Girls* has a lot more in common with *Little Women* than any of its chick lit jr. counterparts. At its heart is the relationship between Lorelai and her daughter, Rory, who are really more like sisters due to the closeness in their ages. Lorelai ran away from home when she got pregnant at sixteen and raised Rory on her own. Thus their relationship mirrors both the one between Marmee and her daughters and those between the March sisters themselves. Thirty-two-year-old Lorelai is a far cry from Marmee, however. She still has a lot of growing up to do herself. But she resembles Marmee in being a single mom who is always there for her daughter. The cozy scenes in *Little Women* where Marmee shares her dreams with Meg and Jo or helps Jo decide what to do about Laurie are echoed again and again in the series as Lorelai comforts and consoles Rory throughout her adolescence and young adulthood.

The mother-daughter/sister bond is at the center of the show, which is dominated by female relationships—including those Lorelai and Rory have with their best friends and with Emily Gilmore, Lorelai's mother. These relationships sometimes turn sour, just as the March sisters' did when Amy burned Jo's manuscript, but they are strong at their core—unbreakable in fact—while their relationships with men come and go. The show includes plenty of male characters, but again

In the television series *Gilmore Girls*, the
relationship between Lorelai and Rory, played by
Lauren Graham and Alexis Bledel, echoes that
between Marmee and her daughters in *Little
Women*. (AF archive/Alamy Stock Photo)

they seem to be on the outside, always trying to get in, like Laurie
looking through the Marches' window. Even when Rory's dad, Christopher, is around, he exists as much in the shadows as does Mr. March.

As I contemplated the legacy of *Little Women* and Jo March (and
listened to my daughter binge-watching the *Gilmore Girls* in the next
room), I realized that Rory is today's Jo for many girls. While my
daughter's most all-absorbing reading experiences have been the
*Harry Potter* and *Hunger Games* series, it is Rory who is helping her
navigate young womanhood. The show's creator, Amy Sherman-
Palladino, has described her conception of Rory in a way that echoes
Alcott's Jo. Sherman-Palladino was interested in portraying a novel
type of girl on television: a girl who did not "look longingly at the

group over by the soda fountain with good shoes," who did not define herself through her relationship to boys or how popular she was, but through her interest in academics.[12] Quite simply, books matter to Rory more than boys. She wants to grow up to be a writer, specifically a journalist. Her idol is the foreign correspondent Christiane Amanpour. And Rory, like Jo, is supported by her family in her aspirations, which in Rory's case extend much farther than Jo's ever could—all the way to Harvard, although she ends up going to Yale.

Ultimately, Rory serves a similar function to the one Jo served for generations of girls: she validates their sense of individuality, their ambition, and their difference from feminine norms. She is happy in her difference, content just to be herself. Although the actress who played Rory, Alexis Bledel, was always supremely beautiful, her character never worried much about her looks. She and her best friend obsessed over music rather than their wardrobes. They were nerds rather than "it" girls. As a result, Rory became as real to the girls who watched the show as Jo was for generations of young readers. Girls grew up with Rory, watching her navigate school politics, academic challenges, spats with her mother, and relationships with good boys and bad boys. Then they returned to the show as adults and understood it on a new level. *Gilmore Girls* was also an experience that mothers and daughters shared. They watched it together every week when it first aired or shared it in reruns or on DVD, just as mothers have read *Little Women* with their daughters or given them the book when they were at the right age.

Yet Rory is also like Jo in the way she has evoked confusion and disappointment from her fans. If Jo ends up becoming a more conventional woman in the end, Rory also seems to lose her way—but even more thoroughly, becoming more and more dolled up in cosmetics and designer clothes as the series progresses. She also becomes absorbed by the ultra-wealthy, class-conscious world of her grandparents, even joining the Daughters of the American Revolution. Worse than that, she has a major meltdown and leaves Yale when her boyfriend's father says she doesn't have what it takes to become a journalist. After some spectacularly poor choices, including stealing a yacht, she sucks it up and goes back to Yale to finish her degree. But our confidence in her has been shaken. As one woman who grew up with the series says about Rory, "The only way to be truly inspired by *Gilmore Girls* is to watch it and want to be Rory, but better."[13]

In 2016, Netflix aired a four-episode, six-hour revival of *Gilmore Girls* titled *A Year in the Life*. The sequel picks up ten years after the series ended, and fans were dying to know how Rory's life turned out. Sherman-Palladino and her co-writer husband had been unable to reach a contract agreement for the show's final season, so this revival was her chance to end the series the way she had wanted to. The new finale has the same effect as the final chapter of *Little Women*, allowing us to jump forward into the future to see what has happened with the characters. We find a thirty-two-year-old Rory, whose career as a journalist has not panned out the way she had hoped. After some success, she has been unable to get a steady job and returns home to Stars Hollow. But as the revival approached, fans were most worked up about the question of which boyfriend—Jess or Dean, the stable one or the unpredictable one—Rory would finally end up with. (No one seems to have wanted her to reunite with the spoiled rich kid Logan, whom she dated at Yale.) Sherman-Palladino was not happy with the rampant speculation. Sounding a bit like Alcott, resenting her fans' desire to see her characters paired off, she said, "It's just such a small part of who Rory is. I don't see people debating 'What newspaper is Rory working for?' 'Did she win a Pulitzer yet?' It's all about Dean and Jess."[14]

Although *Little Women* probably only indirectly influenced the original *Gilmore Girls* series, it clearly inspired aspects of the finale, which references the novel as well as Gillian Armstrong's 1994 film. Like Jo, Rory is struggling to make it as a writer, producing what the market wants, until a male friend playing the role of mentor comes along and gives her writing advice. Jess, echoing Professor Bhaer, tells Rory to write what she knows and what only she can write, so Rory decides to write a book about her life growing up with her mom. And like Jo, Rory is motivated to write from her heart after the death of a loved one, here her grandfather. As Rory thinks back over her life, she sees and hears flashbacks from her life (and from the earlier series) just as Winona Ryder's Jo does near the end of Armstrong's film. Rory calls her book *The Gilmore Girls*, but Lorelai suggests she drop the article, aligning it with the title of the series, just as in Armstrong's film Jo writes the book *Little Women*.[15]

The ending of *A Year in the Life* also brings the series full circle when Rory becomes pregnant—ostensibly by Logan, whom she has been seeing on and off even though he is engaged to someone else—and apparently decides to raise the child on her own, as her mother had done with her. Meanwhile, Jess hovers around the edges. In his last shot, we see him looking through the window at Rory, just as Laurie stood on the outside looking in at the Marches. Although there is no mention of Jess and Rory getting back together, the possibility is suggested. Previously, Rory had run up to Jess to show him the manuscript of her book-in-progress, suggesting that he could be involved in its publication, as Bhaer was in the publication of Jo's book in Armstrong's film. But that is where Sherman-Palladino leaves things. Unlike Alcott, she did not feel compelled to marry off Rory in the end.

What has troubled most viewers, however, is that the show seems to finalize the death of Rory's dreams for a career in journalism by making her pregnant. The new finale causes the same conflicted feelings about Rory's life choices that readers have long had about Jo's—although Jo has more of a choice, whereas Rory is almost a victim of fate. Throughout the series, fans were disappointed when Rory chose boys over her own pursuits and relieved when, in the 2007 finale (not written by Sherman-Palladino), she rejected Logan's offer of marriage and headed out on her own to start her first job as a reporter. She seemed destined to become the world-traveling journalist she always wanted to be. She even met Amanpour in that final episode. Now, it seems, that wasn't how Rory's life was supposed to end up after all. It was supposed to be derailed, as her mother's was, by a baby. It's worth noting that Rory never mentioned a desire for children; nor do we learn how she feels about her unplanned pregnancy after the finale's closing words. The message seems to be that whatever a girl/woman's dreams, her body is still her destiny, that ambition is at odds with a woman's relationships. The two can't coexist.

The extensive discussion online of where Rory ends up was every bit as urgent and complex as the endless analyses of Jo March have been—as if these characters' plots are more than just stories. Rory appears destined to settle down into a life very much like her mother's, and this outcome is just as disappointing for many as when Jo got married and had kids. However, Jo's companionate marriage and chance to run a school are an advance on her mother's life. Nearly 150 years later, in *Gilmore Girls*, Rory got the education her mother didn't, but it wasn't clear whether Rory's life would be much different from her mother's, which was Lorelai's hope for her all along.

Today's girls' stories may show us that Jo has lived on, but her sisters have been largely forgotten. The new Jos tend to stand out as exceptional characters, different from and largely apart from other girls. What *Little Women* did so well was to show readers there was not one way to be a girl or to grow into womanhood, but many ways. One notable successor to Alcott's usage of the ensemble cast is HBO's *Girls*, inspired by another four-girlfriend hit, *Sex and the City*. Hailed by many as a groundbreaking look at the messy realities of young women's lives today, *Girls* is decidedly for mature audiences only, but it has some interesting resonances with Alcott's novel. As Chiara Atik (author of a play called *Women*, billed as a mash-up of *Little Women* and *Girls*) has argued, they "share the same plot, give or take a sex scene or two; they both tell the story of four girls trying (to varying degrees of success) to grow up. . . . The characters of the show are analagous in a way that suggests these four girls—the writer, the responsible one, the sweet one, and the wild child—are time-honored archetypes for American women, rather than products of their creator's imagination. Or maybe American society and American girlhood just haven't changed that much in the past 150 years." Lena Dunham, the show's creator, has indicated that the parallels are intended. As another writer pointed out, however, the two creations diverge in one important way: Alcott's little women grow up while Dunham's girls don't, as their titles alone suggest.[16] Over six seasons, the four friends struggle to find and keep jobs, get published (in Hannah's case), and have healthy relationships with men, but they don't make much progress on the path to adulthood. Taking a rather adolescent view, they seem eager to prove they are grown up simply by being sexually adventurous. Emotional depth and stability, not to mention character development, remain frustratingly out of reach.

The HBO series *Girls*, starring Lena Dunham, is an obvious successor to *Little Women*, although the young women in the series do much less growing up than the March sisters. (AF archive/Alamy Stock Photo)

If nothing else, *Girls* suggests that maturity is harder than ever for young women to attain and define.

When *Girls* came to an end in 2017 after six seasons, audiences wondered if Hannah and her friends would finally grow up. By the end, two of the girls had married and already been divorced, one had been through rehab for drug addiction, one had gotten engaged, and Hannah had given birth and gotten a job teaching writing. The final episode shows her struggling to be a mom, finding it excruciatingly difficult to bond with her newborn son, who is having trouble breastfeeding. After running off into the woods, where she bumps into a teen who has run away from home, Hannah begins to take on a motherly role, first with the girl, a representation of her former self, and then with her son when she returns home. She seems to have finally learned to connect selflessly with another human being.

Lena Dunham's series and *Little Women* tackled the hardest part of girls' stories to tell: leaving girlhood behind and becoming an adult. While the advent of womanhood may be marked differently today, perhaps by moving away from home and starting a career (and too often simply by being sexually active), it would seem that becoming a mother remains the primary marker of womanhood. Rory and Hannah may be staking out new territory from their predecessor Jo March by becoming single mothers, but the message is still clear: you are a girl until you become a mom; only then are you a woman. As Hannah's mom explains to her in the final episode, her child is not a temp job or another dead-end relationship with a guy. She can't quit her son or simply delete his phone number. He is forever.

In Alcott's day, becoming a wife was the dividing line, and motherhood was expected to follow naturally. But today's writers, by showing girls with no interest in marriage who become moms on their own, are also making independence from men a key component of women's maturation. Rory and Hannah are both ultimately connected to their mothers and to a close friend, but not to men. The companionate marriages that Alcott envisioned for her little women remain out of reach for today's fictional heroines.

*Girls* further deviates from *Little Women* in its portrayal of female friendship. Whereas in Alcott's universe the relationships between women are central and the sisterly bond eclipses all others, in Dunham's the friends sleep with each other's boyfriends and in various ways find it impossible to overcome their self-centeredness. The one who seems to have matured the most cuts her ties with the other three, leaving the toxic friendships behind, while the other three remain unable to support each other apart from their own self-interest.


As GIRLS GRAVITATE to more contemporary fare and away from *Little Women*, they are missing a lot. Today's successors to *Little Women* seem to have overlooked two of the most important themes of Alcott's classic: companionate marriage and sisterhood. And many of them are missing the central premise altogether, namely that growing up means becoming a better person, one who can balance her own needs and desires with those of the people she loves.

The trend toward fantasy literature can also make it harder for girls to see their future selves in today's heroines. Hermione's braininess helps Harry Potter defeat the Dark Lord, but at the end of the series, it's not clear where she is headed. In Rowling's conclusion, which flashes forward nineteen years, she reveals only that Hermione has married Ron and had two children. Writers of the Rowling-approved sequel, the play *The Cursed Child* (2016), had an opportunity to flesh out the adult Hermione, and—to no one's surprise—made her Minister of Magic. Typically, however, the adventures that fantasy heroines undertake are portrayed as an interlude before real life begins. Once the world is saved or the evil force is vanquished, the book ends.

When it comes to Alcott's message of girls realizing their potential beyond their looks, contemporary culture still has a lot of catching up to do. Despite the models of Hermione, Katniss, and Rory, girls remain overwhelmed with demeaning images of women. A teacher at McGehee told me that young women today need *Little Women* more than ever, as a counter to the images of womanhood that bombard them. As one concerned mom has vividly written, "Between mean girls and predatory boys, texting and sexting, and mass media that celebrate Miley Cyrus twerking and Kim Kardashian's generous booty, it's hard to help a teenage girl focus on what really matters—like her brain, strength, passion, and conviction; her rights as a human and as a citizen of this country." In response, she has tried to surround her daughter with strong female role models. While her daughter's English teachers have assigned primarily texts about boys, and her daughter's own pleasure reading has tended toward *Gossip Girl* and its ilk, this mother has encouraged her daughter to read *Little Women*, *Jane Eyre*, *The Color Purple*, and Jane Austen's novels.[17] Providing our daughters with an alternative canon of female-centered stories can help ensure that they don't, like so many of my students, get to college or graduate school and wonder why they have read so little about girls' and women's experiences.

What makes *Little Women*, in particular, such powerful reading? It unearths the tensions between family and self, sisterhood and separation, growing up and failing to find one's way. As today's stories show us, these themes remain highly relevant. Atik is right that girl-hood hasn't really changed all that much over the past century and a half. However, Alcott's classic pointed the way not only toward girls' future selves but also toward the future relationships they could have with men and with each other. She imagined her characters moving into a mature womanhood that achieves self-fulfillment as well as shared joys and responsibilities, a storyline today's little women desperately need. Until girls' stories are truly able to follow the lead of *Little Women*, Meg, Jo, Beth, and Amy will continue to live and challenge us to consider the many different ways girls can become women.

# Acknowledgments

THIS PROJECT WOULD not have been possible without the groundwork laid by generations of talented Alcott scholars. I am particularly indebted to Beverly Lyon Clark, author of *The Afterlife of* Little Women, Anne K. Phillips and Gregory Eiselein, editors of the Norton Critical edition of *Little Women*, as well as Daniel Shealy, Joel Myerson, and Madeleine Stern, editors of *The Selected Letters of Louisa May Alcott*, *The Journals of Louisa May Alcott*, and *Alcott in Her Own Time*. The work of biographers John Matteson, Eve LaPlante, and Harriet Reisen has also been extremely helpful. It has been my pleasure to meet many of these scholars, and I very much enjoyed my discussions with Eve, Harriet, and Daniel as I worked on this book.

I am also grateful to those who aided me in securing the time I needed to write this book. Cheryl Torsney and Sharon M. Harris graciously supported my application for funding, and the National Endowment for the Humanities provided invaluable support through a Public Scholar Award. The University of New Orleans also provided supplementary funding.

Many people also aided me in writing this book. Many heartfelt thanks to the NOLA Nonfiction Writing Group, especially Pat Brady, Nigel Hamilton, Randy Delehanty, Carol Gelderman, Lynn Adams, and Molly Mitchell for support and advice. I am grateful as well to Susan Rudy, Constance Adler, Miki Pfeffer, Pamela Toler, Teresa Brader, and Theresa Kaminski for their advice on a portion of the manuscript, and particularly to Beverly Rude, who read the whole thing.

As I developed my thoughts about *Little Women*, I found women of all ages eager to discuss the book with me. Thank you to all of the book's fans who shared their thoughts with me online and in person over the last few years, especially Shawna Ross and Susan Harlan. I was particularly blessed to have a group of women from the New Orleans chapter of the Women's National Book Association read *Little Women*, *Little Men*, and *Jo's Boys* with me and share their many fascinating experiences with and opinions of the books: Constance Adler, Susan Larson, Miki Pfeffer, Teresa Brader, and Carol Gelderman. I was also quite fortunate to meet in London with Susan Rudy, Krissie West, Helen Glew, and Dawn Sardella-Ayres for a delightful evening discussing *Little Women*. My thanks to Susan Rudy for graciously hosting us! Thank you as well to Katheryne Patterson at Lusher Charter School and Erin Fallon and Melissa Lyman at Louise S. McGehee School, both in New Orleans, Louisiana, for facilitating my visits, and to the students in Ms. Patterson's and Ms. Lyman's classes, who discussed *Little Women* and their other reading with me.

I am grateful to the staff of the Library of Congress, the New York Public Library, and the Clifton Waller Barrett Library at the University of Virginia for facilitating my research there. Leslie Perrin Wilson of the Special Collections at the Concord Free Public Library was tremendously helpful with locating Alcott material there. Jan Turnquist at Orchard House in Concord, Massachusetts, was a fount of information and was kind enough to bring me along to an evening reception so that we could talk along the way. Susan Bailey and Jeannine Atkins were kind enough to drive to Concord to meet me during my stay and discuss all things Alcott. Miki Pfeffer drove me out to Fruitlands for a splendid visit.

Research assistant Kristy Lewis helped gather articles and other resources. My thanks to the English Department at the University of New Orleans, particularly the chair, Peter Schock, for providing the funds for a research assistant and for supporting my work generally.

My sincere thanks as well to my agent Barbara Braun, for helping this project to find such a wonderful home, and to my editor, Amy Cherry, for her insight, support, and outstanding editorial advice. Remy Cawley again was an invaluable guide through the process of manuscript preparation. And Christianne Thillen was a superb copy editor who helped me avoid many errors.

Lastly, I appreciate beyond measure the love and support of my family. To Paul and Emma, you have helped me more than anyone to appreciate Jo's feeling that her book "will be all the better for such experiences and illustrations as these," referring to her family. I sincerely believe that mine is better, and my life richer, for having you as my family.

# *Notes*

## Abbreviations

| | |
|---|---|
| ABA | Amos Bronson Alcott (Louisa's father) |
| *Afterlife* | Beverly Lyon Clark, *The Afterlife of* Little Women (Baltimore, MD: Johns Hopkins University Press, 2014). |
| *AIHOT* | *Alcott in Her Own Time: A Biographical Chronicle of Her Life, Drawn from Recollections, Interviews, and Memoirs by Family, Friends, and Associates*, ed. Daniel Shealy (Iowa City: University of Iowa Press, 2005). |
| AMA | Abigail May Alcott (Louisa's mother) |
| *CE* | *Critical Essays on Louisa May Alcott*, ed. Madeleine B. Stern (Boston: G. K. Hall, 1984). |
| *CR* | *Louisa May Alcott: The Contemporary Reviews*, ed. Beverly Lyon Clark (Cambridge, UK: Cambridge University Press, 2004). |
| *EO* | John Matteson, *Eden's Outcasts: The Story of Louisa May Alcott and Her Father* (New York: W. W. Norton, 2007). |
| *JB* | Louisa May Alcott, *Jo's Boys* (London: Hesperus, 2014). |
| *Journals* | *The Journals of Louisa May Alcott*, ed. Joel Myerson, Daniel Shealy, and Madeleine B. Stern (Athens: University of Georgia Press, 1997). |
| *LM* | Louisa May Alcott, *Little Men: Life at Plumfield with Jo's Boys* (Boston: Little, Brown, 1994). |

LMA   Louisa May Alcott

*LMAB*   Madeleine Stern, *Louisa May Alcott: A Biography* (Norman: University of Oklahoma Press, 1950. Reprint, Boston: Northeastern University Press, 1999).

*LMAWB*  Harriet Reisen, *Louisa May Alcott: The Woman Behind* Little Women (New York: Picador, 2009).

*LW*    Louisa May Alcott, *Little Women*. Norton Critical Edition, ed. Ann K. Phillips and Gregory Eiselein (New York: W. W. Norton, 2004).

*LWFI*   *Little Women and the Feminist Imagination: Criticism, Controversy, Personal Essays*, ed. Janice M. Alberghene and Beverly Lyon Clark (London: Routledge, 1999).

*MHIB*   *My Heart Is Boundless: Writings of Abigail May Alcott, Louisa's Mother*, ed. Eve LaPlante (New York: Free Press, 2012).

*ML*    Eve LaPlante, *Marmee and Louisa: The Untold Story of Louisa and Her Mother* (New York: Simon & Schuster, 2012).

*SL*    *The Selected Letters of Louisa May Alcott*, ed. Joel Myerson, Daniel Shealy, and Madeleine B. Stern (Boston: Little, Brown, 1987).

*TW*    Cynthia Barton, *Transcendental Wife* (Lanham, MD: University Press of America, 1996).

## Prologue: "Our Book"

1. Elena Ferrante, *My Brilliant Friend* (New York: Europa, 2012), 68.
2. Christine King Farris, "Why Reading Matters," *What Kids Are Reading and Why It Matters* (Renaissance Learning, 2015), 27. Marley Dias, "Hillary Clinton Faces Her Toughest Interviewer Yet—11-Year-Old Marley Dias," *Elle*, Oct. 6, 2016; elle.com. Carla Hayden, "By the Book," *New York Times Book Review*, Aug. 3, 2017; nytimes.com. Deirdre Bair, *Simone de Beauvoir: A Biography* (New York: Simon & Schuster, 1990), 69. Patti Smith, *Just Kids* (New York: HarperCollins, 2010), 10–11. Cindy Cantrell, "Concord's Orchard House Director Brings Alcott to Japan," *Boston Globe*, Feb. 17, 2003; bostonglobe.com. Anderson Cooper and Gloria Vanderbilt, *The Rainbow Comes and Goes: A Mother and Son on Life, Love, and Loss* (New York: HarperCollins, 2016), 92. Chung cited in *Afterlife*, 107. Steinem quoted in Lisa O'Kelly, "How Was It for You, Girls?" *Observer* (London), Feb. 19, 1995, p. 23. "J. K. Rowling: By the Book," *New York Times Book Review*, Oct. 11, 2012; nytimes.com. Cynthia Ozick, "The

Making of a Writer: Spells, Wishes, Goldfish, Old School Hurts," *New York Times*, Jan. 31, 1982, p. BR24. Rosanna Greenstreet, "Q&A: Caitlin Moran," *Guardian*, May 4, 2013; theguardian.com.

## 1. "Pegging away": The Road to *Little Women*

1. LMA, May, June 1868, *Journals*, 165–66. *LMAWB*, 268–69.
2. LMA to Mary E. Channing Higginson, Oct. 18, [1868], *SL*, 118.
3. Madeleine B. Stern, Introduction, *Journals*, 22–23. Ednah Cheney, *Louisa May Alcott: The Children's Friend* (Boston: L. Prang, 1888).
4. Ralph Waldo Emerson, "Self-Reliance," *Essays and Lectures* (New York: Library of America, 1983), 259. Anne E. Boyd, *Writing for Immortality: Women and the Emergence of High Literary Culture in America* (Baltimore: Johns Hopkins University Press, 2004), 23.
5. ABA, *Conversations with Children on the Gospels*, vol. 1 (Boston: James Monroe, 1836), xxvii, xviii. ABA quoted in Madelon Bedell, *The Alcotts: Biography of a Family* (New York: Clarkson N. Potter, 1980), 245. May Alcott quoted in *EO*, 261. ABA to LMA in *The Letters of A. Bronson Alcott*, ed. Richard L. Herrstadt (Ames: Iowa State University Press, 1969), 379. AMA quoted in *LMAWB*, 23. LMA to AMA, Dec. 25, 1854, *SL*, 11.
6. *United States Review* quoted in Joyce W. Warren, *The (Other) American Traditions: Nineteenth-Century Women Writers* (New Brunswick, NJ: Rutgers University Press, 1993), 1. Elizabeth Stoddard, "Woman in Art.— Rosa Bonheur," *The Aldine* 5 (July 1872): 145. Fanny Fern, *Ruth Hall and Other Writings*, ed. Joyce W. Warren (New Brunswick, NJ: Rutgers University Press, 2005), 116. Hawthorne quoted in Introduction to *Selected Letters of Nathaniel Hawthorne*, ed. Joel Myerson (Columbus: Ohio State University Press, 2002), xv.
7. The phrase "anxiety of authorship" is Sandra Gilbert and Susan Gubar's in *Madwoman in the Attic: The Woman Writer and the Nineteenth-Century Literary Imagination* (New Haven, CT: Yale University Press, 1979). LMA to Louisa Caroline Greenwood Bond, Sept. 17, [1860], *SL*, 61.
8. *LMAWB*, 155–56. LMA to AMA, Dec. 25, 1854, *SL*, 11.
9. LMA, "A Modern Cinderella," *Atlantic Monthly* 6 (Oct. 1860): 427. I discuss this story and her rocky relationship with the *Atlantic Monthly* in Boyd, *Writing for Immortality*, 168–69, 208–10.
10. LMA, November 1859, *Journals*, 95. LMA to Alfred Whitman, Aug. 4, [1861], *SL*, 67. I discuss the *Atlantic*'s treatment of women writers in Boyd, *Writing for Immortality*, 206.
11. Ralph Waldo Emerson, "Experience," in *The Essential Writings of Ralph Waldo Emerson*, ed. Mary Oliver (New York: Random House, 2009), 310. LMA, May 1861; Oct. 1861; Sept., Oct. 1862; Apr. 1861, *Journals*, 105, 106, 109, 105.

12. LMA, May, Feb. 1862, *Journals*, 109, 108.

13. LMA, "Transcendental Wild Oats," in *Alternative Alcott*, ed. Elaine Showalter (New Brunswick, NJ: Rutgers University Press, 1988), 375. LMA quoted in Frederick L. H. Willis, *Alcott Memoirs* (Boston: Richard G. Badger, 1915), 41.

14. LMA to Alfred Whitman, June 22, [1862], *SL*, 70.

15. LMA quoted in LaSalle Corbell Picket, *Across My Path: Memories of People I Have Known* (1916), excerpted in *AIHOT*, 184–85.

16. LMA, Nov. and Dec. 1862, *Journals*, 110.

17. LMA, June and Aug. 1863, *Journals*, 119, 120. Boyd, *Writing for Immortality*, 212.

18. LMA to Moncure Daniel Conway, Feb. 18, 1865, *SL*, 108. Boyd, *Writing for Immortality*, 226–27.

19. LMA, Feb. 1865, *Journals*, 139.

20. LMA, Dec. 1865 and May 1866, *Journals*, 145, 151.

21. LMA to Louisa Chandler Moulton, n.d., quoted in *ML*, 224.

22. LMA, June 1868, *Journals*, 166. Thomas Niles to LMA, quoted in *ML*, 228.

23. LMA, Aug. 1868, *Journals*, 166.

24. LMA, *LW*, 185. LMA, Nov. 1, 1868, *Journals*, 167.

25. LMA, Nov. 1, Nov. 17, 1868, *Journals*, 167. LMA to Samuel Joseph May, Jan. 22, [1869], *SL*, 122.

26. LMA, "Our Foreign Correspondent," chap. 7 of *Little Women*, part two, manuscript, Louisa May Alcott Papers, Vault A35, Unit 1, Folder 5, Concord Free Public Library, Concord, MA.

27. LMA, "Heartache," chap. 12 of *Little Women*, part two, manuscript, Louisa May Alcott Papers, Vault A35, Unit 1, Folder 6, Concord Free Public Library, Concord, MA.

28. LMA, Apr. 1868, *Journals*, 171.

29. Julian Hawthorne, "The Woman Who Wrote *Little Women*" (1922), in *AIHOT*, 200–201. LMA, Aug. 1868, *Journals*, 172.

## 2. "We really lived most of it": Making Up *Little Women*

In writing this chapter, I have consulted the following secondary sources liberally throughout: *AIHOT, EO, LMAB, LMAWB, MHIB, ML*, and *TW* (see Abbreviations). Direct citations have been limited for ease of reading.

1. LMA, May 1868, *Journals*, 165–66. LMA, Aug. 26, 1868, *Journals*, 166.

2. Letter quoted in Sheryl A. Englund, "Reading the Author in *Little Women*: A Biography of the Book," *American Transcendental Quarterly* 12.3 (Sept. 1998): 206. LMA, Apr. 1855, *Journals*, 73.

3. LMA, *LW*, 38–39.

4. *ML*, 68.

5. Quoted in *EO*, 99.
6. Quoted in Daniel Shealy, ed., *Little Women: An Annotated Edition* (Cambridge, MA: Harvard University Press, 2013), 131.
7. The story is recounted in two different sources from friends of the family, with slight variation, reprinted in *AIHOT*, 215 and 225.
8. Eve LaPlante sees Samuel Joseph May as the prototype for Mr. March (personal conversation). She discusses his and AMA's progressive politics extensively in *ML*.
9. LMA, *LW*, 69.
10. Quoted in *EO*, 96.
11. Descriptions of ABA in Frederick H. Willis, in *AIHOT*, 173. AMA to Samuel Joseph May, Dec. 14, 1852, in *MHIB*, 185. AMA quoted in Frederick L. H. Willis, *AIHOT*, 174.
12. *LMAWB*, 128. Annie M. L. Clark in *AIHOT*, 113.
13. LMA, Dec. 10, 1843, *Journals*, 47.
14. *EO*, 202. Anna, letter to ABA, quoted in *EO*, 247. Here and elsewhere, the original spelling has been retained in quotations without the inclusion of [*sic*] to indicate misspellings.
15. LMA quoted in Frank Preston Stearns, *AIHOT*, 87. AMA quoted in *ML*, 119. LaPlante, *ML*, 120.
16. An archivist has discovered that it was common to add a silent "r" to names in New England letters of the period. See "Marmee Dearest," Letter to the Editor, *New York Times*, Jan. 3, 2013; nytimes.com. LMA, *LW*, 68.
17. AMA's advice summarized by LaPlante in *ML*, 282. AMA quoted in *ML*, 138.
18. LaPlante, *ML*, 192. AMA quoted in *LMAWB*, 83. LMA, July 1850, *Journals*, 63. ABA quoted in *LMAWB*, 350.
19. LMA's version of her relatives' impressions of her quoted in *ML*, 254. Lydia Hosmer Wood in *AIHOT*, 165.
20. Clara Gowing, in *AIHOT*, 135.
21. LMA, "Reminiscences," in *AIHOT*, 34. Clara Gowing in *AIHOT*, 135.
22. Clara Gowing in *AIHOT*, 136. LMA, "Reminiscences," in *AIHOT*, 35.
23. LMA, "Reminiscences," *AIHOT*, 36. LMA, December 1863, *Journals*, 122. LMA, "Merry's Monthly Chat with His Friends," in *LW*, 541–43. The girls' names are also taken from life in the story: Nan, Lu, Beth, and May.
24. *ML*, 142–43.
25. LMA, 1852, *Journals*, 67. LMA, "Reminiscences," *AIHOT*, 36.
26. LMA, "Reminiscences," *AIHOT*, 37.
27. *ML*, 151, 153–54.
28. *EO*, 374.
29. LMA, *LW*, 272.
30. Maria S. Porter in *AIHOT*, 61–62. See also LMA, Apr. 1862, *Journals*, 109. LMA, Feb. 1863, *Journals*, 117.

31. LMA, Apr. 1855, *Journals*, 73.
32. Matteson describes Lizzie's likeness to her father and quotes ABA in *EO*, 186. AMA quoted in *LMAWB*, 151. Reisen interprets Lizzie's symptoms as describing "a deep depression bordering on catatonia and requiring hospitalization," *LMAWB*, 151. LMA, *LW*, 253. LMA, 1853 and 1854, *Journals*, 69, 72.
33. LMA, June 1857, *Journals*, 85. For homeopathic remedies, see, for instance, A. Gerald Hull, *The Homeopathic Examiner*, vol. 1 (New York: Henry Ludwig, 1840).
34. LaPlante and Reisen assume rheumatic fever, although her symptoms do not correlate with that disease (see Rachel Hajar, "Rheumatic Fever and Rheumatic Heart Disease a Historical Perspective," *Heart Views* 17.3 [Jul.–Sept. 2016]: 120–26). Barton points out that "physicians could not agree whether Lizzie's afflictions were of the lungs or of the brain," with no mention of the heart, the afflicted organ in rheumatic fever, *TW*, 160. Matteson seems to suggest mental ailment, pointing out that "Lizzie's emotional attachment to the world was diffident and weak," *EO*, 230. Susan Bailey, who is working on a biography of Elizabeth Alcott, is examining the possibility of anorexia nervosa (personal conversation). Doctor's diagnosis in AMA's diary, quoted in *TW*, 161. Symptoms in *LMAWB*, 175. Lizzie's words to her mother a quote from ABA's journal in *ML*, 183.
35. AMA to Samuel Joseph May, Mar. 19, 1858, *MHIB*, 196. LMA, Mar. 14, 1858, *Journals*, 89. ABA's poem quoted in *EO*, 327.
36. LMA to the Alcott Family, [Oct. 1858], *SL*, 34.
37. Anna wrote to Alfred Whitman about Louisa's dream of being a famous author, adding, "Mine you know was to be an actress, Mays to be an artist," quoted in "The Alcotts Through Thirty Years: Letters to Alfred Whitman," *Harvard Library Bulletin* 11 (Autumn 1957), 381. LMA, "The Sister's Trial," in *LW*, 511.
38. LMA, *LW*, 118.
39. May Alcott to Alfred Whitman, Sept. 25, 1868, quoted in "The Alcotts Through Thirty Years," 377. Frederick H. Willis called May "childishly tyrannical," in *AIHOT*, 181. LMA, Feb. 1864 and Apr. 1878, *Journals*, 128, 209.
40. May Alcott to Alfred Whitman, Jan. 5, 1869, quoted in "The Alcotts Through Thirty Years," 377.
41. LMA claims Hawthorne was not Laurie in a letter to Miss Holmes, [ca. 1872], *SL*, 167. Quotes from Frederick H. Willis, in *AIHOT*, 171, 170, 180.
42. LMA to Alfred Whitman, Feb. 13, [1858], *SL*, 42. Alfred Whitman, in *AIHOT*, 108. LMA to Alfred Whitman, Jan. 6, 1869, *SL*, 120.
43. LMA to Elizabeth Powell, Mar. 20, [1869], *SL*, 125. LMA, June 1860, *Journals*, 99.
44. LMA, Apr. 1860, *Journals*, 98. Reisen, *LMAWB*, 193. LMA, *LW*, 84.

45. LMA, "Reminiscences," *AIHOT*, 36. Christine Doyle, "Singing Mignon's Song: German Literature and Culture in the March Trilogy," *Children's Literature* 31 (2003): 56, 58–59.
46. Reisen, *LMAWB*, 3.

## 3. "Fresh, sparkling, . . . full of soul": The Phenomenon of *Little Women*

1. *Eclectic Magazine* in *CR*, 64.
2. Charlotte Yonge, *The Daisy Chain: or, Aspirations. A Family Chronicle* (London: John W. Parker and Son, 1860), 21.
3. A.D.T. Whitney, *Faith Gartney's Girlhood* (Boston: Loring, 1863), 7.
4. LMA, *LW*, 11.
5. *Boston Daily Evening Transcript* in *CR*, 61. *Providence Daily Journal* in *CR*, 62.
6. Daniel Shealy, Introduction, *Little Women: An Annotated Edition* (Cambridge, MA: Harvard University Press), 18. "Books for the Young," *The Spectator* 42 (Mar. 13, 1869), p. 332.
7. "Little Women," *The Graphic*, Nov. 26, 1870, p. 11. Review of *Little Women; or, Meg, Jo, Beth, and Amy*, Part Second, *London Evening Standard*, Nov. 2, 1869, p. 2. "Christmas Books," *Pall Mall Gazette*, Dec. 6, 1870, p. 12.
8. Henry James, Review of *Eight Cousins*, *The Nation*, in *CR*, 247. "New Books," *Charleston Daily News*, June 28, 1868, p. 2.
9. *Zion's Herald* in *CR*, 64. *The Ladies' Repository*, in *LW*, 549. Thomas Niles to LMA, Oct. 26, 1868, in *LW*, 419.
10. LMA to Thomas Niles, [1868], https://www.skinnerinc.com/auctions/2658B/lots/5. Current price of book by Antiquarian Booksellers Association of America, http://www.abaa.org/member-articles/louisa-may-alcott-a-checklist-of-first-editions. *Boston Daily Evening Transcript, National Anti-Slavery Standard*, and [Unknown], in *CR*, 61, 62, 68, 63.
11. Unidentified newspaper clipping in *CR*, 69. Joel Myerson and Daniel Shealy, "The Sales of Louisa May Alcott's Books," *Harvard Library Bulletin* n.s., 1.1 (Apr. 1990): 51. LMA to Thomas Niles, [early 1869], *SL*, 118–19. Shealy, Introduction, *Little Women: An Annotated Edition*, 22.
12. Reviews quoted in *CR*, 78, 72, 84. Frank Preston Stearns in *AIHOT*, 85.
13. *Zion's Herald* in *CR*, 75. For a recent article warning homeschooling parents about the lack of Christianity in *Little Women*, see http://www.homemakerscorner.com/alcott.htm. LMA, *LW*, 281. *Christian Union* quoted in Thomas Niles to LMA, [June 1882], in *LW*, 426.
14. Billings, Hammatt, Little Women [proof of frontispiece illustration for second part], 1868; Sinclair Hamilton Non-book collection (GC053); Graphic Arts Collection Department, Rare and Special Books Collection, Princeton University Library. LMA to Elizabeth B. Greene, Apr. 1, [1869], *SL*, 126.

15. James F. O'Gorman, *Accomplished in All Departments of Art—Hammatt Billings of Boston, 1818–1874* (Amherst: University of Massachusetts Press, 1988), 64.

16. Ibid., 65.

17. Reviews quoted in *CR*, 88, 90. Sales in *Afterlife*, 11.

18. Frank Merrill's drawings, Vault A20, Unit A1, Series I, Drawings, Folders 1 and 2, Concord Free Public Library, Concord, MA. LMA to Thomas Niles, July 20, 1880, *SL*, 249.

19. LMA, *Old-Fashioned Girl* (New York: Puffin, 1991), 215–16.

20. For an extensive list of the changes, see "Textual Variants," in *LW*, 386–408.

21. Susan R. Gannon, "Getting Cozy with a Classic: Visualizing Little Women (1868–1995)," *LWFI*, 116. See Shealy, "Note on the Text," *Little Women: An Annotated Edition*, x. Thomas Niles to LMA, Jan. 5, 1883, in *LW*, 427. The Norton Critical, Penguin Classics, and Broadview editions are based on the original 1868–69 text.

22. "Special Notice," in the back of *Little Women Wedded* (London: Sampson Low, Marston, Low & Searle, 1872). Advertisement for *A Story of Four Little Women* in *Publishers' Circular*, Oct. 1, 1870, p. 616.

23. Gloria T. Delmar, *Louisa May Alcott and "Little Women": Biography, Critique, Publications, Poems, Songs and Contemporary Relevance* (Jefferson, NC: McFarland, 1990), 196. Catalogue of the British Library. Advertisement in *London Evening Standard*, Nov. 9, 1872, p. 8. Ward, Lock, and Tyler also published *Good Wives* serially in its magazine *Beeton's Young Englishwoman* in 1873.

24. Discussed in Sarah Elbert, *A Hunger for Home: Louisa May Alcott's Place in American Culture* (New Brunswick, NJ: Rutgers University Press, 1987), 217–18.

25. Constance Fenimore Woolson to Linda Guildford [1891], in *The Complete Letters of Constance Fenimore Woolson*, ed. Sharon Dean (Gainesville: University Press of Florida, 2012), 464. Anne Boyd Rioux, *Constance Fenimore Woolson: Portrait of a Lady Novelist* (New York: W. W. Norton, 2016), 72–73.

26. Thomas Niles to LMA, Apr. 4, 1869, in *LW*, 422. LMA, 1869, *Journals*, 172, 173, 176.

27. LMA, 1871 and June 1871, *Journals*, 177, 178.

28. LMA, *LM*, 109–10, 115.

29. LMA, "Reminiscences," *AIHOT*, 35. LMA, *LM*, 161–62.

30. LMA, *LM*, 113.

31. LMA, *LM*, 25, 29.

32. LMA, June 1871, *Journals*, 178.

33. LMA, quoted in *EO*, 370.

34. LMA, *JB*, 38. LMA, July 1872, *Journals*, 183. LMA to *Springfield Republican*, May 4, 1869, *SL*, 127, 128.

35. LMA, Sept. and Oct. 1875, *Journals*, 196. LMA, *JB*, 41.

36. The letters are reprinted in *SL*, 275–80, 285–88, 296–97.

37. "Barbara Sicherman: The Persistence of *Little Women*, or Still Timely after All These Years," Nov. 29, 2012; UNCPressBlog.com. Barbara Sicherman, *Well-Read Lives: How Books Inspired a Generation of American Women* (Chapel Hill: University of North Carolina Press), 22. Delmar, *Louisa May Alcott and "Little Women"*, 136, 110.

38. John Barry, "Louisa Alcott Lives for Tots," *Des Moines Register*, Feb. 23, 1933, p. 14. "Louisa M. Alcott Dead," Mar. 7, 1888, *New York Times*; nytimes.com. Spofford quoted in *Afterlife*, 28. Ednah D. Cheney, *Louisa May Alcott, the Children's Friend* (Boston: Prang, 1888).

39. Typescript copy of LMA's will, Louisa May Alcott Papers, Folder 12, Concord Free Public Library, Concord, MA. Ednah D. Cheney, *Louisa May Alcott: Her Life, Letters, and Journals* (Boston: Roberts Brothers, 1889). *LMAB*.

40. "Louisa M. Alcott Centenary Year," *Publisher's Weekly* 122 (July 2, 1932): 23–24.

41. Madame Alexander created the Little Women dolls to coincide with the 1933 film starring Katharine Hepburn. Katharine Anthony, "The Most Beloved American Writer," *Woman's Home Companion* (Dec. 1937): 9–11+; (Jan. 1938): 11–13+; (Feb. 1938): 9–11+; (Mar. 1938): 20–22+.

42. *Afterlife*, 186.

43. *Afterlife*, 186. Results of worldcat.org search for "little women" by Louisa May Alcott and Louisa M. Alcott, and "'little women' retold" in English. A fraction of the results are collections of stories that include portions of *Little Women*. These numbers include e-books, microfilm, and braille books.

44. See *Afterlife*, 16.

45. For translations through the 1960s, see Judith C. Ullom, *Louisa May Alcott: A Centennial for* Little Women. *An Annotated, Selected Bibliography* (Washington, DC: Library of Congress, 1969), 27–31. For post-1970 translations, see *Afterlife*, 142. For *Little Women* in Japan, see Kazuko Watanabe, "Reading Little Women, Reading Motherhood in Japan," *Feminist Studies* 25.3 (Fall 1999): 700; and Aiko Moro-oka, "Alcott in Japan: A Selected Bibliography," *LWFI*, 377–79.

46. This estimate is based on the claim that 5 million copies had been sold by 1968 in Eugenia Kaledin, "Louisa May Alcott: The Success and Sorrow of Self-Denial," *Women's Studies* 5 (Jan. 1978): 262.

4. "See her . . . *living* . . . the immortal Jo!":
*Little Women* on Stage and Screen

1. Anna Steese Richardson, "At the Theater with 'Little Women,'" *Woman's Home Companion* 39 (May 1912): 10.

2. John S. P. Alcott, "The 'Little Women' of Long Ago," in *AIHOT*, 154. "'Little Women and Sundry Big Events," *New York Times*, Dec. 6, 1931, p. X3. "Lovely Play Made from 'Little Women,'" *New York Times*, Oct. 17, 1912, p. 11.

3. "The Playgoer," *New-York Tribune*, Oct. 20, 1912, part 5, p. 2. Bonstelle and theatergoer quoted in *Afterlife*, 71.

4. "Little Women Revived," *New York Times*, Dec. 8, 1931, p. 36.

5. For an overview of the critical and popular reaction, see *Afterlife*, 75–77. Quotes from *New-York Tribune* and *Brooklyn Eagle* on 76 and 76–77. Run of 203 nights recorded in "'Little Women and Sundry Big Events," *New York Times*, Dec. 6, 1931, p. X5. Adolph Klauber, "The Week's New Plays," *New York Times*, Oct. 20, 1912, p. X5.

6. The two silent films and all other film and television adaptations mentioned in this chapter are in the Internet Movie Database, imdb.com. "Little Women and Sundry Big Events." "*Little Women* Leads Poll: Novel Rated Above Bible for Influence on High School Pupils," *New York Times*, May 22, 1927, in *CE*, 84.

7. "Book Notes," *New York Times*, July 16, 1935, p. 17. B. Lamar Johnson, "Children's Reading Interests as Related to Sex and Grade in School," *School Review* 40 (Apr. 1932), 261. "Televiews of Pictures," *New York Times*, Dec. 17, 1939, p. X12. *Afterlife*, 117–18.

8. Charlotte Chandler, *I Know Where I'm Going: Katharine Hepburn, A Personal Biography* (New York: Simon & Schuster, 2010), 82. *Afterlife*, 122. Richard B. Jewell, *RKO Radio Pictures: A Titan Is Born* (Berkeley: University of California Press, 2012), 62, 75–77. Gene D. Phillips, *George Cukor* (Boston: Twayne, 1982), 65.

9. *Afterlife*, 122. Katharine Hepburn, *Me: Stories of My Life* (New York: Random House, 2011), 149.

10. Chandler, *I Know Where I'm Going*, 82. Hepburn, *Me*, 147.

11. Hepburn, *Me*, 149. Cukor quoted in *Afterlife*, 123. Cukor and Hepburn quoted in Anne Edwards, *Katharine Hepburn: A Remarkable Woman* (New York: St. Martin's Griffin, 1985, 2000), 110.

12. Newspaper ads quoted (with ellipses in original) in Edwards, *Katharine Hepburn*, 110. William J. Mann, *Kate: The Woman Who Was Hepburn* (New York: Picador, 2006), 42, 36–37; Hepburn quoted, 40.

13. *Afterlife*, 123. "*Little Women*," *Variety*, Nov. 31, 1933, p. 14.

14. Kate Ellis, "Life with Marmee: Three Versions," in *The Classic American Novel and the Movies* (New York: F. Ungar, 1977), 70. Ellis is also referring to June Allyson's performance in the 1949 film. Mann, *Kate*, 195.

15. Jewell, *RKO Radio Pictures*, 75–76. "*Little Women*," *Variety*, Nov. 31, 1933, p. 14. *Afterlife*, 122.

16. Jewell, *RKO Radio Pictures*, 76. Corbin Patrick, "Katharine Hepburn Triumphs in 'Little Women,'" *Indianapolis Star*, Dec. 3, 1933, part 4, p. 7. See also *Afterlife*, 124–27.

17. "Story Success 'Unexpected,'" *Los Angeles Times*, Apr. 7, 1934, p. 7; "'Little Women' Demand Is Far Ahead of Library Supply," *Hutchinson News* (KS), Jan. 12, 1934, p. 9. Mary Knight, "Paris Styles," *Chillicothe Constitution-Tribune* (MO), Aug. 25, 1934, p. 3.

18. *Afterlife*, 109, 128. "Miniature Women," *The Jack Benny Program*, Feb. 11, 1934; oldtimeradio.com.

19. The shows can be found at oldtimeradio.com.

20. *Afterlife*, 117–18.

21. Quoted in Phillips, *George Cukor*, 67.

22. LMA, *LW*, 13. Carol Gay, "*Little Women* at the Movies," in *Children's Novels and the Movies* (New York: F. Ungar, 1983), 35. For a critique of Allyson's performance at the time, see Bosley Crowther, "Metro Fails to Spare Pathos in 'Little Women' Remake Seen at Music Hall," *New York Times*, Mar. 11, 1949; nytimes.com. "Actresses Have Happy Memories of '49 Film," *USA Today*, Dec. 20, 1994, p. 4D.

23. Quote in C. David Heymann, *Liz: An Intimate Biography of Elizabeth Taylor* (New York: Simon & Schuster, 2011), 72. Allan R. Ellenberger, *Margaret O'Brien: A Career Chronicle and Biography* (Jefferson, NC: McFarland, 2004), 148.

24. LMA, *Little Women*, 124. Bosley Crowther, "Into the Rainbow: 'Little Women' Acquires a Pollyanna Air," *New York Times*, March 20, 1949, p. X1. Stuart Aubrey, "Somewhere under the Rainbow Lies Louisa May Alcott's 'Little Women,'" *Hutchinson News-Herald* (KS), July 17, 1949, p. 22. Philip K. Scheuer, "'Little Women' Revives Era of Gracious Living," *Los Angeles Times*, Apr. 18, 1949, p. 39. "Casting Jewels Before Audiences: A Woman's Picture," *The Age* (Melbourne, Australia), Nov. 5, 1949, p. 9.

25. Jewelry box in advertisement, *Daily Capital Journal* (Salem, OR), May 6, 1949, p. 3. Scarf in *Afterlife*, 133. "'Little Women' Gowns Adapted for Today," *Los Angeles Times*, Mar. 20, 1949, p. 74; Advertisement, *Portsmouth Herald* (NH), Apr. 7, 1949, p. 6. *Afterlife*, 132.

26. Barbara Crossette, "Television Discovers 'Little Women,'" *Tennessean* (Nashville), Oct. 1, 1978, p. 157. Tom Dorsey, "Television Does Justice to 'Little Women,'" *Courier-Journal* (Louisville, KY), Oct. 2, 1978, p. C1.

27. "Third Film Unlike the First Two," *Greenville News* (SC), May 3, 1978, p. 4B. Crossette, "Television Discovers 'Little Women,'" p. 157.

28. Ibid. LMA, *Little Women*, 372.

29. Joan Hanauer, "'Users' Trashy TV, 'Women' Too Sweet," *Pittsburgh Press*, Sept. 30, 1978, p. B4. Dorsey, "Television Does Justice to 'Little Women,'" p. C1.

30. "Wakakusa Monogatari Yori Wakakusa no Yon Shimai (TV)" and "Ai no Wakakusa Monogatari (TV)," *Anime Encyclopedia*, animenewsnetwork.com.

31. "Actresses Have Happy Memories of '49 Film." Tom Stempel, *Frame-*

*work: A History of Screenwriting in the American Film,* Third Edition (Syracuse, NY: Syracuse University Press, 2000), p. 250.

32. Gillian Armstrong, "Director's Commentary," DVD of *Little Women* (1994).

33. Marshall Fine, "Little Women' Is a Surprising Achievement," *USA Today,* Dec. 21, 1994, n.p. Sara Eckel, "Feminist Tale OK with All," *Daily Chronicle* (DeKalb, IL), Mar. 6. 1995, p. 4.

34. Kristine McKenna, "Not So 'Little Women,'" *Los Angeles Times,* Dec. 27, 1994, pp. 8, 9. "'Little Women' Kicks Off a Hollywood Trend," *Entertainment Weekly,* Mar. 11, 1994; ew.com.

35. McKenna, "Not So 'Little Women,'" p. 9.

36. LMA, *LW,* 84.

37. Armstrong, "Director's Commentary."

38. Cindy Pearlman, "The Ballad of 'Little's' Jo," *Kokomo Tribune* (IN), Dec. 15, 1994, p. 36. Susan Wloszczyna, "Classic 'Little Women' Meets Generation X," *USA Today,* Dec. 20, 1994, p. 4D. See also Armstrong, "Director's Commentary."

39. Armstrong quoted as saying, "There are gross preconceptions about female achievers. That's why I always wear my lipstick," in Quentin Curtis, "The Mother of Modern Movies," *Independent on Sunday* (London), Mar. 19, 1995.

40. Bob Strauss, "Actress Thinks 'Little Women' Can Inspire Girls of the '90s," *Courier-Journal* (Louisville, KY), Jan. 15, 1995, p. 95.

41. Roger Ebert, Review of *Little Women,* Dec. 21, 1994; rogerebert.com. Janet Maslin, "The Gold Standard for Girlhood Across America," *New York Times,* December 21, 1994; nytimes.com. "Sisters Are Doing It for Themselves," *Daily Telegraph* (London), Mar. 17, 1995, p. 20. Curtis, "The Mother of Modern Movies." Stephen Amidon, "No Liberties with the Little," *Sunday Times* (London), March 19, 1995, p.6.

42. Rita Kempley, "The Gift of 'Little Women,'" *Washington Post,* Dec. 21, 1994, p. C1. "An Oscar for Victorian Values?" *Daily Mail* (London), Mar. 17, 1995, pp. 42–43. Donna Britt, "Four Genteel Sisters: 'Little Women' Is a Film for the Heart," *Des Moines Register,* Dec. 30, 1994, p. 9.

43. Rated at #9 (Jan. 22, 1995), #10 (Feb. 5, 1995), #13 (Feb. 12, 1995), and #13 (Feb. 19, 1995) on *New York Times* Paperback Best Seller Lists, nytimes. com. Molly Walsh, "Film Gives New Editions of 'Little Women' a Big Boost," *USA Today,* Jan. 16, 1995, n.p. Christopher Hudson, "Never Mind the Book, You Can Read the Film," *Daily Telegraph* (London), Mar. 14, 1995, p. 17.

44. "Alcott Novel on Way; Was Too Steamy in 1866," *Arizona Republic* (Phoenix), Dec. 20, 1994, p. 17. Nancy Roberts Trott, "Unpublished Alcott Novel Is a Real Find," *Akron Beacon Journal* (Ohio), Jan. 3, 1995, p. 1. Ranked #14 on *New York Times* Best Seller List for Oct. 15, 1995; nytimes.com.

45. markadamo.com/little-women.

46. John Rockwell, "Opera Review; Alcott's Sisters Grow from Page to Stage," *New York Times*, Mar. 26, 2003; nytimes.com.

47. Alex Ross, "Sisterhood: Making Opera out of 'Little Women,'" *The New Yorker*, July 22, 2002; newyorker.com. Rockwell, "Opera Review; Alcott's Sisters Grow from Page to Stage." Anthony Tommasini, "Television Review; Lyricism but Few Modern Bits for the March Sisters," *New York Times*, Aug. 29, 2001; nytimes.com.

48. Orla Swift, "Getting 'Little Women' Ready," *News & Observer* (Raleigh, NC), Oct. 10, 2004, p. G1. Michael Kuchwara, "Girl Power Lights Up B'way Shows," *Star-Ledger* (Newark, NJ), Feb. 22, 2005.

49. Swift, "Getting 'Little Women' Ready."

50. Matthew Murray, review of *Little Women the Musical*, *Talkin' Broadway*, Jan. 23, 2005; talkinbroadway.com. David Rooney, "Review: 'Little Women: The Musical,'" *Variety*, Jan. 23, 2005; variety.com. Howard Kissel, "'Little Women' Is a Big Letdown," *New York Daily News*, Jan. 25, 2005. Michael Sommers, "Sister Act: Sutton Foster Glows as Jo in 'Little Women,'" *Star-Ledger* (Newark, NJ), Jan. 24, 2005.

51. *Afterlife*, 153. Elizabeth Weiss, "To Flip a Flop," *The New Yorker*, Jan. 7, 2014; newyorker.com.

52. Sarah Hughes, "Sex and the Middle-Aged Woman . . . a Groundbreaking BBC Drama Tells It Like It Is," *Guardian*, Jan. 14, 2017; theguardian.com.

## 5. "The mother of us all": *Little Women*'s Cultural and Literary Influence

1. Deborah Weisgall, "The Mother of All Girls' Books," *American Prospect*, June 11, 2012; prospect.org.

2. For early respect among scholars and subsequent decline of *LW*'s reputation, see Barbara Sicherman, "Reading *Little Women*: The Many Lives of a Text," in *The Girls' History and Culture Reader: The Nineteenth Century*, ed. Miriam Forman-Brunell and Leslie Paris (Urbana: University of Illinois Press, 2011), 278–79; and *Afterlife*, 43–44. G. K. Chesterton, "Louisa," in *CE*, 213, 214.

3. I discuss the masculinization of the American literary canon in Anne E. Boyd, *Writing for Immortality: Women and the Emergence of High Literary Culture in America* (Baltimore: Johns Hopkins University Press, 2004), 241–46. Edward Wagenknecht, *Cavalcade of the American Novel* (New York: Holt, 1952), 88. Lawrence Buell, in *The Dream of the Great American Novel* (Cambridge, MA: Belknap Press of Harvard University Press, 2014), devotes a chapter to *Adventures of Huckleberry Finn*. *Little Women* is mentioned nowhere in its pages.

4. James quoted in *CR*, 246. British critic quoted in *Afterlife*, 85. "Our

Library Table," *Educational Times* (Apr. 1, 1893), p. 188. For Little, Brown editions in 1907, 1913, and 1908, respectively, see Anne Lindsey Bruder, "Outside the Classroom Walls: Alternative Pedagogies in American Literature and Culture," diss., University of North Carolina at Chapel Hill, 2009, p. 91. "Further Testimony of a Great Picture's Hold on the Public," *Washington Post*, Dec. 24, 1933, p. B2.

5. "Popular Books for Children of Grammar Grade," *Journal of Education* 70.7 (Aug. 26, 1909), 182. G. W. Willett, "The Reading Interests of High-School Pupils," *English Journal* 8.8 (Oct. 1919), 474–87. H. D. Roberts, "Review: A Study of Reading Interests," *English Journal* 15.7 (Sept. 1926), 557–58. "Little Women Leads Poll: Novel Rated Ahead of Bible for Influence on High School Pupils," *New York Times*, Mar. 22, 1927; in *CE*, 84. Edgar Dale, "Books Which Children Like to See Pictured," *Educational Research Bulletin* 10.16 (Nov. 11, 1931), 423–29. Edith Rosenblatt, "Library Surveys Show Reading Trends Here," *Pittsburgh Post-Gazette* (PA), Jan. 4, 1949, p. 7. " 'Trapp Family' Favorite Book at Library Here; Children Select 'Little Women' as Favorite," *Suburbanite Economist* (Chicago), May 31, 1950, p. 5. "Religious Books Are the Most Popular," *Lincoln Evening Journal* (NE), Apr. 28, 1950, p. 6.

6. Quote from a WWII-era poster reprinted as the frontispiece in Molly Guptill Manning, *When Books Went to War: The Stories That Helped Us Win World War II* (Boston: Houghton Mifflin, 2014). "Send in Your Lists," *Courier-Journal* (Louisville, KY), May 3, 1942, p. 39. Pearl S. Buck, "Books About Americans for People in Asia to Read," *Asia: Journal of the American Asiatic Association* (Oct. 1942): 2, 1. "An American Album," *Tucson Daily Citizen* (AZ), Oct. 16, 1942, p. 8. The books chosen were microfilmed by the Office of War Information and sent to Chunking. Last quote from Brett Anderson, "Book Marks," *Pittsburgh Press* (PA), Dec. 20, 1942, p. 39.

7. "School Correspondence Plan Boosts International Friendship," *Los Angeles Times*, Feb. 3, 1949, p. 33. Quote about Franklin Book Program in Louise S. Robbins, "Publishing American Values: The Franklin Book Programs as Cold War Cultural Diplomacy," *Library Trends*, 55.3 (Winter 2007): 642. Choice of *Little Women* as one of first texts in finding aid for "Franklin Book Programs Records," Princeton University Library; http://arks.princeton.edu/ark:/88435/p2676v53g. Hiroshi Kitamura, *Screening Enlightenment: Hollywood and the Cultural Reconstruction of Defeated Japan* (Ithaca, NY: Cornell University Press, 2010), 100–104. Frances Stonor Saunders, *The Cultural Cold War: The CIA and the World of Arts and Letters* (New York: The New Press, 2013), 243. "Interchange," *The Reading Teacher* 25 (Dec. 1971): 287. "Laura Bush Promotes Reading in Russia," *School Library Journal* (Nov. 2003): 25.

8. "Ban Cinderella in Red Hungary," *Des Moines Register*, Dec. 14, 1950, p. 8. Ralph Thompson, "In and Out of Books," *New York Times*, Nov. 14,

1948; nytimes.com. "Hungary Bans 'Little Women' and Strippers Too," *Brooklyn Daily Eagle*, Dec. 14, 1950, p. 15. See also "Louisa Alcott's old book, 'Little Women,' has been banned in Russia," *Democrat and Chronicle* (Rochester, NY), Jan. 30, 1949, p. 18; "Cover to Cover," *Sydney Morning Herald*, Apr. 24, 1949, p. 18.

9. Lavinia Russ, "Not to Be Read on Sunday," in *CE*, 99. "Junior Choice," *Guardian*, Nov. 9, 1999; theguardian.com. Patricia J. Wilson and Richard F. Abrahamson, "What Children's Literature Classics Do Children Really Enjoy?" *Reading Teacher* 41.4 (Jan. 1988), 406–11. Arthur N. Applebee, *A Study of Book-Length Works Taught in High School English Courses* (Albany, NY: Center for the Learning and Teaching of Literature, 1989). "Book Poll Reveals Favorites of Young," *Cincinnati Enquirer*, Jan. 5, 1974, p. 12.

10. For an overview of early feminist criticism on *Little Women* and references, see Introduction, *LWFI*.

11. Deborah Friedell, "The Vortex," *New Republic* (May 16, 2005): 42. Quotes about Library of America at its website, loa.org.

12. Weisgall, "The Mother of All Girls' Books." Lucinda Rosenfeld, "Great Novels About Sisters," in *The Pretty One: A Novel About Sisters* (New York: Little, Brown, 2013); googlebooks. Wharton quoted in Sicherman, "Reading *Little Women*," 285. Paglia quoted in Hermione Lee and Sophia Chauchard-Stuart, "Marmee's Girls," *Independent* (London), Mar. 3, 1995; independent.co.uk. Hilary Mantel, "Author, Author: Looking for Female Role Models in Nineteenth Century Novels," *Guardian*, Jan. 31, 2009; theguardian.com.

13. Carolyn G. Heilbrun, "Louisa May Alcott: The Influence of *Little Women*," in *Women, the Arts, and the 1920s in Paris and New York*, ed. Kenneth W. Wheeler and Virginia Lee Lussier (New Brunswick, NJ: Transaction Books, 1983), 25. Elaine Showalter, *Sister's Choice: Tradition and Change in American Women's Writing* (Oxford, UK: Oxford University Press, 1991), 64. Ursula K. Le Guin, "The Fisherwoman's Daughter," in *Mother Reader: Essential Writings on Motherhood*, ed. Moyra Davey (New York: Seven Stories Press, 2001), 162, 164. Sanchez quoted in *Afterlife*, xvi.

14. Gail Mazur, "Growing Up with Jo," *Boston Review* 13 (Feb. 1988): 18. Lynne Sharon Schwartz, *Ruined by Reading: A Life in Books* (Boston: Beacon Press, 1997), 66–67.

15. Barbara Kingsolver, *High Tide in Tucson: Essays from Now or Never* (New York: Harper Perennial, 1995), 44. Maureen Corrigan, *Leave Me Alone, I'm Reading: Finding and Losing Myself in Books* (New York: Knopf Doubleday, 2007), xxx. Nora Ephron quoted in Liz Dance, *Nora Ephron: Everything Is Copy* (Jefferson, NC: McFarland, 2015), 34. Delia Ephron, *Sister Mother Husband Dog (Etc.)* (New York: Penguin, 2013); googlebooks.

16. Ann Petry quoted in Barbara Sicherman, "Reading *Little Women*," 285. bell hooks, *Bone Black: Memories of Girlhood* (New York: Holt, 1996), 77.

Elizabeth Alexander, "Elizabeth Alexander on the Book That Taught Her About Complicated Women," *The Cut*, Sept. 9, 2017; thecut.com. Bich Minh Nguyen, *Stealing Buddha's Dinner* (New York: Penguin, 2008); googlebooks. Candy Gourlay, comment on Elizabeth Bird, "Denying Children's Literature: When Adult Authors Talk About Youthful Indiscretions," *School Library Journal*, June 14, 2016; blogs.slj.com. Cynthia Ozick, "The Making of a Writer: Spells, Wishes, Goldfish, Old School Hurts," *New York Times*, Jan. 31, 1982, p. BR24. "Why Does Cynthia Ozick Write? 'I Simply Must,' She Says," National Public Radio, July 17, 2016; npr.org. Mazur, "Growing Up with Jo," 18.

17. "Christmas Books; Uncle Wiggily's Karma and Other Childhood Memories," *New York Times*, Dec. 7, 1986; nytimes.com. Erica Jong, "Unzipped," *New York Times Book Review*, Oct. 3, 2013; nytimes.com.

18. Lisa K. Winkler, "Dr. Perri Klass: Doctor, Writer, Professor, Literacy Advocate," *Education Update Online*, Apr. 2007; educationupdate.com. Stacy Schiff, "Our Little Women Problem," *New York Times*, June 18, 2005; nytimes.com. Lamott quoted in *The Book That Changed My Life: 71 Remarkable Writers Celebrate the Books That Matter Most to Them*, ed. Roxanne J. Coady and Joy Johannessen (New York: Penguin, 2007), 99. "What's on Stephenie Meyer's Ideal Bookshelf?" *Guardian*, Nov. 25, 2012; theguardian.com. Weisgall, "The Mother of All Girls' Books." Natalia Sylvester, "Re-reading *Little Women*," Jan. 13, 2016; nataliasylvester.com.

19. Susan Cheever, Introduction to *Little Women* (New York: Modern Library, 2000), xiv–xv. Jane Smiley, Introduction to *Little Women* (New York: Penguin, 2012), vii. Anna Quindlen, Introduction to *Little Women* (New York: Little, Brown, 1994), n.p.

20. Carl Rollyson, *Amy Lowell: A New Biography* (Lanham, MD: Rowman & Littlefield, 2013), 9. Mary Gordon, *Circling My Mother* (New York: Anchor Books, 2008), 110. Madeleine Blais, *The Heart Is an Instrument: Portraits in Journalism* (Amherst: University of Massachusetts Press, 1992), 246. "Anne Tyler: By the Book," *New York Times Book Review*, Feb. 5, 2015; nytimes.com. Steinem quoted in Lisa O'Kelly, "How Was It for You, Girls?" *Observer* (Philadelphia), Feb. 19, 1995; philly.com. Sara Paretsky, *Writing in an Age of Silence* (London: Verso, 2009), 5. Bloom quoted in Julie Vadnal, "Amy Bloom on the Audacity of Little Women," *Elle*, Mar. 31, 2010; elle.com.

21. Carson McCullers, *The Mortgaged Heart: Selected Writings* (Boston: Houghton Mifflin, 2005), xxiv, 233. Susan Sontag quoted in "Christmas Books; Uncle Wiggily's Karma." Maxine Hong Kingston quoted in Jody Joy, "To Be Able to See the Tao," in *Conversations with Maxine Hong Kingston*, ed. Paul Skenazy and Tera Martin (Oxford: University Press of Mississippi, 1989), 62. "Jhumpa Lahiri: By the Book," *New York Times Book Review*, Sept. 15, 2013; nytimes.com. Margaret Atwood, "Letter to America," in *Moving Targets: Writing with Intent, 1982–2004*

(Toronto: Anansi Press, 2004), 324. Shaena Lambert, "How My Writing Allowed Me to Heal," *Huffington Post*, Jan. 9, 2014; huffingtonpost.ca. Emma Donoghue, "Once upon a Life: Emma Donoghue," *Guardian*, Sept. 5, 2010; theguardian.com. Adriana Lanzi, "The Influence of Little Women in Argentina"; academia.edu. For further examples of American authors, see the following sources: Edna Ferber, Bess Streeter Aldrich, Ida B. Wells, and Sarah Teasdale cited in *Afterlife*, 15. Mary Antin quoted in Sicherman, "Reading *Little Women*," 288. H.D. in Annette Debo, *The American H.D.* (Iowa City: University of Iowa Press, 2012), 182. Shirley Jackson, *Raising Demons* (New York: Penguin, 2015). Rita Dove quoted in Rob Crisell, "The Power of Poetry," *Highlights* 50.9 (Sept. 1995): 10. "Francine Prose: By the Book," *New York Times Book Review*, Jan. 3, 2013; nytimes.com. Ann Hood, "Ann Hood: The Books We Love," *Parade*, Aug. 5, 2016; parade.com. Shirley Geok-lin Lim, "'Ain't I a Feminist?' Reforming the Circle," in *The Feminist Memoir Project: Voices from Women's Liberation*, ed. Rachel Blau DuPlessis and Ann Snitow (New Brunswick, NJ: Rutgers University Press, 2007), 450. Vanessa Hua, "At Home at the Library," *San Francisco Chronicle*, July 7, 2016; sfchronicle.com. "Danielle Steel: By the Book," *New York Times Book Review*, Feb. 11, 2016. Judith Krantz quoted in "Christmas Books; Uncle Wiggily's Karma." Jennifer Weiner, "Jennifer Weiner on Finding Her Way Back from Sadness," *Huffington Post*, July 7, 2014; huffingtonpost.com. Julia Alvarez, *Something to Declare: Essays* (Chapel Hill, NC: Algonquin Books, 2014), 139. Mary Jo Salter, "Louisa May Alcott's American Girls," *New York Times Book Review*, May 15, 2005; nytimes.com. Robb Forman Dew quoted in J. Peder Zane, ed., *The Top Ten: Writers Pick Their Favorite Books* (New York: W. W. Norton, 2010), 57. Bobbie Ann Mason quoted in Marie Arana-Ward, "Speaking for the Country," *Washington Post*, Dec. 20, 1998, p. X10. Isabelle Holland quoted in *LWFI*, xv. Laurie Hertzel, "Q&A with bestselling author Deborah Harkness," *StarTribune* (Minneapolis), Aug. 13, 2014; startribune.com. "J. Courtney Sullivan: By the Book," *New York Times Book Review*, Aug. 2, 2012; nytimes.com. "One Minute with Kim Edwards, Novelist," *Independent* (London), Mar. 4, 2011, p.25. Donna Britt, "Four Genteel Sisters: 'Little Women' Is a Film for the Heart," *Des Moines Register*, Dec. 30, 1994, p. 9. Margo Jefferson, *Negroland* (New York: Pantheon, 2015). Deborah Feldman, "Once upon a Life: Deborah Feldman," *Guardian*, Aug. 29, 2010; theguardian.com. Mitali Perkins, "Grow Up with Us, You'll Be Fine" and Alice Schertle, "Up the Bookcase to Poetry," in *A Family of Readers: The Book Lover's Guide to Children's and Young Adult Literature*, ed. Roger Sutton and Martha V. Parravano (Somerville, MA: Candlewick Press, 2012). Karen Cushman in *Once upon a Heroine: 450 Books for Girls to Love*, ed. Alison Cooper-Mullin and Jennifer Marmaduke Coye (New York: McGraw-Hill, 1998), 150. Susanna Daniel, *Jane Yolen* (New York: Rosen, 2004),

16. Bonnie Kunzel and Susan Fichtelberg, *Tamora Pierce* (Westport, CT: Greenwood, 2007), 256. Eileen Myles in Emily Temple, "The Books That Made Your Favorite Writers Want to Write," *Literary Hub*, Apr. 26, 2017; lithub.com.

22. "J. K. Rowling: By the Book," *New York Times*, Oct. 11, 2012; nytimes.com. Rowling interviewed in "The Women of Harry Potter," *Deathly Hallows, Part 2*, DVD extras. Rosanna Greenstreet, "Q&A: Caitlin Moran," *Guardian*, May 4, 2013; theguardian.com. "Books That Changed Me: Holly Smalle," *Sydney Morning Herald*, Mar. 17, 2013; smh.com. Gabrielle Donnelly, "Little Women and Me," gabrielledonnellyauthor.com. Kate Mosse, "The Little Women Who Never Grow Old: Kate Mosse Delights in a New, Annotated Edition of Louisa May Alcott's Defining Tale," *Times* (London), June 1, 2013, p. 43.

23. Louise Jury, "The Life-Changing Novels Every Woman Should Read," *Independent* (London), Sept. 13, 2004; independent.co.uk. Carol Clewlow, "Sisters Stealing a March on Time," *Herald* (Glasgow), Mar. 20, 1995, p. 15. Enid Blyton, *The Story of My Life* (London: Grafton Books, 1952), 47. Jacqueline Wilson, "The Ten Best: Books to Read Aloud," *Independent* (London), May 7, 2006; independent.co.uk. Arifa Akbar, "One Minute with Francesca Simon, Children's Author," *Independent* (London), Oct. 21, 2011, p. 23. Doris Lessing (and Carol Ann Duffy) in "'Get your head out of that book!'—The Children's Stories That Inspired Leading Writers," *Guardian*, May 9, 2015; theguardian.com. A. S. Byatt in *The Pleasures of Reading: 43 Writers on the Discovery of Reading and the Books That Inspired Them*, ed. Antonia Fraser (New York: Bloomsbury, 2015), 136, 140. Zadie Smith thought "Hepburn played the greatest, most empathic and beautiful Jo March there ever has been or ever will be," suggesting her admiration of the character; see Smith, "The Divine Ms H," *Guardian*, July 1, 2003; theguardian.com. Helen Oyeyemi in Megan O'Grady, "The Fantastic and *Mr. Fox*: Helen Oyeyemi on Her New Folktale-Inspired Novel," *Vogue*, Sept. 28, 2011; vogue.com. See also P. D. James, *Time to Be in Earnest* (New York: Random House, 2007); googlebooks; Germaine Greer in O'Kelly, "How Was It for You, Girls?"; Sue Townsend in *The Pleasures of Reading*, 220; Shena Mackay, Lynne Truss, and Julie Burchill in Lee and Chauchard-Stuart, "Marmee's Girls"; Catherine McPhail in Amanda Keenan, "Half-a-Million Books to Be Handed Out Free Today as World Book Night Spreads the Beauty of the Printed Word," *Daily Record*, Apr. 23, 2013; dailyrecord.co.uk; Carole Cadwallader in *Afterlife*, 142; Jennie Colgan in JoJo Moyes, "The Healing Power of Jane Austen," *Telegraph*, Mar. 30, 2010; telegraph.co.uk; Zoë Heller, "Five Best: Zoë Heller Chooses Memorable Portraits of Sisters," *Wall Street Journal*, Mar. 27, 2010; wsj.com; "Guest post: Holly Webb Talks About the Inspiration Behind Her Newest Characters," June 18, 2013; librarymice.com.

24. Deirdre Bair, *Simone de Beauvoir: A Biography* (New York: Simon &

Schuster, 1990), 69. Simone de Beauvoir, *Memoirs of a Dutiful Daughter* (New York: Harper Perennial, 2005), 89. Last quote from Bair, *Simone de Beauvoir*, 69. Lavinia R. Davis, "American Ambassadors," *New York Times*, May 8, 1960; nytimes.com. Elena Ferrante, *My Brilliant Friend* (New York: Europa Editions, 2012). *Afterlife*, 108. Ghada Hashem Talhami, *Historical Dictionary of Women in the Middle East and North Africa* (Lanham, MD: Scarecrow Press, 2013), 297. Jennifer Dann, "Twelve Questions with Emily Perkins," *New Zealand Herald*, Sept. 11, 2012; nzherald.co.nz.

25. Stats on sequels, retellings, etc., in *Afterlife*, 177. See Lois Lowry, *Anastasia at Your Service* (Bantam Doubleday Dell Books for Young Readers, 1982), *Anastasia, Absolutely* (Bantam Doubleday Dell, 1995), *The Willoughbys* (Yearling, 2008), *Like the Willow Tree: The Diary of Lydia Amelia Pierce* (Scholastic, 2011), and *The Silent Boy* (Houghton Mifflin Books for Children, 2003, 2012).

26. Gabrielle Donnelly, *The Little Women Letters* (New York: Simon & Schuster, 2011), 349.

27. "Previous Books: Frequently Asked Questions," kingsolver.com.

28. Kate Saunders, "A Book That Changed Me," *Independent on Sunday* (London), July 5, 1998, p. 32. Chelsea Cain, "Fairest of Them All," *New York Times Book Review*, June 5, 2009; nytimes.com.

29. See Clark, who also mentions more, in *Afterlife*, 181–82, 256. Sherry Jones comments on the likeness of her four sisters to the March sisters in Nancy Bilyeau, "Bloody Good Interview: Sherry Jones on "Four Sisters, All Queens," May 9, 2012; bloodygoodread.blogspot.com.

30. Amy Bloom, *Lucky Us: A Novel* (New York: Penguin Random House, 2014); googlebooks. A. S. Byatt, *The Game: A Novel* (New York: Knopf Doubleday, 2012); googlebooks. See Jennifer Weiner's novels *Little Earthquakes* (New York: Washington Square Press, 2004), *The Guy Not Taken* (New York: Washington Square Press, 2006), and *Who Do You Love* (New York: Washington Square Press, 2015).

31. The Open Syllabus Project database; explorer.opensyllabusproject.org.

## 6. "A divided house of a book": Reading *Little Women*

1. Margo Jefferson. "Books of the Times; Little Women, Growing Up Then and Now," *New York Times*, Dec. 21, 1994; nytimes.com. Alice Kaplan, *Looking for* The Stranger: *Albert Camus and the Life of a Literary Classic* (Chicago: University of Chicago Press, 2016), 2.

2. LMA, *LW*, 36, 275–76, 12.

3. [Larcom, Lucy?], *Our Young Folks*, in *CR*, 79; see also 61–82. [Review of *Little Women*, Part I], *Harper's New Monthly Magazine*, in *CE*, 83.

4. G. K. Chesterton, "Louisa Alcott," in *CE*, 213. LMA, *LW*, 368.

5. Reviews from [*Northern Christian Advocate?*], *Hartford Daily Courant*, and *The Galaxy*, in *CR*, 81, 77, 78.

6. Review of 1912 play quoted in *Afterlife*, 78. Quentin Letts, "A Night Out as Warm and Wholesome as Hot Milk," *Daily Mail* (London), Oct. 14, 2004, p. 6.

7. LMA, *LW*, 368.

8. Lavinia Russ, "Not to Be Read on Sunday," in *CE*, 100.

9. LMA, *LW*, 30, 65, 369.

10. Quotes in *Afterlife*, 126, 131.

11. James Baldwin, "Everybody's Protest Novel," *Notes of a Native Son* (Boston: Beacon Press, 1955; reprint, 1984), 14. The essay was first published in *Zero* magazine in Paris and in *The Partisan Review* in the United States in June 1949.

12. Brigid Brophy, "A Masterpiece, and Dreadful," *New York Times Book Review*, Jan. 17, 1965.

13. Elizabeth Janeway, "Meg, Jo, Beth, Amy and Louisa," in *CE*, 97. Russ, "Not to Be Read on Sunday," in *CE*, 99.

14. Sean O'Faolain, "This Is Your Life . . . Louisa May Alcott," in *CE*, 106.

15. Mary Gaitskill, "Does Little Women Belittle Women?" *Vogue* (Jan. 1995): 36. Miranda Kiek, "Why I Love . . . the Dribbly Kiss in Little Women," *Guardian*, Aug. 21, 2013; theguardian.com. Laura Miller, "A Good Book Should Make You Cry," *New York Times*, Aug. 22, 2004; nytimes.com.

16. Foster quoted in Orla Swift, "Getting 'Little Women' Ready," *News & Observer* (Raleigh, NC), Oct. 10, 2004, p. G1. Anna Quindlen, "She Was Jo, and That Was That," *New York Times*, Mar. 3, 1991; nytimes.com. "Little Women at Seacoast Rep This August," *Broadway World*, July 22, 2016; broadwayworld.com.

17. LMA, *LW*, 93.

18. Perri Klass, *Other Women's Children* (New York: Random House, 1990), 231. "Gloria Steinem's Wandering Childhood," *Wall Street Journal*, Oct. 27, 2015; wsj.com.

19. Review from the *Cincinnati Times Star* quoted in Susan R. Gannon, "Getting Coy with a Classic: Visualizing *Little Women* (1868–1995)," in *LWFI*, 120.

20. LMA to *Woman's Journal*, [ca. Oct. 11, 1879], *SL*, 237–38. LMA, *JB*, 70.

21. LMA, *LW*, 207, 235.

22. Elizabeth Vincent, "Subversive Miss Alcott," in *CE*, 223, 224. F. Scott Fitzgerald, "Bernice Bobs Her Hair," in *Novels & Stories 1920–1922* (New York: Library of America, 2000), 365.

23. Elizabeth Janeway, "Meg, Jo, Beth, Amy and Louisa," in *CE*, 98.

24. "Letters," *New York Times Book Review*, Nov. 3, 1968, p. 56.

25. Gerald Nachman, "After 'Wuthering,' What?" *New York Times*, Oct. 4, 1970, p. D13.

26. Karen Lindsay, "Louisa May Alcott: The Author of *Little Women* as Feminist," *Women: A Journal of Liberation* 2 (Fall 1970): 35.

27. Stephanie Harrington, "Does *Little Women* Belittle Women?" in *CE*, 110, 111, 112.

28. Nachman, "After 'Wuthering,' What?"

29. Patricia Meyer Spacks, *The Female Imagination*, in *CE*, 117, 116, 119. Nina Auerbach, *Communities of Women: An Idea in Fiction* (Cambridge, MA: Harvard University Press, 1978), 55, 68.

30. Judith Fetterley, "*Little Women*: Alcott's Civil War," *Feminist Studies* 5.2 (Summer 1979): 382. Two other feminist analyses of the 1970s are Kate Ellis, "Life with Marmee: Three Versions," in *The Classic American Novel and the Movies* (New York: F. Ungar, 1977), 62–72; and Thomas H. Pauly, "*Ragged Dick* and *Little Women*: Idealized Homes and Unwanted Marriages," *Journal of Popular Culture* 9 (Winter 1975): 583–92.

31. Numbers of articles based on the "selected bibliography" of Alcott criticism in *LWFI*, 406–17. I have counted those works that focus on *Little Women* and rounded up for the 1990s since *LWFI* was published in 1999. "Cultural work" from Jane Tompkins's *Sensational Designs: The Cultural Work of American Fiction, 1790–1860* (New York: Oxford University Press, 1985). See also *Afterlife*, 147. Gregory Eiselein, "Reading a Feminist Romance: Literary Critics and *Little Women*," *Children's Literature* 28 (2000): 243.

32. Carolyn G. Heilbrun, "Louisa May Alcott: The Influence of *Little Women*," in *Women, the Arts, and the 1920s in Paris and New York*, ed. Kenneth W. Wheeler and Virginia Lee Lussier (New Brunswick, NJ: Transaction, 1982), 21, 23. Angela M. Estes and Kathleen Margaret Lant, "Dismembering the Text: The Horror of Louisa May Alcott's *Little Women*," *Children's Literature* 17 (1989): 101, 115. Beverly Lyon Clark, "A Portrait of the Artist as a Little Woman," *Children's Literature* 17 (1989): 88.

33. Gaitskill, "Does *Little Women* Belittle Women?" 44, 38. Caryn James, "Amy Had Golden Curls; Jo Had a Rat. Who Would You Rather Be?" *New York Times*, Dec. 25, 1994; nytimes.com.

34. Brenda Maddox, "Making Little Women of Us All," *Times* (London), Jan. 18, 1995, p. 23. Roberts, Grant, and Forgan quoted in Lisa O'Kelly, "How Was It for You, Girls?" *Observer* (London), Feb. 19, 1995, p. 23. Hermione Lee and Sophia Chauchard-Stuart, "Marmee's Girls," *Independent* (London), Mar. 3, 1995; independent.co.uk. Julie Bindel, "I Know We've Had Our Spats," *Guardian*, May 13, 2009; theguardian.com.

35. Greer and Steinem quoted in O'Kelly, "How Was It for You, Girls?"

36. Deborah Friedell, "The Vortex," *New Republic* 232 (May 16, 2005): 42–43. Stacy Schiff, "Our Little Women Problem," *New York Times*, June 18, 2005; nytimes.com. Elaine Showalter, "Little Women," Letter to the Editor, *New York Times*, June 22, 2005; nytimes.com.

37. Barbara Sicherman, "Reading *Little Women*: The Many Lives of a Text,"

in *The Girls' History and Culture Reader: The Nineteenth Century*, ed. Miriam Forman-Brunell and Leslie Paris (Urbana: University of Illinois Press, 2011), 289. Catharine R. Stimpson, "Reading for Love: Canons, Paracanons, and Whistling Jo March," in *LWFI*, 75.

38. LMA, *LW*, 128. Elizabeth Lennox Keyser points out Jo's contradictory desires in *Whispers in the Dark: The Fiction of Louisa May Alcott* (Knoxville: University of Tennessee Press, 1993), 70. Michelle A. Massé, "Songs to Aging Children: Louisa May Alcott's March Trilogy," in *LWFI*, 332.

39. LMA, *LW*, 379.

40. LMA, *LW*, 327.

41. LMA, *LW*, 337, 99.

## 7. "A private book for girls": Can Boys Read *Little Women*?

1. *What Kids Are Reading: The Book-Reading Habits of Students in American Schools* (Renaissance Learning, 2010 edition). This and the other reports are difficult to locate because renaissance.com provides the current edition only; those I previously found are no longer available.

2. *What Kids Are Reading: The Book-Reading Habits of Students in American Schools* (Renaissance Learning, 2014 and 2016 editions); and *What Kids Are Reading: The Book-Reading Habits of Pupils in British Schools* (Renaissance Learning, 2016 report).

3. For criticism of Common Core lists of exemplar texts, see Rick Chambers, "The Common Core Text Exemplars: A Worthy Canon or Not?" *Voices from the Middle* 21.2 (Sept. 2013): 48–52; and Lindsay Cesari, "Weeding the Common Core Standards," May 4, 2011; noshhinghere.blogspot.com. Quote from Susan Ohanian, "Grade 8 Common Core ELA Sample Questions," Aug. 11, 2012; susanohanian.org.

4. "Please, Do Not Teach Little Women!" Aug. 21, 2011; usedbooksinclass.com. Cesari, "Weeding the Common Core Standards."

5. David Curtis, "Little Women: A Reconsideration," *Elementary English* 45 (Nov. 1968): 878.

6. David Denby, *Lit Up: One Reporter. Three Schools. Twenty-Four Books That Can Change Lives* (New York: Macmillan, 2016), 73. See Sandra Stotsky, "Literary Study in Grades 9, 10, and 11: A National Survey," *Forum* 4 (Fall 2010): 2–77.

7. See the surveys conducted in Barbara G. Samuels, "Young Adult Literature: Young Adult Novels in the Classroom?" *English Journal* 72.4 (Apr. 1983): 86–88; and Stotsky, "Literary Study in Grades 9, 10, and 11." Although Stotsky documents a consistency in the most frequently taught titles, their frequency has diminished considerably, as indicated in table 6, p. 17.

8. For how boys became the focus of education research, see Marcus

Weaver-Hightower, "The 'Boy Turn' in Research on Gender and Education," *Review of Educational Research* 73.4 (Winter 2003): 471–98. For an overview of initiatives in different countries, see Roberta F. Hammett and Kathy Sanford, Introduction to *Boys, Girls, and the Myths of Literacies and Learning* (Toronto: Canadian Scholars' Press, 2008), 1–20. Peg Tyre, "The Trouble with Boys," *Newsweek* (Jan. 30, 2006): 44–52. For critical articles, see Caryl Rivers and Rosalind Chait Barnett, "The Myth of 'The Boy Crisis,'" *Washington Post*, Apr. 9, 2006; washingtonpost.com; Cara Okopny, "Why Jimmy Isn't Failing: The Myth of the Boy Crisis," *Feminist Teacher* 18.3 (2008): 216–28. One recent article on the crisis is Elizabeth Perlman, "School Gender Gap Crisis: Boys 'Twice as Likely to Fall Behind Girls,'" *Newsweek*, July 18, 2016; newsweek.com.

9. Librarian quoted in Jeff Kinney, "Kid Lit Unbound," *Time*, July 18, 2011; content.time.com. Michael Sullivan, "Why Johnny Won't Read," *School Library Journal*, Aug. 1, 2004; slj.com. A few examples of boys being actively discouraged from reading books about girls: Awnali Mills, "Boy and Books," *The Librarian Is on the Loose*, June 16, 2015; librarianontheloose.wordpress.com; Elizabeth Bluemle, "He Won't Read Books About Girls," *ShelfTalker*, Apr. 5, 2012; blogs.publishersweekly.com; Josie Leavitt, "It's Not a Boy Read or a Girl Read," *ShelfTalker*, Dec. 1, 2011; blogs.publishersweekly.com. One librarian bucking the trend is Karen Yingling, "Challenging Gender Norms with 'Boys Read Pink' Celebration," *School Library Journal*, May 18, 2016; slj.com.

10. First quote from Nicole Senn, "Effective Approaches to Motivate and Engage Reluctant Boys in Literacy," *Reading Teacher* 66.3 (Nov. 2012): 217. Quote about more boy books than girl books in libraries in Myra Pollack Sadker et al., "Sex Bias in Reading and Language Arts Teacher Education," *Reading Teacher* 33.5 (Feb. 1980): 534. Quotes from textbook and about teachers' and librarians' assumptions in Elizabeth Segal's "'As the Twig Is Bent . . .': Gender and Childhood Reading," in *Gender and Reading: Essays on Readers, Texts, and Contexts*, ed. Elizabeth A. Flynn and Patrocinio P. Schweickart (Baltimore: Johns Hopkins University Press, 1986), 180. On preference for boy books in education courses, see Pamela J. Farris et al., "Male Call: Fifth-Grade Boys' Reading Preferences," *Reading Teacher* 63.3 (Nov. 2009): 181. In Stotsky's "Literary Study in Grades 9, 10, and 11: A National Survey," only three of the twenty most frequently assigned titles could be said to represent female points of view unfiltered by a male author: *To Kill a Mockingbird*, Lorraine Hansberry's *A Raisin in the Sun*, and Laurie Halse Anderson's *Speak*, the last being the only one that focuses on women's issues. *Speak* was ranked twentieth, with only 3 percent frequency; see table 2, p. 14.

11. Elizabeth Dutro, "'But That's a Girls' Book!' Exploring Gender Boundaries in Children's Reading Practices," *Reading Teacher* 55.4 (Dec. 2001–Jan. 2002): 377.

12. The discussion that follows is drawn from Segal, "'As the Twig Is Bent,'" 165–86.

13. Roosevelt quoted in *LWFI*, xv; Phelps and Woollcott in Segal, "'As the Twig Is Bent,'" 176; and Kipling in *Afterlife*, 15. Quote about boys reading at turn of the century from the *Bookman* (1897) in *Afterlife*, 29. Cather quoted in M. Catherine Downs, *Becoming Modern: Willa Cather's Journalism* (Selinsgrove, PA: Susquehanna University Press, 1999), 72.

14. Alison Flood, "Study Finds Huge Gender Imbalance in Children's Literature: New Research Reveals Male Characters Far Outnumber Females, Pointing to 'symbolic annihilation of women and girls'," *Guardian*, May 6, 2011; theguardian.com. Alison Flood, "Children Are Being 'Indoctrinated' Says *Chocolat* Author," *Guardian*, Sept. 17, 2015; theguardian.com.

15. Sarah P. McGeown, "Sex or Gender Identity? Understanding Children's Reading Choices and Motivation," *Journal of Research in Reading* 38.1 (Feb. 2015): 43.

16. See, for instance, McGeown, "Sex or Gender Identity?"

17. See Elizabeth Dutro, "Boys Reading *American Girls*: What's at Stake in Debates About What Boys Won't Read," in *Boys, Girls, and the Myths of Literacies and Learning*, ed. Roberta F. Hammett and Kathy Sanford (Toronto: Canadian Scholars' Press, 2008), 69–90; quote on 80–81.

18. Shannon Hale, "No Boys Allowed: School Visits as a Woman Writer," Feb. 26, 2015; shannonhale.tumblr.com (ellipses in original). Lauren Barack, "When Boys Can't Like 'Girl Books,'" *School Library Journal*, Mar. 5, 2015; slj.com. Caroline Paul, "Why Boys Should Read Girl Books," Mar. 29, 2016; ideas.ted.com.

19. On masculine identity requiring the repression of empathy, see Beth A. Quinn, "Sexual Harassment and Masculinity: The Power and Meaning of 'Girl Watching,'" *Gender and Society* 16.3 (June 2002): 386–402. On reading and empathy, see Raymond A. Mar and Keith Oatley, "The Function of Fiction Is the Abstraction and Simulation of Social Experience," *Perspectives on Psychological Science* 3.3 (May 2008): 173–92.

20. Bluemle, "He Won't Read Books About Girls."

21. Carolyn G. Heilbrun, "Louisa May Alcott: The Influence of *Little Women*," in *Women, the Arts, and the 1920s in Paris and New York*, ed. Kenneth W. Wheeler and Virginia Lee Lussier (New Brunswick, NJ: Transaction Books, 1983), 25. The Bechdel test, whether two female characters in a given film or literary work have a conversation about something other than a man, was first mentioned in 1985 in Alison Bechdel's comic strip *Dykes to Watch Out For* and has since been popularized. Jan Susina describes his friend's interest in reading *LW*

in "Men and *Little Women*: Notes of a Resisting (Male) Reader," in *LWFI*, 166.

22. Susina, "Men and *Little Women*," 164, 165, 167.

23. Philip Charles Crawford, "Of Sissies, Invalids, and the Mysterious Boy in the Window," *Horn Book Magazine*, 83.5 (Sept. 2007): 473.

24. Luis Negrón, "The Pain of Reading," *New York Times*, Oct. 6, 2012; nytimes.com. Leo Lerman, in *CE*, 113–14. Armond White, "*Little Men* Is a Class-Conscious Coming-of-Age Story," *Out Magazine*, Aug. 5, 2016; out.com.

25. Kidder quoted in Bill Bradfield, ed., *Books and Reading: A Book of Quotations* (Mineola, NY: Dover, 2012), 31. James Parker and Charles McGrath, "Is There Anything One Should Feel Ashamed of Reading?" *New York Times Book Review*, Apr. 7, 2015; nytimes.com. Sean O'Faolain, in CE, 106.

26. Daniel Shealy, ed., *Little Women: An Annotated Edition* (Cambridge, MA: Harvard University Press, 2013); John Matteson, ed., *The Annotated Little Women* (New York: W. W. Norton, 2015). Roger Ebert, Review of *Little Women*, Dec. 21, 1994; rogerebert.com. Gabriel Byrne mentioned in Gillian Armstrong, "Director's Commentary," DVD of *Little Women* (1994). "John Paul Stevens: By the Book," *New York Times Book Review*, Apr. 3. 2014; nytimes.com. George Orwell, "Riding Down from Bangor," *The Collected Journalism, Essays, and Letters*, vol. 4, ed. Sonia Orwell and Ian Angus (Boston: Nonpareil Books, 2000), 243. Peter Craven, "Love and Longing in the Crinoline and Bonnet Set," *The Age* (Melbourne), Oct. 4, 2008, p. 27. Melvyn Bragg, "Little Women," *Children's Literature in Education* 9 (1978): 95. "*Little Women* Still Has Big Fans," *Parade Magazine*, Dec. 19, 1994, p. 15.

27. Stephen King, "Blood and Thunder in Concord," *New York Times Book Review*, Sept. 10, 1995; nytimes.com. Dorris quoted in *Conversations with Louise Erdrich and Michael Dorris*, ed., Allan Richard Chavkin and Nancy Feyl Chavkin (Oxford: University Press of Mississippi, 1994), 218. Matthew Bell, "Fellowes Denies Plagiarism in 'Downton Abbey,'" *Independent* (London), Oct. 30, 2010; independent.co.uk. (The scene he allegedly borrowed was that in which Jo puts salt on a dessert instead of sugar, which Mrs. Patmore does as well in season 1.) Marc McEvoy, "Interview: John Green," *Sydney Morning Herald*, Jan. 21, 2012; smh.com.au.

28. "Risque Book—Porridge—BBC Classic Comedy," Nov. 12, 2007, BBC Worldwide Channel; youtube.com. "The One Where Monica and Richard Are Just Friends," *Friends*, 1997, season 3, episode 13. "The Man in the Flannel Pants," *The Simpsons*, 2011, season 23, episode 7. *Girls*, 2013, season 2, episode 6.

29. Jane Roland Martin, *The Schoolhome: Rethinking Schools for Changing Families* (Cambridge, MA: Harvard University Press, 2009), 76. Mark Adamo, composer's commentary at end of video of Great Performances broadcast of *Little Women* opera, 2001.

## 8. "Being someone":
## Growing Up Female with *Little Women*

1. Robin Wasserman, "What Does It Mean When We Call Women Girls?" *Literary Hub*, May 18, 2016; lithub.com.

2. Margo Jefferson, *Negroland* (New York: Pantheon, 2015), 216–17, 210. Judith Beth Cohen quoted in Sue Standing, "In Jo's Garret: *Little Women* and the Space of Imagination," in *LWFI*, 179.

3. Elizabeth Freeman, "Key Limes: Amy," *Los Angeles Review of Books*, July 18, 2016; lareviewofbooks.org.

4. Mary Wollstonecraft, *Mary and the Wrongs of Woman* (1798, repr.; Oxford, UK: Oxford University Press, 2009), 67. Margaret Fuller in *The Portable Margaret Fuller*, ed. Mary Kelly (New York: Penguin, 1994), 330.

5. "Growing down" in Annis Pratt, *Archetypal Patterns in Women's Fiction* (Bloomington: Indiana University Press, 1981), 14. "Tam[ing] girls into women" in Holly Blackford, "*Little Women* on the Big Screen: Heterosexual Womanhood as Social Performance," in *Sisterhoods: Across the Media/Literature Divide*, ed. Deborah Cartmell et al. (London: Pluto Press, 1998), 32. For the prevalence of romance, see Kelsey McKinney, "It's Frustratingly Rare to Find a Novel About Women That's Not About Love," June 9, 2013, *Atlantic Monthly*; theatlantic.com.

6. John Demos and Virginia Demos, "Adolescence in Historical Perspective," in *Childhood in America*, ed. Paula S. Fass and Mary Ann Mason (New York: New York University Press, 2000), 132–38. Colin Heywood, *A History of Childhood: Children and Childhood in the West from Medieval to Modern Times* (Malden, MA: Blackwell, 2001); googlebooks.

7. Crista DeLuzio argues that the form of adolescence as torn between family and independence was especially typical for girls, whereas boys tended to be released from family responsibility quite early and unproblematically. See *Female Adolescence in American Scientific Thought, 1830–1930* (Baltimore: Johns Hopkins University Press, 2010), 10–11. LMA, *LW*, 14.

8. Suzanne Fagence Cooper, *Effie: The Passionate Lives of Effie Gray, John Ruskin, and John Everett Millais* (New York: St. Martin's Griffin, 2010), 23.

9. LMA, *A Long Fatal Love Chase* (New York: Dell, 1995), 3, 8.

10. Nicholas L. Syrett, *American Child Bride: A History of Minors and Marriage in the United States* (Charlotte: University of North Carolina Press, 2016), 52, 53, 2. The year 1861 was the last for which statistics were available. Unfortunately, percentages for the ages of sixteen and seventeen are not provided, only raw numbers.

11. Matthew Waites, *The Age of Consent: Young People, Sexuality, and Citizenship* (New York: Palgrave Macmillan, 2005), 69.

12. Robert Douglas-Fairhurst, *The Story of Alice: Lewis Carroll and the Secret

*History of Wonderland* (Cambridge, MA: Belknap Press of Harvard University Press, 2015); Carroll quotes on 233, 151.

13. Deborah Gorham, *The Victorian Girl and the Feminine Ideal* (1982 repr.; New York: Routledge, 2012), 101.

14. LMA, *LW*, 11, 12, 132, 134.

15. Ibid., 76, 232.

16. *Shortchanging Girls, Shortchanging America* (Washington, DC: American Association of University Women, 1991, 1994).

17. Anne Thompson, "'Little Women' Kicks Off a Hollywood Trend," Mar. 11, 1994, *Entertainment Weekly*; ew.com.

18. "Paperback Bestsellers," Aug. 16, 1998," *New York Times*, Aug. 16, 1968; nytimes.com. Kathleen Sweeney, *Maiden USA: Girl Icons Come of Age* (New York: Peter Lang, 2008), 97.

19. Sweeney, *Maiden USA*, 106. Jane Victoria Ward and Beth Cooper Benjamin, "Women, Girls, and the Unfinished Work of Connection: A Critical Review of American Girls' Studies," in *All About the Girl: Culture, Power, and Identity*, ed. Anita Harris (New York: Routledge, 2004), 20. Mary Pipher also indicated that black, Hispanic, and poor girls might be more resilient in *Reviving Ophelia: Saving the Selves of Adolescent Girls* (New York: Ballantine, 1994), 281.

20. Pipher, *Reviving Ophelia*, 39.

21. *Report of the APA Task Force on the Sexualization of Girls* (Washington, DC: American Psychological Association, 2007).

22. Pipher, *Reviving Ophelia*, 283–84. Anna Quindlen, Introduction, *Little Women* (New York: Little, Brown, 1994), n.p.

23. Pipher, *Reviving Ophelia*, 43.

24. LMA, *LW*, 35, 225.

25. Ibid., 306, 305. Sarah Blackwood and Sarah Mesle, "No One Likes Meg," *Avidly*, July 18, 2016; avidly.lareviewofbooks.org.

26. LMA, *LW*, 199, 192, 299, 297.

27. Ibid., 317. Caryn James, "Amy Had Golden Curls; Jo Had a Rat. Who Would You Rather Be?" *New York Times*, Dec. 25, 1995; nytimes.com.

28. Judith Fetterley, "*Little Women*: Alcott's Civil War," *Feminist Studies* 5.2 (Summer 1979): 379. Michelle A. Massé, "Songs to Aging Children: Louisa May Alcott's March Trilogy," in *LWFI*, 337. David H. Watters, "'A Power in the House': *Little Women* and the Architecture of Individual Expression," in *LWFI*, 198. Angela M. Estes and Kathleen Margaret Lant, "Dismembering the Text: The Horror of Louisa May Alcott's *Little Women*," *Children's Literature* 17 (1989): 113.

29. LMA, *LW*, 118.

30. See discussion of Lizzie Alcott's illness in chapter two. Lois Keith, *Take Up Thy Bed and Walk: Death, Disability and Cure in Classic Fiction for Girls* (New York: Routledge, 2001), 62. Sandra Gilbert and Susan Gubar, *Madwoman in the Attic: The Woman Writer and the Nineteenth-Century Literary*

*Imagination* (New Haven, CT: Yale University Press, 1979), 483. Janice M. Alberghene and Beverly Lyon Clark write, "Shy Beth is so fully self-effacing that she dies," Introduction, *LWFI*, xvii.

31. LMA, *LW*, 254.
32. Ibid., 294–95.
33. Ann B. Murphy, "The Borders of Ethical, Erotic, and Artistic Possibilities in 'Little Women,'" *Signs* 15.3 (Spring 1990): 572, 571. See also Fetterley, "Little Women: Alcott's Civil War," where she says, "Beth registers the cost of being a little woman; of suppressing so completely the expression of one's needs; of controlling so massively all selfishness, self-assertiveness, and anger" (379).
34. My discussion of anorexia nervosa here is informed by Joan Jacobs Brumberg, *Fasting Girls: The History of Anorexia Nervosa* (New York: Vintage, 2000); and Megan Warin, *Abject Relations: Everyday Worlds of Anorexia* (New Brunswick, NJ: Rutgers University Press, 2010), especially chap. 6.
35. LMA, *LW*, 191. For the history of "fasting girls" as symbols of religious devotion, see Brumberg, *Fasting Girls*. LMA, *LW*, 97. Strangely, though, Beth is described as "retir[ing] to her room, overcome with emotion and lobster," after the funeral (98), so she is supposed to have eaten something, although she was never mentioned as being at the table. The lobster was also of "meagre proportions" (97), so she couldn't have eaten much of it.
36. Brigid Brophy, "A Masterpiece, and Dreadful," *New York Times Book Review*, Jan. 17, 1965, p. 44. LMA, *LW*, 39, 12.
37. LMA, *LW*, 12, 14, 13.
38. Ibid., 138, 176, 51.
39. Ibid., 230, 237, 257, 255.
40. Ibid., 273.
41. Ibid., 281.
42. Ibid., 287, 286.
43. Ibid., 372.
44. Gail Mazur, "Growing Up with Jo," *Boston Review* 13 (Feb. 1988): 18.
45. Michelle A. Massé, "Songs to Aging Children: Louisa May Alcott's March Trilogy," in *LWFI*, 327.
46. LMA, *LW*, 84.

### 9. "Wanting to be Rory, but better": *Little Women* and Girls' Stories Today

1. Peggy Orenstein, *Girls and Sex: Navigating the Complicated New Landscape* (New York: HarperCollins, 2016). Shauna Pomerantz and Rebecca Raby, *Smart Girls: Success, School, and the Myth of Post-Feminism* (Berkeley: University of California Press, 2017).
2. John Ezard, "Little Women—and Boys—Losing Touch with Classics,"

*Guardian*, Feb. 1, 2003; theguardian.com. "The Big Read Top 100," BBC, Sept. 2, 2014; bbc.co.uk. "The Nation's Favourite Books" in *Times* (London), Mar. 1, 2007, p.25. Robert McCrum, "The 100 Best Novels: No. 20—*Little Women* by Louisa May Alcott (1868–9)," *Guardian*, Feb. 3, 2014; theguardian.com. "The Cat in the Hat is America's Favorite Book from Childhood," Mar. 11, 2016; "The Bible Remains America's Favorite Book," Apr. 29, 2014; theharrispoll.com. See chapter seven for discussion of *What Kids Are Reading* reports.

3. Elaine Dutka, "'Beauty and Beast' Writer Is as Feisty as Her Heroine," *Orlando Sentinel*, Jan. 25, 1992; articles.orlandosentinel.com.

4. Dorian Lynskey, "Why *Frozen*'s 'Let It Go' Is More Than a Disney Hit—It's an Adolescent Aperitif," *Guardian*, Apr. 10, 2014; theguardian.com.

5. "World Book Day: Heroines Fight Off Heroes in Poll," BBC News, Feb. 22, 2016; bbc.com.

6. Cindy Hudson, "Book Review: *The Summer I Turned Pretty* by Jenny Han," *Mother Daughter Book Club*, June 29, 2020; motherdaugther bookclub.com.

7. Joanna Webb Johnson, "Chick Lit Jr.: More Than Glitz and Glamour for Teens and Tweens," *Chick Lit: The New Woman's Fiction*, ed. Suzanne Ferriss and Mallory Young (New York: Routledge, 2006), 141–57. Much of this paragraph is also informed by Johnson's article. My thanks as well to former McGehee student Elizabeth Gay for sharing with me her senior thesis, "An Analysis of Chick Lit," which discusses *Little Women* and the *Gossip Girl* books. "Review: Little Women, Louisa May Alcott," Nov. 2014; girlwithherheadinabook.co.uk.

8. Cecily von Ziegesar, *Gossip Girl* (New York: Little, Brown, 2002), 3.

9. Naomi Wolf, "Young Adult Fiction: Wild Things," *New York Times*, Mar. 12, 2006; nytimes.com. Emily Nussbaum, "Psst, Serena Is a Slut. Pass It On," *New York Magazine*, n.d.; nymag.com.

10. See, for instance, Hannah Schiff, "12 Things Rory Gilmore Taught Us About Growing Up," *Buzzfeed*, Nov. 2, 2014; buzzfeed.com; and Hannah Steinkopf-Frank, "What I Learned from Growing Up with Rory Gilmore," *Bitch Media*, Nov. 7, 2014; bitchmedia.org. A later example is Betsy Morais, "My Life with Rory Gilmore," *The New Yorker*, Dec. 1, 2016; newyorker.com.

11. Ritch Calvin, Introduction, "'Where You Lead': *Gilmore Girls* and the Politics of Identity," in *Gilmore Girls and the Politics of Identity: Essays on Family and Feminism in the Television Series*, ed. Ritch Calvin (Jefferson, NC: McFarland, 2008), p. 15. Kaitlyn Tiffany, "The New Gilmore Girls Is Weirdly Hostile Toward Fans, Women, and Storytelling in General," *The Verge*, Nov. 28, 2016; theverge.com.

12. Calvin, "Introduction," p. 5.

13. Kaitlyn Tiffany, "Gilmore Girls' Depressing, Regressive Ending: Was It Fine?" *The Verge*, Nov. 30, 2016; theverge.com.

14. Quoted in Eliana Dockterman, "Gilmore Girls Creator Amy Sherman-Palladino Wishes You Weren't So Obsessed with Rory's Boyfriends," *Time*, Nov. 2, 2016; time.com.

15. Kathryn VanArendonk, "How *Gilmore Girls: A Year in the Life* Is Just Like *Little Women*," *Vulture*, Nov. 29, 2016; vulture.com. Leah Thomas, "Rory Writing a Book on 'Gilmore Girls' Is the Perfect Way to Wrap Up Her Story and the Series," *Bustle*, Nov. 25, 2016; bustle.com.

16. Chiara Atik, "Girls and Little Women: How Hannah Horvath Is Like Jo March," *Vulture*, Jan. 21, 2014; vulture.com. Lena Dunham, responding to the article, wrote on Twitter, Jan. 22, 2014, "This rules. We definitely had Ray reading Little Women for a reason." Kit Steinkellner, "Little Women Is Not Like Girls," *Book Riot*, Jan. 29, 2014; bookriot.com.

17. Alexandra MacAaron, "Raising a Feminist Teen in the Age of Texting and Twerking," *Women's Voices for Change*, Dec. 17, 2013; womensvoicesforchange.org.

# Index

Note: Page numbers in *italics* indicate illustrations.